Bo's
Lasting
Lessons

BO'S LASTING LESSONS

The Legendary Coach Teaches the Timeless Fundamentals of Leadership

BO SCHEMBECHLER
AND JOHN U. BACON

**BUSINESS
PLUS**

NEW YORK   BOSTON

Business Plus
Hachette Book Group USA
237 Park Avenue
New York, NY 10017
Visit our Web site at www.HachetteBoookGroupUSA.com.

Business Plus is an imprint of Grand Central Publishing. The Business Plus name
and logo is a trademark of Hachette Book Group USA, Inc.

Printed in the United States of America

First Edition: September 2007

10 9 8 7 6 5 4 3 2 1

Library of Congress Cataloging-in-Publication Data

Schembechler, Bo.
    Bo's lasting lessons : the legendary coach teaches the timeless fundamentals
of leadership / Bo Schembechler and John U. Bacon. — 1st ed.
        p. cm.
    Includes index.
    ISBN-13: 978-0-446-58199-8
    ISBN-10: 0-446-58199-2
1. Leadership. 2. Management. I. Bacon, John U., 1964- II. Title. III. Title:
Lasting lessons.
    HD57.7.S344 2007
    658.4'092—dc22   2007011312

Interior design by Charles Sutherland

To Bo:
A great leader.
A great mentor.
A great friend.

Contents

Foreword

Everyone knew the public Bo: the man on the sidelines berating referees, screaming at players, and smashing his headset against the AstroTurf. All true, of course. But the public Bo had little to do with the Bo I came to know—the same one his family, friends and former players loved so much.

I first met Bo in 1974, when I was a ten-year-old kid attending a Michigan hockey game. In the second period the PA announcer paged "Bo Schembechler" to meet someone under the north stands. My buddy and I figured, How many Bo Schembechlers can there be? We left the game to find him.

Sure enough, there he was, chatting up some old friends, while we waited nearby, nervously rolling up our programs. When he saw us standing there, he interrupted his conversation to bellow, "Now what can I do for you young men?" He signed our programs with care—no small feat when your last name is twelve letters long—and thanked us for supporting the Wolverines.

They say your character is what you do when you think no one is watching. I've seen Bo pass that test a thousand times, but none was more important to me than that first encounter. If he had ignored me thirty-two years ago, I wouldn't be writing this today. Since I became a sportswriter fifteen years ago, I've learned the hard way that meeting your childhood heroes as an adult is usually a bad idea. But getting to know Bo has been one of the highlights of my life. As they say, some men are like mountains: The closer you get to them, the bigger they are.

I walked into Bo's office for the first time in August 1996 to interview him for a long piece I was writing on Fielding Yost, Michigan's legendary coach. I was pleasantly surprised to discover Bo knew Michigan's history, chapter and verse—a rarity these days—and could quote Yost at length.

Unlike most retired coaches, whose final days are usually sad, lonely ones, Bo was busier than ever, raising millions for U-M Hospital, performing countless favors for his former assistants and players, giving speeches around the country, and traveling the world with his wife, Cathy. The story of their courtship, in Chapter 31, is one of my favorites.

Seeing all this, I had the temerity to ask if he might let me follow him around for a week. Incredibly, he agreed. After that feature was published in *The Detroit News* in November 1996, Bo asked me if I wanted his papers. I couldn't believe he was serious. After we loaded sixteen boxes onto a U-Haul, it didn't take a genius to realize what a gift he'd given me. I knew there was a biography in those papers, but the more I talked to him, the more convinced I became we had to write another book first, on leadership. It took me a little longer to convince him, however, because he was having such a good time doing everything else.

In the intervening years, I stopped by every month or so to talk to Bo about this or that, but mainly just to visit. I would bring up the subject of the proposed book once in a while, and he would always say no. To avoid being a pest, I asked if I should stop bringing it up. "No," he said, "keep trying." Shortly after Bo's former athletic director, Don Canham, died in the spring of 2005, Bo told me, "It's time."

Winston Churchill once said "Meeting Franklin Roosevelt was like opening your first bottle of champagne." Meeting Bo every week was like busting open a whole crate of the stuff. Contrary to his "football-mad" reputation, Schembechler was interested in just about everything—from the Ann Arbor bus system to teacher training to deficit spending—and he had personal opinions about all of it, too. Bo never stopped learning. This past semester he audited a class on politics with Cathy at the Gerald Ford School of Public Policy, where he would often admonish his younger classmates to take their hats off. Bo was a voracious reader, with a weakness for Tom Clancy books. He also loved music, from Cole Porter to Tina Turner (the latter thanks to Cathy). He hummed constantly. It resonated in his chest, occasionally bubbling up to form a verse, which he sang in a deep baritone—"With YOU, I've gone from RAGS to RICHES. I feel like a MILL-ion-AIRE"—then he'd return to humming while filing some papers.

Above all, Bo was interested in people. He hated talking about himself, but he loved talking about you. When he met my father at a book signing ten years ago, he said, "I know all about YOU!" Needless to say, my dad has never forgotten it.

When Bo was in town he'd drive to Schembechler Hall around 10 A.M., park in "Reserved Space 01," and trundle down the second-floor hallway to his office. Schembechler might have been a great coach, but he would have made a terrible spy, with a complete inability to whisper, sneak up on anyone, or speak anyone's name in lowercase letters. "Hey, MARY!" he would roar at the far end of the hallway. "Howya doin'? Hey, BIG JON FALK! What's the good word?"

Before Bo could sit down, the phone started ringing. He would lean forward, snap up the handpiece and shout, "Hel-LO! This is HE! Heyyyyy! How the hell are ya?" then lean back in his chair, flashing his famous teeth-clenched grin.

When he finished, no matter what kind of mood he was in, he would slam the handpiece down on the receiver as if he were spiking a football—BANG!—every time. Of the dozens of phones in Schembechler Hall, only Bo used the ancient, chunky model, and it was a good thing: Those fancy, sleek kinds wouldn't last any longer in Bo's hands than his old headsets.

The chances were good the call was from one of his former Michigan players, a dozen of whom called or stopped by every day. Whether they were All-Americans or walk-ons, Schembechler invariably remembered their names, their positions, their hometowns and what they were up to the last time they talked. Not surprisingly, almost all of them kept in touch. If you played for Bo, you had two fathers.

His voice is still ringing in their ears, long after they've graduated. "Early is on time, and on time is late!" "There is NO substitute for hard work!" "You know what the right thing to do is—so just do it!"

He wrote their recommendations, attended their weddings and visited their hospital rooms. If he could do anything to help, he would—just like that—including visiting two players in prison, and working to get them back on their feet after they got out.

They all say the same thing: "You may not always have liked it, but with Bo, you always knew exactly where you stood." Bo insulted you to your face (I was flattered to be added to his long list of victims) and praised you behind your back. In a society that favors image over substance and glad-handing over sincerity, Bo's bedrock values seem almost extreme to us now.

Schembechler was a man who knew exactly who he was, but seemed mystified by the public's view of him. "Hey, I'm not Jonas Salk," he often said. "Football coaching should not have so much status attached to it."

Bo didn't get it. His appeal was not based on his victories, but on his values—which were as simple as they were timeless.

It was those values, not his victories, that inspired me to ask him to write this book, but it took me six years to convince him that people wanted—even needed—to hear him now more than ever. "Bacon, nobody cares what I say, because nobody remembers who I am!"

I know, I know. He was a hard man to argue with, even when you knew you were right. But he actually believed it.

When Bo was still coaching, he helped out the Special Olympics by playing basketball with mentally challenged kids. He loved it because they had no idea who he was, and they didn't care. "I was just some old guy who came down to play basketball with them."

That's pretty much how Schembechler saw himself: Just some old guy who once coached football.

We knew better.

John U. Bacon
Ann Arbor, Michigan
January 2007

Introduction

Bacon's been after me to write this book ever since I gave him my personal papers ten years ago. But whenever he brought up the idea of writing one final book, I always said no. I mean, hey, I'm not Jonas Salk. I'm just a football coach. Besides, I already wrote a book with Mitch Albom a couple decades ago—and it was a bestseller. So why would anyone want to read another book by me?

"Because you've got a lot more to say," Bacon kept telling me.

About what?

"About being honest and direct and confident. But most of all, about how to *lead*!"

Now *that*, I admit, I know something about! But there are already lots of books out there about leadership. Check out any bookstore, and you'll see a new self-proclaimed expert every month—guys who write about "Altering Your Optics" and "Knowing Your Core Competencies" and all that stuff. Maybe there's something to it. I don't know. But the problem is, most of those guys have never actually *led*.

Well, I have. I spent twelve years working for three Hall of Fame coaches—Doyt Perry, Ara Parseghian and Woody Hayes—then led Miami of Ohio for six years and the University of Michigan for twenty-one. I've seen a lot, and I've done a lot.

I didn't do it with fancy theories. I did it with fundamental values—values I learned from my parents and my mentors and passed on to my players. Values that they have passed on to their employees and their children and even their grandchildren. Values that are as vital today as they were when I started coaching half a century ago.

I *believe* in these values. But I didn't believe anyone would want to hear me talk about them after I retired in 1990. Boy, was I wrong about that! I started getting calls to give speeches around the country to corporations, to hospitals, to schools and to service groups. They all want to know the same things: how to get their careers started, how to build a team, how to become better leaders. I thought it'd slow down, but I get more calls every year, from more groups, offering more money. If I wanted to, I could give a speech every day of the year, and get more money for one hour of talking than I earned my entire first year of coaching the Wolverines.

Hey, I'm as surprised as you are. I figured they'd forget about me, but it's been just the opposite. I'm giving speeches now to people who weren't even old enough to see me coach, and they eat it up. Now, you have to ask yourself: Why do they want to listen to some old football coach tell his stories?

Maybe it's because our leaders today—the people who are running our corporations, our government, our schools—seem lost. After we discovered that some of our so-called best and brightest don't know the difference between right and wrong, maybe I shouldn't be so shocked that even young people are dying to hear someone tell it to them straight. And mean it.

So what do I have to say that hasn't been said? I'll be the first to tell you there's nothing revolutionary in what I have to say. Heck no. The lessons I want to teach are simple as can be, but they must not be that *easy,* because not many people in this world seem to be able to follow them anymore.

Hey. I'm just a football coach. I'm not going to try to tell you how your industry works. But I know how to do the things *everyone* needs to know if they're going to be successful. I don't care if you're running a Fortune 500 company or a Girl Scout troop. You need to know what to do from the day you become a leader to the day you step down. How to pick the right mentors, and how to lay down your laws when it's your turn at the top. How to hire your people—and fire them, when you have to. How to train them, motivate them and mold them into a team. How to get them to execute what you want, perfectly, every time. How to handle conflicts and crises and troublemakers and guys who just aren't getting it. How to keep outsiders from meddling with your program, and insiders from undermining it. How to handle sudden setbacks, crushing pressure and constant criticism. How to handle failure—and how to handle success. Even when to call it quits, and how to do it the right way.

And trust me: There's a right way and a wrong way to do *all* these things.

The key to all these lessons is in the details, the application, the execution. Okay, you want to be honest. Who doesn't? But how do you communicate that to your people? How do you *show them* that you're going to be honest—no matter what it costs you?

You want to be fair with your people? Fine. But what are you willing to *sacrifice* to do it? Do you have the courage to send your top performer packing just because he broke one of your rules?

Everyone wants to set goals, but do you have the *guts* to let *your people*, not *you*, set the standards for your team? I did, it works, and I can show you how.

It's not just *wanting* to do the right thing. It's *knowing how to do it*!

I can tell you this: The fundamental values that worked for me coaching football work everywhere else, too—in business, in medicine, in law, in education. I know this because I've seen my players succeed in all those fields, using the same principles they learned playing on our team. Guys like Jimmy Hackett, the CEO of Steelcase, and Dave Brandon, the CEO of Domino's Pizza, both tops in their fields. *And these principles never change.* They are the key to success, *real* success, and that's what this book is all about.

I'll be honest. I don't know how much longer I'm going to be around. When you have your first heart attack at age forty, you're probably living on borrowed time.

My body isn't worth a damn anymore, and all my records will be broken one day. I know this—but it doesn't bother me, because these values will outlast everything else I've done.

I'm seventy-seven now, and it's time I told you what I've learned.

Bo Schembechler
Ann Arbor, Michigan
October 2006

I

PREPARE TO LEAD

1

You Better Start with Your Heart

Let's start with first things first: *passion*. Because without that, nothing else I'm going to tell you in this book is going to be worth a damn. It just won't do you any good.

Because the fact is, you're never going to be able to lead others effectively unless you put your whole heart into what you're doing. If it's just a job to you, it's going to be just a job to them. And trust me: You're not going to fool them.

So you need to find something you really love to do, because otherwise you're going to hate it. And if you hate your work, you'll never put in the kind of effort the guys at the top are putting into it. You'll lose!

Once you figure out what you love to do, don't worry about the money or the prestige or anything else. Those things won't make you happy if you hate your job.

For me, it was easy to figure out what I loved—football! The game got me at an early age, so when people talk about all the sacrifices I'm supposed to have made pursuing this crazy life—in time, in money, in status—I have to laugh. They weren't sacrifices to me. I got to coach! And that's all I ever wanted to do.

I'm from Barberton, Ohio, and went to Oakdale grade school, where we had baseball, basketball and track teams, but no football. So you could only play football if you were willing to get to the high school and practice with the freshman team—and it wasn't easy. You had to go down the hill, across the tracks, over the canal and walk five miles to get to Barberton High on the north end of town. And if you were going to get there on time, you had to run.

Nobody else in my class would go with me, but as soon as the school bell rang each day, I started running down that hill and across town for freshman football practice, and I kept it up for two years. When I was in eighth grade, near the end of the football season, the Oakdale basketball coach wanted me to quit freshman football because I was a starter on his team, too. I said, "No way. I've got to play in the last football game!" So that's what I did.

They drove us over to Akron in this dump truck with two benches in the back for the players to sit on. A dump truck! It took us an hour to get there and an hour to get back, with the wind and the rain and the cold coming in, whipping all around. This was no school bus—heck no. That would have felt like a *Cadillac* to us!

We get there, and no one's in the stands. No one. I mean, the Akron parents weren't even showing up for this one. Guess they were smarter than we were.

You consider the whole thing—the daily run to practice, the

distance to our games, the dump truck, the empty stands—and you'd have to say we were a little crazy to do this. But I loved it. I *knew* I'd rather be in the back of that damn dump truck going to play some football game in the freezing cold in front of nobody than standing in a nice warm gym wearing shorts playing in front of a big crowd.

Football is what I loved.

By the time I got to tenth grade, I'd already played freshman football for three years. There was no question I was going to be a starter on the high school varsity. But the question was where our coach, Karl Harter, was going to put me. Our two big plays were the reverse and the reverse pass. You've got to have right-ies to run those plays, and fast ones, too.

Well, I was a lefty, so there's one strike. And we had guys who could run a lot faster than I could. There's two strikes. So I went to Coach Harter and said, "Where do you need the most help?"

"Guard."

"Then put me at guard!" Hell, I didn't care. I just wanted to play. And I started the next three years.

If you want to know why I've always loved the big lugs on the line the most—well, you can thank Coach Harter for that.

Even then, I knew—and I don't know how to put this without sounding like a jerk—but I knew I had a way with people, and the reason I had a way with people is because I liked 'em. And the reason I chose to coach football instead of baseball or basketball is because, of all the athletes out there, the football players were the ones I liked and respected the most. And I think that showed in the way I coached them.

When I graduated from Miami of Ohio, I knew I was going to be a coach. I was as sure of that as anything I knew—and nothing was going to stop me! To be honest, I always thought I'd be a high school coach—and that was fine with me. I didn't care about money or fame or any of that. I just wanted to coach.

And let me tell you, now that I'm looking back on the whole thing: I made the right call!

2

Seek Mentors, Not Money

When you're just starting out, it's better to make peanuts for a great leader than it is to get some big salary from a mediocre one.

But one of the biggest mistakes I see young coaches make—and young businessmen and doctors and lawyers, too, for that matter—is thinking their first job should make them rich or famous. When you're in your twenties, those things shouldn't matter. Maybe they never should. They didn't to me. But especially when you're young, big money doesn't matter. Big names don't either.

Good organizations matter. Good bosses matter.

It would've been a big mistake for me to take a job as an offensive coordinator for some hotshot who really didn't know what he was doing—and there are plenty of them out there—than to make nothing running errands for Woody Hayes when he was just starting out at Ohio State, struggling to build a winning program, and no one really knew who he was.

And I know this because that's exactly what I did.

If you want to become a great leader, you need to *prepare*

yourself to become a great leader, and the best way to do that is to *study* great leaders. I worked for Doyt Perry at Bowling Green, Ara Parseghian when he was at Northwestern, and Woody Hayes at Ohio State. Every one of those guys is a Hall of Fame coach. I worked sixteen-hour days doing everything they asked me to, and I didn't get paid squat.

But it was the best training any coach in America ever received. I studied them, I watched them every second, I knew them cold.

This is what I learned.

When Woody Hayes left Miami of Ohio in 1951, right after my senior year, to take the head coaching position at Ohio State, I didn't have to think too long to accept his offer to go with him. This was the first of my two stints with Woody, which formed the bookends of my twelve years as an assistant coach.

But back then, there was no such thing as a graduate assistant, so he got me a job down at the tax department in Columbus, where I handed out the stamps that served as sales tax rebates for church groups, charities and other nonprofits. I got paid $100 a month. I wasn't paid a cent to coach.

When the coaches needed coffee, I got the coffee. When they needed someone to get their laundry, I got it. When they had to pick up recruits at the airport, I picked them up. I did all their grunt work, and I did it without complaining.

What did I get in return? I learned how to recruit, I learned how to run a practice, I learned everything I could, from top to bottom, from one of the greatest coaches who ever lived. I even learned a thing or two about alumni relations.

Ohio State had no athletic scholarships in the early 1950s, so the alums would get the players jobs in town. Well, Woody's first year at Ohio State was one of the worst in Ohio State history. The Buckeyes finished 4-3-2, and adding insult to injury, they lost to a mediocre Michigan team, 7–0.

Not long after we got back to Columbus, Woody decided to have a staff meeting at his house, a modest little home at 1711 Cardiff Road. He had one of those old Bell & Howell 16mm projectors, and while we were watching the film from the Michigan game, he was getting hotter and hotter, until he finally picked the damn projector up and heaved it against the wall, smashing the whole thing to bits. "I will not subject the people of Columbus to that kind of football!"

Now, I'm just a wide-eyed twenty-two-year-old kid, sitting in the back of the room—and I'd already played two years for Woody at Miami of Ohio—but that made quite an impression on me. He was serious!

A few days later we were back in our coaches conference room, when one of the staffers opened the door and said, "Woody, the alums are going to cut all the players' jobs downtown!"

We were stunned. "All the jobs?"

"All of them."

Obviously, the alums weren't happy—but they didn't realize who they were dealing with. "Well, if that's the case," Woody said, "then I have a message for them: Screw 'em! I'll pay the players myself!" He wasn't kidding. Woody was ready to mortgage his house and pay their tuition himself, right then and there, and I never doubted for a second he'd do it. But when the alums heard about his resolve they decided that would make them look pretty bad, so they backed down.

The next year, the Buckeyes go 6-3, they beat a 12th-ranked Michigan team, 27–7, and the alums were on Woody's side from then on. Before he was done, he rewarded them with thirteen Big Ten titles and five national crowns.

What did I learn? If you cave in to outside pressure—I don't care if it's alums or stockholders or special interests—you're done as a leader. Woody was willing to risk everything, even his home, to do it his way.

As soon as I finished that 1951 season, I served two years in the United States Army. I boarded a bus to Cleveland headed to Camp Rucker, Alabama, where the air feels like a wet rag on your face, then coached at Presbyterian College in Clinton, South Carolina, for one season.

The next year, 1955, Doyt Perry—who'd been one of Woody's assistants at Ohio State—got the top job at Bowling Green, and he asked my old buddy Bill Gunlock and me to join him. That didn't take a lot of thinking, either.

Now, Doyt was the sweetest guy who ever came down the pike—everyone loved him—but one day, Bill and I got into a big argument with Doyt about some defensive scheme or other on our way to the office. The two of us were walking up the steps behind Doyt, going on and on about why we should use this strategy we'd come up with, until finally Doyt got to the top of the steps and whipped around with his finger pointing right at us. "Now I know you two guys are a lot smarter than I am and you know more football than I'll ever know and you have a million great ideas. But I've got some news for you: *I am the head coach!*"

Bill and I looked at each other—and we both laughed! We didn't have any doubt about who was in charge after that. There was a lot of clarity in Doyt's message. That settled that, and we never questioned him again.

You can be sure I took that lesson with me to Ann Arbor. Just ask my assistants.

The following season, 1956, I left Doyt and Bowling Green— with his blessings—to become an assistant for Ara Parseghian at Northwestern University. I had made it to the Big Ten! I knew that's where I wanted to be, and I was working for a great coach. Of course, everyone remembers Ara when he led Notre Dame to a couple national titles, but a lot of people don't realize he led the Wildcats to some of their best seasons before that.

Ara was not a big ego guy, he was great with players, he was a wonderful motivator, and he understood the game so well he could come up with things no one else had thought of. He was probably the most imaginative coach I'd ever seen, always adapting his plays to his players instead of the other way around like most coaches do. Heck, we used to call his practice field "The Laboratory," because that's where he'd try every trick in the book on Mondays, testing this and experimenting with that, just to see what might work that Saturday.

Before Ara arrived, Northwestern hadn't had a winning season in five years, but in his first year Northwestern went 4-4-1, and everyone was encouraged. But in Ara's second season, 1957, everything went to hell. We lost nine games—every single game we played! For a coach, that's just about the most difficult situation you have to face.

We could keep our opponents down to one or two touchdowns, but we couldn't score for our lives. And I was working with the offense!

Losing creates all kinds of other problems too—poor morale, nagging injuries, lackluster effort. The players were spending more time in the PR office than in the weight room. It was just a mess. I never experienced anything like that in all my years of coaching—and thank God for that.

I learned an awful lot from Ara in my first year at Northwestern, but I learned a heckuva lot more from him that second season, when we lost 'em all. And what I learned was how a real leader leads when things aren't going his way.

Ara treated the staff as though we were winning every game. He never gave the slightest inclination that we were the problem. He not once blamed any assistant or any player for any loss we suffered that year. NOT ONCE.

"Stick with it, guys, and we'll get through this," he'd tell us. "We're going to be okay." We all kept busting our butts for Ara, working past midnight, doing everything we could to get that guy a victory.

I'm not saying there wasn't some bitching among the *players*. When you're losing every game, every player thinks he deserves more playing time. But I promise you this: There was a whole lot less bitching on that team than I've heard on teams that won half their games—and there was absolutely no, but *no*, bickering among the coaches.

And that wasn't even the most impressive thing Ara did that year.

Stu Holcomb was Northwestern's athletic director, and his son Chip was a backup quarterback on the varsity. In the middle of this losing streak, Stu kept cranking up the pressure for Ara to start his son. At one of our staff meetings, Ara laid the situation on the table. Then he asked us point-blank: "What do you think?" The thing is, there wasn't anybody on the staff pounding on the table to make a quarterback change just because we were losing. We knew there had to be a ton of pressure on Ara to put Stu's son in, but our quarterback wasn't the problem. And that's exactly what we told him when he asked us. He just nodded.

Another coach—maybe most coaches—would have caved in to their boss just to save their hides. But Ara held firm. He didn't change quarterbacks, or even consider doing it. And every one of us who walked out of the coaches room that day felt the same way I did: Ara Parseghian is a stand-up guy. He is a *leader.* I want to work for this guy!

And that's why that losing season didn't break Ara's back: Because he's a confident guy, and he knew he could coach. His staff remained dedicated to him and his program the entire season.

You'd think my two years at Northwestern would have been a horrible experience, but it wasn't. It was a *great* experience, because Ara had put together a stellar staff—they're all still good friends of mine, especially Alex Agase—but mostly, it was because *Ara* was there.

The result? Put this down: Ara Parseghian lost every game that year, but the next year his team went 5-4—Northwestern's first winning season in eight years.

When Ara took the Notre Dame job five years later, in 1963, he left Evanston as one of only three coaches in the last *century* of Northwestern football to post a winning record. And of course, from there he won two national titles and Coach of the Year at Notre Dame. Don't tell me he didn't deserve it.

But that 0-9 year? He didn't get any awards for that, but let me tell you: THAT was the most impressive year of his coaching career.

When Woody came calling for me the second time, in 1958, the Buckeyes had just won their second national title under him—the same season Northwestern hadn't won a game at all. Still, I had a hard time deciding whether to leave Ara. Think about that. I'm working for the *worst team in the country,* and *the national champs* want to hire me, and amazingly, I'm debating it! In fact, I had made up my mind to turn down Woody and stay with Ara when Alex Agase invited me to play some pool in his basement.

Alex is a big bear of a man—he played linebacker for the Cleveland Browns—and he got around to business pretty quickly. A politician, he isn't.

"I hear Woody's offering you a job," he said. He took his shot—crack!—and sat down. "What are you going to do?"

I picked up my cue and lined up my shot. "Alex, I'm turning it down. I like the guys here, I like what Ara's doing, and Northwestern is going to be successful."

Alex stood up—he's a lot bigger than I am—and said, "Now you listen to me, you dumb sonuvabitch. Don't you *dare* turn that job down. You're going to Ohio State!"

I swear to you I was not going to go leave until that moment— but Agase could be pretty persuasive! I left Ara and Northwestern to return to Ohio State as Woody's assistant in 1958, and I stayed there until I became the head coach at Miami in 1963.

Now, here's the kicker. In my first year back with Woody, the Buckeyes were coming off a national championship year and Northwestern, the team I just left, was of course coming off that 0-9 season. And I'll be damned if Ara's Wildcats don't beat Woody's Buckeyes, 21-0—Ohio State's only loss all year! In fact, as soon as I left Northwestern, Ara's teams won three out of four against Ohio State.

Well, that'll teach me.

My second year back in Columbus, 1959, Ohio State goes 3-5-1 and finishes eighth in the Big Ten—Woody's worst season ever. You have to wonder: How did I keep getting hired? I must have been the worst luck charm in the world.

*   *   *

I have to tell you an aside, to prove my point about money not being the most important thing. In 1962, I'm making $6,000 a year coaching for Woody. He'd tell us, "I don't care what I make, so I don't care what you make, either."

Get this: By the mid-1970s, Woody had already won five undisputed national titles, he was one of the most successful coaches in America, and probably the most famous person in the entire state of Ohio. And he was making $29,400—lowest in the Big Ten. And you know who was making the second-lowest? Yours truly. You can check it. And neither one of us cared. What we cared about were Big Ten titles, and no one else in our league went to the Rose Bowl during the decade we were both coaching.

Well, even if Woody didn't care about money, the Ohio State administrators did. They were embarrassed by Woody's salary, so they went directly to Woody, three years in a row, and damn near *begged* him to take a raise—and he still wouldn't do it! President Ford had asked every American to do everything he could to keep inflation down, and Woody figured that included him.

So when he told us way back when that he didn't care what any of us made, including him, I guess you'd have to say he meant it.

During my second stint with Woody, a businessman in town asked me out to lunch and offered to double my salary if I would work for him as a real estate appraiser.

I didn't hesitate. "Hey, I'm already doing what I always wanted to do. If it's outside of football, I'm not interested. But," I told him, "Bill Gunlock's working with me, and he's got four kids and no money, so you might want to talk to him."

Bill won't know it until he reads this book, but because of that lunch, that businessman sought out Bill, he hired him, and Bill applied all the things we learned coaching football to business, and did very well for himself. When I called Bill in 1989 to tell him I was about to retire from coaching, and I was feeling good about it, he said, "That's funny, because I'm about to sell my company and retire, too."

"Really? For how much?"

Let's just say it was many millions.

"Why you son of a bitch!"

Even if I gave ten speeches a day, I couldn't catch Bill in a thousand years. But I don't care, so long as Bill keeps picking up the tab for our dinners. We both got what we wanted.

The simple question is: Are you doing what *you* always wanted to do? I always think of that poor SOB who gets up every day to go to a job he doesn't even like. Well, hell's fire. How do you do that? I have no idea—and I know Woody didn't either. We wouldn't trade our coaching careers for anything in the world.

After my slow start as Woody's assistant, we won a national title my fourth year back, in 1961. But what I learned from Woody was this: He was the greatest teacher and the hardest worker I have ever seen in my entire life, to this day.

Where Ara was humble and innovative and easy to work with, Woody could be arrogant, stubborn and just plan difficult. Very difficult. But this was a very complex man, with the most brilliant intellect I've ever seen.

Woody was not innovative. He didn't waste any plays trying to fool you. That was not his game. No, his strategy was to teach his team *fundamental techniques* better than anyone else, and win game after game through simple, mistake-free football.

He coached the kind of teams that you simply did not want to get behind in the first half, because he was going to make it just about impossible for you to come back in the second half. You couldn't move! He'd just grind you down—and man, was that demoralizing when you were on the other end of it.

That's another lesson I took to Ann Arbor—much to Woody's chagrin, I'm sure.

I remember when Lee Corso was Indiana's head coach in the 1970s—this was before he went on to become a college football expert—and he tells us at the preseason Big Ten meeting in Chicago one year that unless we opened up the recruiting season to run year-round, eight of the ten coaches in the league photo that season were going to be gone in two years.

I just laughed. I told Corso, "If we had year-round recruiting, maybe you'll outwork me—*maybe*—but I guarantee you this: *No one* in this league will *ever* outwork Woody Hayes. It's just not possible!"

Put all those things together, and what do you get? I worked my tail off, I didn't make a dime, but I learned everything I needed to know from three of the greatest leaders the game has ever seen.

Smartest move I ever made.

3

Wait for the Right Opportunity

What did I do with all this knowledge I acquired from Doyt and Ara and Woody?

I didn't use it to sell myself, that's for sure. I used it to become the best assistant coach I could be. I had no qualms about being an assistant coach, and I thought I was the best offensive line coach there ever was!

I have never applied for a job in my entire life. I have never, not once, prepared a résumé. I just figured if I worked hard and got really good at this, someone's going to say, "This guy is good," and I'd get plenty of opportunities. And I was right.

Don't worry about marketing yourself. Just be good at what you're doing now and enjoy it, and things will take care of themselves. Yes, I know in some fields you have to get your résumé out and all that, but I think it's overestimated. In most businesses, word gets around pretty fast—and hey, that's what headhunters are for.

That was the final lesson I learned from my days as an assistant coach: Don't waste your time and energy looking for the next job. Take care of the job you've got now. If you're good at what you're doing now, they'll find you. Trust me, word will get out there, and they'll find you.

They always do.

And when that happens, don't jump at the first offer, just because you think it's a promotion. Being an assistant for a great organization is better than being the head honcho at a place where you're being set up for failure. You've got to wait for the right opportunity, working for the right people—because if you're impatient, you're going to regret it.

I left Woody and Ohio State to become the head coach at Miami of Ohio in 1963, and that was a darn good job. The cradle of coaches! You're talking Colonel Earl Blaik, Paul Brown and Weeb Ewbank, not to mention my coaches, Sid Gillman, Woody and Ara.

In my six years as head coach in Oxford, Ohio, we won 70 percent of our games and a couple league titles—and it didn't take too long at a place like that before bigger schools started calling.

I never made a pitch for any job, because I figured if they didn't already know about me and what I was doing, they wouldn't have called me in the first place. And I certainly wasn't going to beg for any job, no matter how good it looked, because I already had a good one at Miami.

After we won our conference title in my third and fourth seasons at Miami—1965 & 1966—Wisconsin called. From the outside, it seemed like a pretty good job. Wisconsin's a good school in a great league. It was about ten o'clock on a Sunday

night when I walk into this meeting room to face twenty guys
sitting around—and some board member falls asleep, right there
in front of me! Now what does that tell you?

They also had a student on the committee, and this kid asks
how I would handle Clem Turner, a Cincinnati kid, who was
always in trouble. Well, how the heck do I know how I would
handle Clem Turner? I've never met him! And that's exactly
what I told that kid. But I'm thinking, Who the hell's running
this show?

The whole thing lasted maybe forty minutes, and the *second*
I was out that door I walked right to the nearest pay phone and
called Ivy Williamson, the Wisconsin athletic director, and told
him to withdraw my name from consideration. Keep in mind, I'd
already learned they were going to hire a guy named John Coatta
from Notre Dame, so the whole thing was just a big dog-and-
pony show, anyway. And I didn't appreciate that, either.

But I knew one thing: I didn't want that job, whether they
wanted me or not.

Now here's a funny thing. After I'm back home in bed, at about
five in the morning, the phone rings. It's Bob Knight, who was
the head coach at West Point at that time, when he was maybe
twenty-five years old. We'd met a few times at Ohio State, when
I was an assistant under Woody and Knight was on the Buckeyes'
national championship basketball team.

Knight says, "Bo, you went up to Wisconsin and interviewed
for that job. You know they've been after me for the basketball
position, so what do you think?"

"I can't tell you what to do," I said, "but I have to tell you, I
was unimpressed. If I was in your shoes, I wouldn't go to Wisconsin. But that's just my personal opinion."

Knight turned it down, for the same reasons I did.

But hot damn, can you imagine both of us coaching at Wisconsin? That would've been something! And that's another lesson, too, now that I think of it: When you're interviewing candidates, they're judging you, too, and word gets out. Wisconsin lost out on two up-and-coming coaches because they simply didn't have their act together.

Same week I returned from Madison—hell, it might have been the same night Bob called—I got a call from the North Carolina athletic director to come down to Chapel Hill. His timing couldn't have been worse. I had only been interviewed once, and I was already sick of the whole thing. I told him I wasn't going, but he asked me at least to look over the situation. I finally agreed to come down and talk. Just talk. I get to Chapel Hill on a Sunday, I've got a really negative attitude already, and then they bring in the president dressed like he's been working out in the yard all day.

"Here we go again," I'm thinking. "Same thing!"

But it was a good situation. It felt like Miami, only bigger. This was the only job before Michigan I wanted. If they had offered it to me, I probably would have taken it, and I think we could have succeeded there, but they finally gave it to Bill Dooley.

After that, I'd had enough. I wasn't going to jump for just anything. I interviewed with Tulane and Pitt, and was offered both jobs, but turned them down. When Vanderbilt and Kansas State called, I said no on the spot. No more visits.

All those schools were bigger than Miami, and most of them were in great conferences like the Big Eight, the ACC, the SEC. But if you've already got a great job—and I did—you can afford to be patient, even picky. Like I said before, not every so-called promotion is a step up.

The process also made me realize I was a Big Ten guy, through and through. It's the league I admired the most, the conference I knew the best. I had already been recruiting Big Ten country for years. It was no accident, when I was at Michigan, that so many of our players came from Ohio.

So that was it. The Big Ten, that's where I wanted to coach, and I was going to hold out until I got it.

Just a few weeks after I finished my sixth year at Miami, in December of 1968, I got a call from Bump Elliott, who had been an All-American at Michigan on Fritz Crisler's national title teams in the late 1940s, and had just completed his tenth season as the Wolverines' head coach. He was moving up to associate athletic director under Don Canham, the former track coach, who was starting his second year as Michigan's athletic director.

I was definitely interested in Michigan—how could you not be?—but when Canham called, I told him I wasn't going through any of the crap I'd gone through at Wisconsin. He assured me there wouldn't be any of that nonsense with him, and that was what I wanted to hear.

I met with exactly three guys: Bump, Canham and Marcus Plante, the faculty rep who had once been president of the NCAA. That's it. They didn't need some silly committee or student rep to check me out, and I didn't need any dime-store tour of the campus to appreciate what Michigan had to offer. I knew them and they knew me.

Things happened real fast—a good sign. Canham called me a couple days later and said, "Bo, I'm offering you the job at Michigan."

And brilliant me, all I say is, "Good." That's it. Just, "Good." How do you like that?

When he asked when I could come up to finalize the deal, I said, "Right now." Turned out "right now" was the day before Christmas, so I drove up there the next evening, on Christmas Day. Clearly, we were both interested in each other.

Being the hard-driving negotiator that I am, when the issue of salary finally came up, I said, "I don't care about money." Boy, talk about music to Canham's ears! This is a guy who inherited a quarter-million-dollar deficit, and, shall we say, knew how to squeeze a nickel.

Canham asked me, "What are you making at Miami?"

"Nineteen thousand a year. But they've promised me a $1,000 raise."

"Then I'll give you $21,000."

We had no contract. Just a handshake. And for twenty-one years, that was always enough between Don and me. Another good sign.

Canham realized the people at Miami could have thrown a little more money at me to keep me, but they couldn't compete with Yost's hole in the ground—the biggest stadium in the nation—or the prestige of Michigan.

Canham knew that he was offering something special, and so did I.

I took it happily.

I was a lot less concerned about Canham giving me more money than making sure he was committed to giving my assistants a living wage, improving the facilities, and paying to develop game film—a big thing in those days. When you're starting out, it's not money you need, it's *support*! And Canham gave us all those things without flinching.

The most important thing Don Canham gave me, though, was control over my program. He couldn't have given me that autonomy unless he had it himself, and the interview process proved that. I only had one person to please, and that was Donald B. Canham. And that held true every year I worked at Michigan. I don't think ADs have that kind of control anymore, and they probably never will again.

Bottom line: When I was starting out, I wasn't worried about money or prestige or any of that stuff. I waited until I found a position where I could succeed—and then I went to work.

That's why I tell young coaches, my former players, anyone who'll listen: For God's sakes, quit worrying about your next job. Just do the best you can at the job *you have now,* and the offers will come.

And when they do, if you have confidence in yourself, you don't have to feel that you can't turn it down if it isn't quite right for you because you fear you'll never get another offer. You will.

Wait for the right opportunity, and turn down all the rest. It will make all the difference.

II

Take Charge

4

Throw a Bucket of Cold Water

When you take over a new operation, some people will tell you that you ought to lie low, and look around before you do anything. But that's not me—because I just don't think it works.

I say, whatever your philosophy, whatever your standards, whatever your expectations, you establish those on Day One. Don't waste a second! Let them adjust to *you*, not the other way around. You can always soften up if you need to, but you can't get tougher later on. It's a lot better to throw a bucket of cold water on them on your first day than it is to try to coax them into the cold water, toe by toe. Because they won't do it that way.

Your people aren't stupid, and they're not lazy, either. They'll respond—and faster than you think.

Now, Ann Arbor isn't Oxford, Ohio. It's bigger, more liberal, more active. In 1960 John F. Kennedy introduced the idea of the Peace Corps on the steps of Michigan's student union, and a few years later LBJ announced the Great Society during graduation in

Michigan Stadium. When I got here in January 1969, Ann Arbor was at its hottest. Antiwar demonstrations, racial protests, students taking over the president's office—you name it.

I'll never forget the day Will Perry, our sports information director, came down that first year and said, "There's something new going on, and you need to know about it. *The Michigan Daily* has a woman sports editor, and she's covering football."

"You've got to be kidding me."

"No, Bo, it's true."

"Well, what am I going to do? I can't let her in that locker room."

A few days later, down comes the cutest little thing you ever saw. Robin Wright. Her dad was a professor here, local girl. So, how are we going to handle this?

Here's what we did. We made a deal that I would talk to her in the entryway between the locker room and the meeting room every day after practice. Every day, she waited right there for me. I told her how practice went, and she wrote her story for the next day's paper. And even then you could tell, this girl was a sharp one.

She's a big star now at *The Washington Post,* covering the White House, the war, you name it. We've stayed in touch, and get lunch together when she's back in town. Just a few years ago, I was on my bicycle machine, working away, watching TV, when she comes up on the screen, making a speech about the Middle East to a packed house. She still looked cute as the dickens. She ran down all the countries, and she was right on every one of them!

But boy, I was so proud of her, the little girl who used to be the sports editor of the *Daily.* Ha! How do ya like that?

Some of the things happening on Michigan's campus I didn't like so much. At one point during my first season they invited

Dr. Benjamin Spock, Timothy Leary and a bunch of other guys to host an antiwar rally—in our stadium! Leary started burning draft cards, and dropped one on our "M" at midfield and burned a black spot right on our brand-new Tartan Turf. When I saw that—boy was I hot!

You see, I was already a certified "old school" guy from Ohio, trained by Woody Hayes no less—and I had a lot to prove as a coach. So you've got these two trains headed toward each other—this new coach and this wild campus—and something had to give. And it wasn't going to be me!

When Don Canham took over the athletic department from Fritz Crisler in 1968, the year before he hired me, he inherited a $250,000 debt, a half-empty football stadium, and facilities that were about to collapse.

Heck, Canham had trouble finding a room big enough to fit the whole football team. No fancy football buildings back then. So we met in the media room of Crisler Arena, but that was so cramped that whenever we met for Sunday film sessions and the like, we'd get together in a makeshift classroom we created under the stands of the baseball park. We entered by pulling the garage door up, and pulled it down behind us when we left. Michigan football!

It was January, dark and cold, with snow and slush every-where. After the players shuffled through the door and into their chairs, I wasn't too impressed with what I saw: a lot of guys slumped down in their seats, chewing gum, wearing mustaches and muttonchops and huge Afros. A bunch of guys who lived at a house they called the Den of the Mellow Men—can you believe it?—sauntered in ten minutes late, and weren't too apologetic about it. It so happened that the residents of that house included

Thom Darden, Reggie McKenzie, Glenn Doughty, Billy Taylor and Mike Taylor, all big stars. Would I back down, for fear of not alienating a mother lode of talent like that? We'd see.

There was reason to wonder if they'd listen to me. When Canham hired me, one of the Detroit papers' headlines read, "BO WHO?" Don got a lot of letters from disgruntled alumni, too, one of whom said my name sounded like "some German butcher's."

These guys had talent, more than most people gave them credit for. But they played football like it was a recreational sport—and that's exactly how they looked when they walked in that day. They never viewed their team as a championship-caliber squad. How else can you explain how Michigan had won just one Big Ten title in the previous eighteen years? Michigan football! I'm sorry, casual football just does not fly—not when you're playing in the Big Ten and have to face Woody Hayes at the end of every season.

From the very start, my entire focus was to beat Ohio State. That was a tall order, because they were the returning national champs, ranked number one in the nation, and had just beaten Michigan the year before, 50–14. In the waning minutes of that game, when the Buckeyes scored their last touchdown to make the score, 48–14, Woody went for the two-point conversion, just to twist the knife. When a reporter asked him afterward why he went for two, he said, "Because the rules wouldn't let me go for three." Boy, that's gotta burn you! And those guys remembered that, very bitterly. But they didn't seem ready to do anything about it.

Time for a change.

The first thing I did was tell them how we are going to conduct ourselves at meetings. "From this day forward, you will sit up straight—no slouching—with both feet on the floor. You will have no hats on, and you'll be looking straight ahead, paying attention, staring at me just like I'm staring at you. And from now on you'd better be on time—every time!" I didn't phrase it as a request, or a question—because it wasn't one. It was intended as a command. Period. And that's how it was received.

For punctuation, I stared at the Mellow Men when I said it—and some of them stared right back! I didn't care. I wasn't there to make friends that day—and it's a good thing, because I'm sure I didn't. I figured this was the easy stuff, and if we couldn't show up on time, looking right and acting right, we weren't going to be able to do anything else.

I didn't stop there. I already knew a lot of the players lived "off campus"—*far* off campus, in Ypsilanti. Rent was cheaper there, and we had a lot of players who were married or about to get married—guys like Dan Dierdorf, Henry Hill, Garvie Craw and Jimmy Betts, some of our best players—and a few of them already had kids. Even worse, to my way of thinking, no one in the athletic department knew where they lived, how to get ahold of them, or what they were up to. Sorry, you just can't have that, either.

"From now on," I said, *"everyone* is going to live in the city of Ann Arbor. Freshmen *and sophomores* are going to live in the dormitories, upperclassmen will live in apartments near campus, and married students will live in university married housing."

Boy, that created a stir. The freshmen didn't know exactly what was going on, but they could tell the seniors were alarmed. No one had told them where they were going to live before that. No one even thought of it. They started sitting up straight after I said that.

But if I said one thing that day that resonated with everyone, it's when I squelched any illusions of favoritism, racism or any other -isms by saying, flat out, "I'm going to treat you all the same. Like dogs!" When I adjourned the meeting they knew—

whatever was going to happen—that the next season was not going to be recreational touch football.

I wasn't there to tell them how great they were. I was there to change the tone of that team. From the looks on their faces after I finished, you'd have to say I succeeded.

The issue of race on an American college football team, especially one in Ann Arbor, couldn't be avoided. When I told the players they'd all be treated the same—like dogs—my sense is that I probably scared the white players, but reassured the black ones. What they wanted was a fair shot—something they had a hard time getting at most schools. Keep in mind, in 1969, the Southern schools were just starting to integrate their teams, and even in the North, it was common practice at many schools to recruit no more than three or four black players—God knows why.

When I went to coaches conferences, other coaches often asked me how I coached the black players. "What do you mean? I coach my players all the same." I didn't make it any harder for them, and I didn't make it any easier. I didn't see much room for discussion on this point.

The black players on the team responded to that. That's all they asked for. So when the Black Action Movement on the Michigan campus asked them to be part of a sit-in during halftime, they told the organizers they wanted no part of it. When Jesse Jackson came to campus, he tried to convince my players they were being exploited. They told him they weren't, at least not on the football team. I felt good about that.

I made only one exception for the black players. The day after my first team meeting, when I told everyone they'd better shave, Jim Betts came into my office to talk to me. "Coach, you've got to understand, for the black players, the mustache represents a part of our heritage."

"You have *got* to be kidding me."

"No, Coach, I'm sincere."

We went back and forth a few times, but Jimmy wasn't budging—and what the hell did I know? I was from Barberton, Ohio.

The next day, I met with the team again. "It has come to my attention that the black players on this team feel they cannot with a good conscience shave their mustaches, because they feel it is a part of their heritage."

I let that sink in.

"So, I am allowing them to keep their mustaches. But as for you white players—you have no heritage! So shave 'em off!"

That broke the tension in the room.

Now, get this. For years I kept asking Betts, "Honestly, were you pulling my leg?"

Finally, twenty years later, he said, "Coach, I have to confess: I'd just grown that mustache, I was proud of it, and I had to think of some reason you'd let me keep it!"

"You dog!"

A few days later I met with each player individually in my office. This was something we would do with every player twice a year, every year, after the season ended and again after we completed spring football, but those guys had never done it before. They didn't know what to expect.

One of the first guys who walked in was Dick Caldarazzo, a senior offensive guard. I'd seen the tapes and I knew he was good. But that's not what I was going to tell him.

"You're too small to play offensive guard," I said. "What're you, 5-8?"

"I'm 5-10."

"My guards at Miami were 6-2, 225," I said. "You didn't play here last year, did you?"

"Actually, I started last year."

"You've got to be kidding me."

He was holding up pretty well, despite my best efforts to get a rise out of him, so I reached for the A-bomb. "You know, Woody always told me never to start an Italian." Now, to be honest, this didn't make any sense to me. I certainly didn't believe it—and I don't think Woody did either—but I was just trying to get under this guy's skin.

It worked. Caldo sat up, looked me in the eye and said, "Coach, when we put the pads on this spring, the cream will rise to the top."

Good answer, I thought—but that's not what I said.

"We'll see about that, Mr. Caldarazzo. You're dismissed."

Next up was Caldo's buddy, Garvie Craw. He was Michigan's star fullback, and one of the guys I'd just made move into married housing. Because I was certain Caldarazzo had already clued him in, I took a slightly different approach.

"First, I've seen the tapes, Craw, and I think you're a helluva player."

"Thanks, Coach." He exhaled.

"And I hear you're in the bars a lot."

"But Coach, I'm twenty-one years old. I'm *allowed* to be in the bars."

"I don't care. If I hear you're in a bar again, you're off the team."

BAM! That got his attention.

Those were fun, but the best was Dan Dierdorf, our star offensive tackle. If you know your football, you know Dierdorf. The guy did it all, in college and in the pros—including once sneaking out the back door to avoid my assistant coach!

Here's the story. When I was coaching at Miami, I wanted Dierdorf something awful, but everyone else did, too, and I knew we probably didn't have much of a chance at signing him. But I'd be damned if I wasn't going to try!

Now, Dan had already made up his mind that he was going to play for Bump Elliott at Michigan, but back then they didn't have press conferences to announce this stuff. He probably told his parents over breakfast, and that was it. But when my assistant coach, Jerry Hanlon, was in Dierdorf's hometown of Canton, Jerry met with Dan's coach. When his coach walked down to the gym to tell Dierdorf an assistant coach from Miami was there to see him, Dan did the mature thing. He slipped out the back door of the gym and went home. Nice.

Of course, Hanlon tells me this, which didn't impress me, but I figured I'd never see Dierdorf again. And I am *certain* Dierdorf thought the same thing. Ha!

Well, I can just imagine Dierdorf's reaction when he heard I was replacing Bump. Dierdorf had just finished his sophomore season, and he was a little more mature, so he decides if he handles it like a man, maybe all would be forgiven. Dierdorf screws up his courage and marches down to my office to introduce himself. Well, as luck would have it—some things you just can't wish for—at the exact same time I'm marching the other way down the hallway. I caught him a little off-guard, but he hurried to regain his composure.

He sticks his hand out, flashes his famous "Dierdorf for Mayor" smile, and gives me some happy crap about just how *thrilled* he is that I'm his new head coach.

I reach out right past his outstretched hand and grab his gut. "You are *fat,* you are *mine,* and I *never* forget!"

Give me a picture of Dierdorf's face at that moment and I

won't ask for anything else. God, that was something! This big, tough guy, so confident, looking like I just dropped a grenade down his pants. THAT was great!

Safe to say, I had Dan's attention, too.

The player interviews were nothing compared to the shock they got once we started working out . . . in *January*.

The rap on these guys around the league was that they were soft. And man, that's a terrible thing to hear. You can call one of my teams slow, short and weak with terrible coaching—but don't *ever* tell me my team is soft.

We were going to fix that, too.

As soon as I arrived, we set up a rather—shall we say—*demanding* off-season regimen, four days a week. Now every team works out in the off-season, but we were ahead of our time—because we had to be.

We had about 110 players at the first session, and normally I'd say that's great—you'll see in later chapters how important the walk-ons have been to our program—but these guys were soft and sloppy, and some were just smart-alecks. Maybe they thought it'd be cool to say they were on the Michigan football team, but they weren't committed to it. So at our very first winter workout, I stood up and said, "We have too many bodies here and not enough serious football players. We need to get our numbers down to eighty or so." That got a few looks, too. So be it. I meant it.

Working them to death wasn't easy when we had no place to do it. We had no weight room, no workout area, not even a place to meet—nothing—and certainly no football building. Michigan football!

In the basement of the Intramural Building we had a boxing

ring and a wrestling mat. In the balcony above the locker rooms at Yost Field House—this is when it was still set up for track, not hockey—we had one of those Universal machines, a few dumbbells lying around and a single bench press. Michigan football!

Well, that was not going to stop me from whipping these guys into shape.

Every day we rotated guys through the pathetic little weight room at Yost, we put them in the boxing ring, and we put a few more on the wrestling mats, working on agility drills. It got pretty hot down there, especially during the slap-and-stomp drill, where two guys faced each other and tried to tap the other guy on his back and step on his toes at the same time. Fights broke out almost daily.

What the guys seem to remember most about that first winter, though, is the running. We did so much running—sprints, stairs, the mile—that we put buckets at each station so the guys could get sick without messing up the floor. Those buckets got good use.

We had them run the steps of the football stadium, the basketball arena and Yost Field House—whatever was available. We had them hop up and down the aisles on two feet, then on one foot, and then charge up the aisles carrying their teammates on their backs.

I announced that they all had to run at least one mile under six minutes in order to secure their spot on the team, but some of the linemen couldn't even do that. The six-minute mile! Whenever that drill came up, they'd try to hide behind the pillars at Yost. Michigan football!

Man, Bobby Baumgartner—a great blocker, a GREAT kid—couldn't run a six-minute mile to save his life. And he wasn't alone. Well, I had a surprise waiting for them.

*   *   *

There was method to my madness: We were in horrible shape, and I wanted to catch up on our conditioning before we got into spring ball, when I wanted to spend our time on our skill work.

We lost a few players during the winter workouts, but not many. I'm sure they figured we couldn't possibly run as much during spring ball—and they were right. In spring ball, we focused on hitting—every day, every session, full pads—and that's when guys really started dropping. In the middle of one of these sessions, when guys were dropping ten pounds of sweat blocking and tackling, you could see some of them look longingly at that damn track. It suddenly looked like an oasis.

Things got so hard that I had to put up that famous sign, "THOSE WHO STAY WILL BE CHAMPIONS." If you toughed it out, you'd be rewarded. I gave my word.

Well, not everyone stayed, of course. We probably lost twenty or thirty guys. Some of them came to my office to quit face-to-face, and some just disappeared, never to be seen again. One guy wrote on the sign, "And those who leave will be doctors, lawyers, and captains of industry." I had to chuckle at that—though it didn't seem so funny when I had to shell out $150 to replace the sign. Naturally, the guy who did it just slinked away—and, I hear, ended up being a lawyer. But you probably guessed that already.

I was prepared for some attrition. I can honestly say we did not lose a guy who really could have helped us. I didn't lose any sleep over anyone who quit that spring.

The guys who stayed were great. After we finished spring ball and had our blue-white scrimmage in Michigan Stadium—oh, you could see it in their eyes, the pride they all felt because they knew no group of young men, outside of the Marines on Parris Island, had worked harder than they had. Whatever happened from that point on, we would never, ever hear again that we were a soft team. In just four months, we had fixed our biggest problem.

I knew we were really getting somewhere at the end of spring ball when I asked my coaches, "Is there anybody down at Miami who could start on this team?"

They thought about it, then said, "No, there isn't. Not now."

"Then gentlemen, we've got a football team here."

I wasn't done with them. After they all went home for the summer, I wrote them letters, every one of them. "Be ready for a tough season," "Come back in shape or you'll pay the price," "Here's what you'll have to do to be champions." Things like that. Plus, a warning. "I have all of your times for the mile, and if you come back slower, I'll know what you did this summer. If you can't break six minutes, you'll be dealing with me."

This scared Bobby Baumgartner so much, he quit his summer job working construction for the city of Chicago to stay in town and work on the mile.

Almost everyone came back that August in good shape, so they must have believed me. Caldarazzo, a guard, could run a 5:30, almost as fast as the backs. Smart move, Caldo—because we were about to move Reggie McKenzie from tackle to guard, and he had Caldo by fifty pounds and half a foot. Caldo's mile time saved his job. Mike Hankwitz, our second tight end behind Jim Mandich, ran the fastest time on the team, just barely over five minutes. I felt that warranted starting two tight ends, which showed everyone how seriously I was taking conditioning.

When they returned, everyone could break six minutes,

too—except for Baumie and a few of his buddies. Cripes! I had already told everyone they weren't going to dress unless they broke six minutes. Now what was I going to do?

We only had three weeks until our opening game against Vanderbilt. Making matters worse, the first week back we were doing three practices a day—the NCAA won't let you do this anymore—so the only time these linemen could work on their mile time was six o'clock in the morning. Those poor guys would drag themselves out of bed at 5:30, and trundle down to the track at Ferry Field in the dark. I'd start my stopwatch at 6 A.M., and I stopped it at precisely 6:06:00. If you weren't across the line by then, you earned an invitation to run extra sprints after *each one* of our three daily sessions, then come back the next morning to try again.

That didn't make them any faster, just more tired, so each morning their times were getting worse: 6:07, 6:08—6:10.

This track, Ferry Field, has been Michigan's track for over a century, and countless Olympians have run there. In 1935, Jesse Owens, running for Ohio State, set three world records and tied a fourth *in a single day*—a feat that will never be equaled. Canham, a track man, built a monument on the site to commemorate the historic day—which I guarantee you is the only shrine built for a Buckeye on our campus. (I'm pleased to report that Michigan won the meet anyway.)

And it was that same track these six tub-o-lards could not get themselves around in under six minutes. God, it was a disgrace to that noble oval!

They finally realized if they didn't stop this vicious cycle soon, they'd get slower and slower and end up running all year. So they got together, they got determined, and they focused on making their best effort at the end of our first week.

They showed up a little earlier than usual. It was still dark out, but the rising sun slowly burned off enough of the morning fog so you could just see to the far end of the track. The six slow-pokes stretched out, peeled off their sweat suits, and gathered at the starting line with pale expressions.

A bunch of their teammates came down to cheer them on. I stood at my post with my stopwatch and clipboard.

"On your mark. Get set. Go!"

They didn't exactly take off like bats out of hell, but they clearly intended to get a good head start. I called their marks after each lap—1:20! 2:51! 4:27! —and the excitement built when everyone realized they just might do it. But they were already showing fatigue, and the fourth and final lap always killed them.

Their teammates started yelling, and running alongside them to keep them going. God, their faces looked horrible, and their form was worse. But there they were, chugging around the final turn, fighting like hell.

"You've got twenty seconds!" I yelled.

"TEN SECONDS!" A couple of them shouted out in pain—but they kept going.

"FIVE SECONDS!"

"THREE! TWO!"

They leaned forward, they dove, they collapsed, they crossed the line. They had made it.

"FINAL TIME—5:58. YOU DID IT!"

Their teammates mobbed them, picked them up, hugged them. Once they got their breath, the linemen started jumping up and down like they'd just won an Olympic gold medal. The whole team loved it. I loved it!

No one else in the Big Ten knew we were doing crazy drills in the bowels of dark, cold gyms, and running the world's ugliest laps in the morning fog, but *we* knew what we were doing. We were getting somewhere.

*   *   *

One of the biggest myths of that '69 team is that we took
a bunch of no-talent guys and turned them into champions.
That's just not true. From that team eleven players became All-
American—eleven! And while I like to think our coaching staff
helped them get there, brother, you can't get blood from a stone.
And let's be clear: I didn't recruit ANY of those guys. Ol' Bump
had not left the cupboard bare.

If we did one thing that helped, it was making sure whoever was
practicing best during the week was playing on Saturday. I didn't
care if you were a sophomore or a senior, a walk-on or an All-American, and I sure as hell didn't care if you were black or white, or
anything else. If you played your position the way I wanted you to
play it, you'd start. That simple. No games. No favorites.

That may sound pretty obvious to you, but you'd be amazed
how often coaches will play the guy who's got a scholarship, or
who's the media darling, or who's his personal favorite, over the
so-called no-names. You do that, and you demoralize the rest of
the team. Everyone figures there's no point knocking themselves
out to challenge the first-stringer, because it's rigged! And the
starter figures, why knock myself out when I can't lose my job to
these schlubs no matter what I do?

No, that's not how you do it. When the ball's snapped you put
the best in there, whoever it is. And if you don't, you're cheat-
ing the team. Ask the guys on our team, and they'll tell you they
didn't fear the guy starting for Iowa. They feared the guy playing
behind them in practice, because he was fighting for their job.

This was especially important my first year, when they had to
find out for themselves if they could trust my word. Once they
saw guys go up and down the depth chart, based solely on their

performance, they started to believe in what we were doing, and we got better performances out of all of them.

Even though the '68 Wolverines had been ranked fourth in the country before getting shellacked by Ohio Sate, we weren't ranked at all entering the 1969 season. We opened the season at home against a good Vanderbilt team, and beat the Commodores, 42-14, in front of 70,000 fans. We were rewarded the next week with 21,000 fewer fans for our game against Washington. Forty-nine thousand fans! Michigan football!

We beat the Huskies, too, 45-7. Now we were ranked 13th in the nation, and our guys were starting to think all that hard work might have really paid off.

Well, hell. Missouri came into our building and just whooped us, 40-17—the most points any team ever scored off one of my Michigan defenses.

I wasn't panicked—I was ticked off! We had to hurry to get our heads on straight for our Big Ten opener against ninth-ranked Purdue, probably the second best team in the Big Ten. They had Mike Phipps at quarterback—who finished second for the Heisman that year—but we beat 'em soundly, 31-20. Heck, that game might have *cost* Phipps the Heisman.

Right when I started to think we were rolling, the week of practice before the Michigan State game was just atrocious. Man was I mad! Even before the game, I didn't like what I saw. Sure enough, we went up to East Lansing and just laid an egg, 23-12.

Part of this was my fault for not realizing how big the Michigan State rivalry really was. I never made that mistake again—we won seventeen of the next twenty MSU games—but that didn't solve any of our problems in 1969. We were 3-2, with two bad losses, and if we lost to anyone else in the next five games we

would be out of the Big Ten race, with no chance to be champions. And I would have broken my promise.

I honestly had no idea how we were going to respond up
in Minnesota. During that first players meeting months earlier,
I made it clear that if you missed our Tuesday or Wednesday
full-contact practices, you wouldn't play on Saturday. After the
State game, we had some legitimately injured players, like Glenn
Doughty, a great guy and a wonderful athlete. Even Glenn,
though, probably had the misconception that he could just jump
in the game on Saturday. That was a mistake.

There was also a bunch of guys who were hurt—a little
bruised and banged up—but not injured, where practicing can
make it worse. Some of those guys didn't get the distinction, and
missed practice with minor stuff. John Gabler, one of our two
wingbacks, just had a crappy attitude that week, and that ticked
me off. Another guy I benched for drinking

So on Thursday night, after telling them I was fed up,
I posted the travel list on the locker room door at Yost, and
walked away. We left a dozen guys back in Ann Arbor, including Gabler, so that meant we had only one wingback making
the trip—and we were a wingback offense. I was hanging it out
there pretty good.

After I posted the list, one of my coaches asked me, "Are you
sure you know what you're doing?" To be honest, maybe I did,
and maybe I didn't. But really, what were my options? Do I play
malcontents? Do I take guys who didn't practice and play them,
and show everybody my word isn't worth a damn? No!

Let me tell you the God's honest truth: Even if we got beat
up there in Minnesota, I would *still* have felt better about
taking the squad I took than I would have if we'd won that
game with a bunch of guys who hadn't practiced all week,
guys who let their teammates down, guys who didn't take my

word seriously. I was still *dying* to beat Minnesota—it was a make-or-break game—but I didn't need to have my decision vindicated by a victory. I wasn't playing games. I was just enforcing my word.

In fact, I already felt better when I got to Minneapolis, *before* we played the game!

We couldn't do anything in the first half against the Gophers, and returned to the locker room down, 9–7. Worse, our quarterback, Don Moorhead, had a pretty serious hip-pointer. I assumed he was out.

I remember this like it was yesterday. At that exact moment, I said to myself, "What do you think it'd be like, you idiot, if you had brought the guys you left in Ann Arbor?" And then I thought, "At least the guys we've got here will give it their all."

Moorhead looked me straight in the eye—a look I'll never forget—and said, "Coach, I'm going to play."

Our doctor shrugged. "If he says he can . . ."

Now, you talk about one tough sonuvabitch! Right there, we had turned a corner. The guys left that locker room jacked! We went out there and just *ripped* the Gophers. We scored 28 points, we shut them down, and we ran off the field with a 35–9 victory.

That might have been the best plane ride home I've ever taken my entire life. When we flew up to Minnesota, we were in disarray with a lot of unanswered questions. When we flew back, we were a TEAM, with a lot of answers. And if you thought you were going to beat that bunch—man, you better bring your lunch!

After that game I honestly believed we were not going to lose another game all season. And the guys on that squad will tell you the same thing. Heck, they started believing they were going to upset the mighty Buckeyes *a month before the game.*

At our first meeting ten months earlier, the players probably thought I was some kind of lunatic. After spring ball, they started to believe maybe we were on to something, and when we showed no favoritism when the season started, they started coming around. Before that Minnesota game, I'd say the players were probably about 90 percent sold on our program—but that game put the exclamation point on our methods. That game sealed it. We had 'em!

After Minnesota, instead of looking for ways to get out of practice, everybody was looking for ways to get into the lineup. Our practices were full tilt, just fantastic. Guys believed in the program, and in each other. It was great!

From that point on, we were a runaway freight train, and if you were in our way—watch out. We beat Wisconsin, 35-7, we shut out Illinois, 57-0, and we whipped Iowa in Iowa City, 51-6. Over those four games, we outscored our opponents 178-22. Now *that* is playing some football—Fielding Yost stuff!

Next up: the defending national champion, number-one-ranked Buckeyes of Ohio State. They came into Ann Arbor riding a 22-game winning streak. They hadn't lost a game in two years. They hadn't even been behind in a single game all season, not even for a second. *Sports Illustrated* said the only game worth watching that fall was Ohio State's offense against Ohio State's defense in a Tuesday practice down in Columbus.

Well, we'd see about that. I would challenge the statement—made by almost everybody at the time, and even some today—that Ohio State was that much better than we were. I have too much respect for the guys on that Michigan team to believe that. Dan

Dierdorf, Jim Mandich and Tom Curtis are already in the College Football Hall of Fame, and Thom Darden will be soon. I'm sorry, our guys could play a little football.

But if you were to script a scenario to create the greatest upset of the decade, we had it. We were unranked and unknown going into the season, we stumbled twice early on, but we were on the rise and peaking at exactly the right time. Outsiders knew we were getting better, but they didn't recognize that, by the Ohio State game, *we were as good as any team in the nation, including the Buckeyes.* And the best part was, no one knew but us!

I'm telling you, our guys were so sharp, so confident, and so jacked up, Ohio State had no idea what they were in for. The day before the game, when the Buckeyes were coming off the field from their walk-through practice and we were about to run on the field, a fight broke out in the tunnel. Must have been twenty or thirty guys involved, pretty much everyone who was in the tunnel at the time. Woody and I had to run back from the field to break it up. When we finally got them all separated, our own Cecil Pryor yelled, "And we're gonna kick your ass tomorrow, too!" They no longer feared the Buckeyes!

On the day of the game, I heard a couple of their players missed their team bus, which suggests a certain arrogance, perhaps. Meanwhile, we've got Jim Mandich crying in the tunnel of our stadium—*before* the game—while he was still waiting to run out and touch the banner. That's how emotionally charged we were. All that pain, all that suffering, all that work we'd done in the off-season—it fueled everything we did.

By the time the Buckeyes realized we had come to play, it was too late. We were already rolling, and there was nothing they could do to stop us. And that was no fluke! We didn't get lucky—we flat out *kicked their asses*! It was nothing less than the greatest game of my life—and I have to believe everyone on our team would say the same.

After we won, 24–12, my phone started ringing off the hook. *Sports Illustrated, The New York Times,* ABC, you name it, they all wanted to talk to us about "the upset of the decade." It's still probably the most celebrated victory in Michigan history. "Boy, that was a stunning, stunning, upset!" they all said. But it wasn't to us—because we *expected* to win!

The Minnesota game convinced everyone *inside* the program of what we were all about. But it was the Ohio State game that convinced everyone *outside* that locker room that the Wolverines will play with anyone, anywhere, anytime, because we're one of the elite teams in the country. And we have been, ever since.

In the Rose Bowl we played a Southern Cal team we should have beaten easily—but dammit, I had to have my first heart attack the day before the game. The coaches couldn't tell the players what was happening until game day, and when they got the news, many of them were in tears.

It's a safe bet they wouldn't have been in tears a year earlier, when they first met me. In our opening game against Vanderbilt, I was just the guy they had to put up with. But by the USC game, I had become someone they counted on. And I wasn't there. They didn't even know if I was going to be all right. Dierdorf told me it was the only time the Big Ten team came through that tunnel walking, not charging out. We were seven-point favorites, but we lost, 10–3.

To this day, I have never seen that Rose Bowl game. I couldn't watch it that day in the hospital, and when I came back, I never wanted to see that tape. I just hoped to go on and coach some more. And I was lucky to be able to do that for twenty more seasons.

The funny thing is, the guys on the 1969 team probably stay in touch better than any team I coached. As much as they hated the workouts then, they all brag about it now.

They stayed. They were champions. And I kept my promise.

And we have kept that promise ever since.

5

Respect Your History

It's one thing, when you start in a new position, to throw a bucket of cold water on your *people* to let them know things are going to be different around here from now on. That's just smart.

But it's something completely different to do the same thing to the *institution* you're taking over. That's just stupid!

Let me explain. One of the most common mistakes new leaders make—and I just can't for the life of me understand this one—is to ignore the *history* of the organization they just took over, or even to disrespect it. That, to me, is the mark of a weak leader—and one who's probably not going to last very long.

Let me be as clear as I can be about this: When you become the leader, do *not* start your reign by dismantling or ignoring the contributions of those who came before. The history of your organization is one of your greatest strengths, and if you're new to the organization, it's your job to learn it, to respect it and to *teach* it to the people coming up in your company.

Sure, it's easy to appreciate Michigan's football history—the best, I'd say, in college football. But even if I had gone to Wisconsin, they have a good history, too. Ditto North Carolina. In fact, *anywhere* I might have gone *had* to have some history, or it wouldn't still exist! And that goes for any organization you might join, too.

When I arrived in Ann Arbor, I was an outsider—born and raised in Ohio, played at Miami, coached at Ohio State for Woody Hayes, for crying out loud—but I already knew a lot about Michigan. And after I got here, I made it my business to learn more, and fast.

When I was thirteen years old, my family drove to Michigan's Upper Peninsula for a fishing trip. It was mid-August, and we had to return a little early because I had to be back in Barberton for football practice. On the way back down, I made my dad stop in Ann Arbor so I could see Michigan's famous football team. Now, my dad wasn't a big football fan—he didn't know a thing about Fritz Crisler or his great teams—but he was willing to indulge me. So he parked on State Street, and I got out by myself and walked right up to the practice field—right where we built our first football building in the early 1970s, right where Schembechler Hall is today.

When I looked through that iron gate, those guys were huge, bigger than life! Even their practice uniforms looked shiny and special to me. The one guy who really impressed me was Lenny Ford. I already knew who he was—I'd read about him in the papers and heard his name on the radio—but seeing him right there, in front of me, was really something.

I can even remember exactly what I was thinking when I looked at all those players out there: Someday, that's going to be me! I was too shy to say anything then, but the rest of the way home I went on and on in the back seat about the great Michigan tradition, naming every All-American of theirs I knew. I probably drove my folks nuts, but I was in heaven.

I always wanted to go to Michigan. We had a Michigan alumnus down in Barberton talking to me, but I wasn't good enough to play for the Wolverines, and I knew it. I guess they knew it, too!

Twenty-seven years later, when I became Michigan's new football coach, the first person to visit me was William D. Revelli, the legendary band conductor. "Anything you need from me or the band," he said, "all you need to do is ask."

That impressed me. So when the freshmen arrived that August, I asked Dr. Revelli to teach them how to sing "The Victors." But brother, let me tell you: He didn't just teach them "The Victors." He taught them Michigan tradition!

I gathered the freshmen at Yost Field House, when in walks Dr. William D. Revelli, in full uniform. Marvelous man. Marvelous! I loved that guy.

"Gentlemen," I said, "you are now going to hear about the greatest college fight song from the greatest band director in the history of college football."

Now I'm sure the freshmen were thinking, What the hell is this? These are big, young, tough guys, after all, and Revelli's a lean, short, distinguished-looking older gentleman—a band director right out of central casting.

But when Revelli marched up to the front of that room, he commanded those football players exactly the way he commanded his band. In about *five seconds,* he had those big lugs in his back pocket! He rose to the podium, tapped his baton, looked right into their eyes and said, "JOHN PHILIP SOUSA CALLED THIS THE GREATEST FIGHT SONG EVER WRITTEN. AND YOU WILL SING IT WITH RESPECT!"

Wow! He had those guys out of their seats, and standing up STRAIGHT! And they sang that song right. I liked his speech so much, I invited Dr. Revelli back every year to teach the new guys what Michigan tradition was all about.

God, he was beautiful.

I also reached out to Bump Elliott, my predecessor, who was instrumental in my getting the job. He's a man of great class. How many former coaches go out of their way to make sure the guy taking over their job has everything he needs to succeed? That was Bump.

If he wanted to, Bump could have made life very difficult for me. Hell, he could have set me up for failure. His players loved him, really loved him—and remember, that first year I was coaching all *his* players. I was an outsider, they didn't owe me anything, and it wasn't like I was making life easy for them, either. Bump was a former Michigan All-American, and a whole lot nicer than I was! They could have complained to him—he was still working in the athletic office—and I bet some of them tried, but he would have none of it. He made it clear to everyone that he was on my side.

Bump showed me what he was made of a dozen times, never interfering, always supporting me, in public and in private. That was a great gift—one I remembered years later when it was my turn to pass the torch.

I made a lot of mistakes, but one thing I got right, after we started having some success, was never once claiming that I alone had put that team together—because I hadn't. And at no time did I ignore the guys who played here before I arrived, either. It was *their* tradition, not mine, that I was now in charge of, and I was going to show them I respected what they'd built here. That's why a lot of those guys are my friends today, great guys like Bob Timberlake and Ron Johnson, who kept Michigan tradition alive before I ever showed up.

I also went out of my way to get to know Fritz Crisler, who had been Michigan's coach from 1938 to 1947—he won a national title his last year—and the athletic director from 1941 to 1968, right before I got to Ann Arbor. He coached that Michigan team I saw when I was a kid peeking through the iron fence. Crisler invented Michigan's famous winged helmet, the modern field goal posts, and the platoon system, which created specialists for offense and defense. Without that, football as we know it today would not exist. This guy was a giant. I was pretty busy my first year in Ann Arbor, but I found time to go over to his house and sit in his basement, to listen to his theories and hear his stories.

I got to know the tradition that is Michigan. I studied it, I followed it, I got to know the people who created it, young and old. I don't think you can operate any other way. And I taught Michigan's tradition to my players, and to my coaches. Yost's Point-A-Minute teams, Crisler's Mad Magicians, the great players—Willie Heston, Bennie Oosterbaan, Bob Chappuis—the great stadium, the fight song, the rich history. I made it a point to learn about all of it, and pass it on.

Remember this: WHEN YOU ARE THE LEADER, YOU ARE THE ORGANIZATION. You are the company, the school, the team. You are it. Now if you want to act like some kind of jerk where guys who worked for the program and led the program and sacrificed for the program are not welcome to come back— well, you're not going to have much of a program. And you certainly won't have a family. But if you respect your history, you'll get a lot more in return.

When I coached at Ohio State and even at Miami, we had really good facilities. When I got here, I was shocked. Our locker room was on the second floor of Yost Field House. We sat in rusty, folding chairs and hung our clothes on nails hammered into a two-by-four bolted into the wall. Those were our "lockers"!

My coaches started complaining. "What the hell is this?" they said. "We had better stuff at Miami."

I cut that off right away. "No, we didn't," I said. "See this chair? *Fielding Yost* sat in this chair. See this nail? *Fielding Yost* hung his hat on this nail. And you're telling me we had better stuff at Miami? No, men, we didn't. We have *tradition* here, *Michigan* tradition, and *that's* something no one else has!"

Well, that settled that! And that's exactly what I taught our players.

After we knocked off the unbeatable Buckeyes in 1969, it was my duty to give away the game ball. I had a lot of good choices. There was Garvie Craw, who ran for two touchdowns. There was Barry Pierson, our senior defensive back, who grabbed three interceptions that day, ran back a punt to the Ohio State three-yard line, and turned in one of the single greatest performances I've ever seen.

But once everyone quieted down, I asked Bump Elliott to come up, and handed the game ball to him. Everyone got choked up, including Bump. Some guys were out and out crying—and I don't remember when I felt better about anything I've done in my entire life.

*   *   *

The night we won that game, Fritz Crisler was in a bed at U-M Hospital, watching on TV. As soon as the players and fans charged the field going crazy, Fritz grabbed a pen and paper and wrote me this letter.

SATURDAY NIGHT, 1969

MY DEAR BO,

I have had a lot of football thrills in my lifetime, but the masterpiece you and the Michigan team turned in this afternoon will stand prominently in the list. In game preparation against seemingly overwhelming odds, I have never seen a team better conditioned, technically, physically and mentally, to reach such a high inspirational peak, as you and your staff had those kids this afternoon. It was the greatest upset I have ever witnessed. The achievement will have a long life in the contribution to the richness of Michigan's enviable football history and tradition.

Even callous me shed a few uncontrolled tears from sheer pride and joy as the game ended. My very best to you and the team, always always.

Fondly,

Fritz Crisler

How much does that letter mean to me?

I have it framed on the wall, right next to my TV, so whenever I'm watching a game, like Fritz was that night, it's right there. I've read it a thousand times.

You tell me how much that letter means to me.

6

Do the Right Thing— Always

E very coach, every executive, every leader: They all know right from wrong. Even those Enron guys. When someone uncovers a scandal in their company, I don't think they can say, "I didn't know that was going on." They're just saying they're too dumb to do their job! And if they really *are* too dumb, then why are they getting paid millions of dollars to do it? They know what's going on.

It all boils down to basic honesty. Without *that,* you won't accomplish a single thing that's worthwhile.

In the college coaching business, like every other business, the temptations are everywhere. You can break recruiting rules, give out cars, even fudge grades. But if you're honest, and you know what you believe, these things really aren't that tempting at all.

*   *   *

My most searing lesson on honesty came from my dad, when I
was just ten. He was a captain in the Barberton fire department,
one of two candidates for chief. Whoever scored highest on the
civil service exam was probably going to get the job.

My dad liked to go down to the local Elks Club and play cards
with his buddies, some of whom were in the department, too.
You know, small-town stuff. One day he shows up, one of his
buddies hands him a manila envelope, and tells him, "Here, this
is for you."

"What is it?"

"It's the answers for the civil service exam."

"Why are you giving this to me?"

"Because the other guy already has them. It's only fair."

"I can't do that," he said. He left. And when he came home,
he cried. I'll never forget it. He wanted that job desperately—
hell, he deserved it!—but he couldn't do that. He couldn't cheat.
Well, apparently, the other guy could. My dad took the test
straight up, scored maybe a 96 or a 97, and missed out by a point
or two to the other guy.

Well, the other guy got the job, and my dad didn't fight it. But
he did walk into that guy's office, and tell him, "I know how you
got that job. And I will *never* work for you!"

And he didn't. He became a fire inspector, and did that job
the rest of his life.

Brother, if that lesson doesn't stick with you, nothing will. I
admired my dad greatly for that. And still do, to this day.

When Bacon was packing up to leave my office one day, he
gave me an assignment. Before he returned the next week, he
asked me to remember some big moral dilemma, like my dad's,

that I had faced, and tell him how I handled it when he returned the next week. Well, a week later, after Bacon set up his computer in my office, he said, "So, what did you come up with?"

"I thought about your question, but I swear to you, I cannot recall a single moral dilemma in all my years of coaching. I really can't! And the reason is: We always knew what the right thing to do was, so we just *did* it. And we slept well at night! Really, it was that simple."

If you really want to have your integrity scrutinized, all you need to do is testify in a federal courtroom. They will grill you over every decision you ever made in your life, and you'll know exactly where you stand pretty fast. So will everyone else.

I know this because I was called to testify in Chicago in 1989. Two of our players, Garland Rivers and Bob Perryman, had signed with a couple agents, Norby Walters and Lloyd Bloom, when Rivers and Perryman were still on campus here a few years earlier. Now, that's not only against our school rules, the Big Ten rules and the NCAA rules, it's also against federal law for those agents to sign college players when they're still in school.

They were not only great players—Perryman was an excellent runner, and Rivers was an All-American defensive back—I really liked those guys. But once you cross that line, there's nothing I can do to save you. At least, there's nothing I'm *going* to do to save you.

The second I caught wind of this, I called them into my office, and I asked them straight up: "Did you sign with these agents?"

Now, these guys were seniors, and they knew damn well that if I was asking the question, I already knew the answer, so they 'fessed up.

"Yes, Coach, but they lied to us!"

"Well, what'd you expect? And what makes me even *madder* is that I've warned you about agents *every year* at our players meeting, and you've heard it four times by now! Did you think I was kidding? Did you think I was covering that every time for the hell of it? And now you're screwed. I am hereby officially rescinding your scholarships and everything else this university has given you. You're a disgrace to this program, to this university—and to your teammates, who've played it by the book. Now get the hell out of here." I can't recall ever being more disappointed in a player than I was that day.

Unfortunately, it wasn't that simple. A few years later, in 1989, those two agents got prosecuted by the U.S. attorney in Chicago, Anton Valukas, and that's what brought me to Chicago's Federal District Court.

Anyone who's seen a courtroom TV show knows the catch: The defense attorneys get to cross-examine whoever takes the stand. Valukas, who's now a famous attorney in a big Chicago law firm, was afraid the agents' attorneys were going to attack me—and the other coaches they'd called to testify—for taking a lot of money ourselves. Their whole plan, Valukas figured, was to convince the jury that the entire institution of college football was just a big corrupt money grab anyway, with every coach exploiting the players for their own personal gain. So if these agents gave our players a few bucks while they were still playing for us, what's the difference?

There wasn't any question I was on Valukas's side. Those agents needed to be dealt with, and severely. But when he called me to come down a day early to prepare for the trial, I was serving as both Michigan's head football coach and athletic director. I was busy! And it just happened to be the very week I fired Bill Frieder as Michigan's basketball coach. (More on that later.) Our basketball team was about to enter the NCAA basketball tournament in a couple days with a new coach at the helm, Steve Fisher, and we were about to start spring football—probably the most hectic week of my career.

So that's what I told him. I'd testify, but I wasn't going down there a day early to prepare their case with them.

Well, as my dumb luck would have it, Valukas is a friend of Dick Caldarazzo, our tough little lineman from that great 1969 team. Caldo lives in Chicago now, where he's a very successful lawyer and businessman, and we've stayed in close touch. When Caldo called me, I started grumbling, until he cut me off at the knees.

"Hey, wait a second, Coach. What'd you always tell us? How do you win games? You gotta practice if you're gonna play! If you don't practice on Tuesday, you're not playing against Minnesota on Saturday! Man, there were times you told us to get off the practice field on Tuesday, because we'd already lost Saturday's game with our crappy practice performance. Coach, it's the same thing here. You've got to prepare."

Damn you, Caldo! He had me, and he knew it. Don't you just hate it when your words come back to bite you in the backside?

As soon as I finished talking to Fisher's basketball team, I hopped on a plane to Chicago. We met in the U.S. attorney's office in the Federal Court Building the night before to go over all the questions the agents' attorney—a guy named Dan Webb, who's now the most expensive defense attorney in Chicago—was probably going to use to grill me the next day.

Valukas's guys started by asking me about the money involved in college football.

"What was your coaching salary when this happened?"

"It was about $80,000 from the university, plus about $50,000 from the TV show."

"Really? That's it?"

One of the prosecutors, serving as the "demo team" for the defense attorneys, kept at it. "What's your shoe contract worth?"

"We get $250,000, but I don't take that money," I told them. "Every penny goes into a trust fund to pay college tuition for my assistant coaches' kids."

"Well, what about your summer football camp?"

"The camp brings in about $180,000, and I divide it among the assistant coaches, because frankly, I think they're underpaid. I don't take anything."

They were flabbergasted. The other coaches they had talked to had all kept the money for themselves.

Then they started asking about Garland Rivers and Bob Perryman.

"These two former players of yours, they weren't really students, and they weren't going to graduate, were they? They were just football players, right?"

"Like hell they were!" I said. "They were doing okay in school, and they would have graduated, if they had stayed."

"But they had 1.4 grade point averages."

"You guys don't know how to read an academic transcript! Here, let me show you." I took the copies from them. "Look. They have a 2.0, and a 2.1, respectively. Not honor students, maybe, but they're more than eligible, and they were on track to graduate with degrees from the University of Michigan if they hadn't left."

The guy asked me, "How do you remember all this? It was three years ago."

"Because I had all these transcripts in a file case right next to my desk, and I pulled them out whenever I met with the kids. And we met at least twice a year to go over all these things."

They looked at each other and nodded: This guy's ready.

The next day I walked into this Federal District courtroom. They had Father Ted Hesburgh, Notre Dame's president, on the stand before me, and he was great. Then I took the stand, and I answered all the prosecutor's questions—boom, boom, boom—just like I had the night before in Valukas's office. Before we met, the prosecutors were hoping the defense wouldn't ask me any of these things. But they liked my answers during the practice session so much, they decided to ask me all of those questions themselves.

After the prosecutors finished, the judge said, "We'll excuse the jury, and take a short recess."

Now, the way this courtroom was designed, the jury had to walk right past the witness stand and the judge's bench to leave. When the jury was walking past the witness stand, two of them actually gave me a high-five!

After the recess, when we got called back in and I returned to the witness stand, the judge asked if the defense wanted to question the witness. Dan Webb and his attorneys huddled around their table and finally decided, No, we're not going to be cross-examining this guy. Let's get him off the stand as fast as we can!

Man, I was prepared. I was *prepared*! And those guys didn't ask me any questions! Probably smart, I guess.

So that was that, and those agents were busted, just like they should have been. They won on appeal later on, but that's not my business.

Even though we won that day, I felt defeated. On my way out, Chuck Gowdy, a Chicago TV reporter, stopped me by the elevator and stuck a microphone in my face.

"What about the Michigan football program? Will this hurt?"

"Sure," I said. "It hurts to have this kind of thing happen to players in our program. But I'm not worried about that. Our program will be fine. Right now, all I know is, I just lost two good friends. And that's sad."

And that was the truth.

I've not seen them since, and that hurts. It could have been so much better if everyone had just been honest from the start. That's all it would have taken.

7

Lay Down Your Laws

Having attended countless business meetings, it never ceases to amaze me how few leaders know how to conduct one.

First, if you don't have anything important to say, don't schedule a meeting for the heck of it. When you *do* have something worthwhile to address, know what your message is—and just as important, know what you want them to get out of it. Otherwise, you're just wasting everyone's time—and people hate that.

The person who knows how to run a meeting will get twice as much out of his people, because when the meeting's over, they'll be ready to act on the message. That's what a meeting's *supposed* to accomplish!

The most important meeting you will ever have with your people is your first one—because it is absolutely *vital* that everyone knows exactly what your values are, from Day One. In this first meeting you need to establish who you are, what you're going to do, and how you plan on doing it.

I never wanted to leave *anything* out of the first meeting. My typed outline for that meeting lists twenty-three categories of expectations—with 197 bullet points under those categories—and I addressed every single one of them, from parking tickets to plagiarism to press relations. If it took two hours, I didn't care. I never looked at my watch. If they needed to know it, I was going to cover it. That way no one could ever say, "You never told us about that!" Because I had—on Day One.

Three weeks before our season opener every year, we would meet as a team for the first time. The players already had their physicals, they'd moved in, they were ready for our first practice the next day. So at seven o'clock, right after our first training table dinner, we gathered in our old football headquarters, a squat, one-story cinder block building right on State Street. That building might not have been much to look at, but it was close to my heart, because it was built only for us. It was the first building big enough to hold the entire team. No more meeting underneath the stands of the baseball park. And when I was coaching at Michigan, it's where we did our most important work.

Our meeting room was pretty narrow, with a low ceiling and fluorescent lighting, but it was deep, so we could fit 150 people in there, wall to wall. Man, that was a bunker! And we loved it. I had a table and a lectern at the front, and the first row was so close I could reach out and touch those guys. No place to hide in that room.

When the players walked in, they picked up a thick Michigan football binder with everything they needed to know to be a Wolverine inside. Well, almost everything. Instead of spoon-feeding them the opening speech by printing it out, I had them write down everything I said so they would *remember* it. And it worked.

Before the meeting even started we established that, from now on, early is on time, and on time is late. That's why we locked the door right at seven o'clock. No more Mellow Men sauntering in ten minutes late! No more excuses.

No matter how many stories they'd heard about me, there was always someone who didn't think they were true. They were mistaken. I have to confess right now I secretly *hoped* some knucklehead would show up late, because it allowed me to hammer home a central point of Michigan football: *You will be on time, always!*

We always had the seniors sit in the front rows, followed by the juniors and sophomores. The freshmen might try to sit closer, but they'd get educated pretty quickly by one of the upperclassmen. There's a lesson in that, too: I don't care if you're an eighteen-year-old Parade High School All-American, and the senior is a no-name walk-on. Right now you're a freshman, and even if the senior at your position can't carry your jockstrap— well, he's a senior, he's paid his dues. He's a *leader,* and you're not. Not yet. You can sit in the back. Plenty of room for you there.

Sometimes, especially in my first years, the white guys would sit with the white guys, and the black guys with the black guys. Well, I wasn't having any of that, either, so I'd simply point and say, "You sit over there. And you sit over here," and so on, until they got another message: You are not black and white anymore. You are Michigan Wolverines. And that's all that matters from now on.

Once the room was set up exactly the way I wanted it, I'd walk to the lectern and start by laying down the basics, same way I did in 1969.

"Gentlemen, the first thing we are going to cover is how we will conduct ourselves in a Michigan football meeting. That means:

- "Your feet are flat on the floor.
- "Your eyes are looking right at me.
- "You are leaning forward to pay attention.
- "You are not chewing any gum, any tobacco, any dip.
- "And no hats!"

To us, those things are not trivial. It's the basis for everything that follows. As I went over this list, you could see the new guys adjusting their bodies with each point, and the seniors chuckling at them. They'd learn.

"If you plan to succeed as a Michigan football player, you need to understand our meetings are just as important as our practices. They *are* practices, mental exercises where we learn to *eliminate mistakes*! And trust me, when we take the practice field, we know *immediately* who was paying attention and who wasn't. So, if you have a question, you better ask it now."

Next, we had the freshmen stand up and introduce themselves. "Hi, I'm Joe Schlunkhead, from Akron, Ohio." Those kids were nervous—are you kidding me?—and their voices were cracking, but it was a good reminder to the veterans how special it was to be in that room.

"Now we're going to talk about the football building, this cinder block box, our home. This is *our* building and we are going to take care of it. That means you toss your tape in the trash, you put your weights where they belong, and you never leave anything on the floor for someone else to clean up. There *is* no one else! We're it!

"Sloppiness in this building breeds sloppiness on the field. When a sloppy guy lines up, he'll jump offsides. When he goes out for a pass, he'll run a bad route. And when he carries the ball, he'll fumble it. Why? Because he's sloppy! Now I realize that seventeen-to-twenty-two-year-old men are inherently sloppy, so we're going to make you something you are not—NEAT!

"Next, we're going to cover all the little things that you need to know to avoid bugging the hell out of me—because I can think of few things more important to the survival of a Michigan football player than *not bugging the hell out of me*!"

My list was very long, and I organized it into categories like the dorm, academics and the like, but this sampler will give you the gist:

- "No bicycles inside the building.
- "Chin straps fastened at all times.
- "No cutting in the chow line.
- "The only guy here who can use foul language is me!
- "Do not bring your parking tickets to me. Coach Burton can get you a parking sticker, and if you're not smart enough to ask for it and to use it, the ticket is yours to keep. You may consider it your welcoming gift from the city of Ann Arbor.
- "What happens to a typical student if he doesn't pay his rent? He gets kicked out of the house. Well, that's exactly what will happen to you, too, and I'll back the landlord!
- "You pull a fire alarm in the dorm, they'll kick you out—and I'll support them, too!
- "Stay out of the bars. Every member of the staff and team must be morally BETTER than any student or faculty member on this campus, because we are being watched twenty-four hours a day. No matter what you think of me, you will never hear of me being in a bar,

or drunk or in a fight. Now I know you've definitely seen me act like a jackass on the sidelines, but that's different!"

The thrust of all these rules was simple: There is a right way and a wrong way to do everything, and at Michigan Football, we're going to do everything the right way. We'll spell it out for you in bold, then we expect you to do it. Laying it all out here saved us a lot of time later in the season, when we needed to focus on Ohio State, not laundry.

I'll take just one of these points, and show you what we did with it to give you a feel for how this meeting worked.

"Section V, Number 7: Dress properly!

"As a member of the Michigan football team, you will dress properly wherever you go. In the dorms, you will always wear shirts and shoes. I don't care what the other students are doing. I don't coach them! In the weight room, you will always wear University of Michigan football T-shirts—no tank tops. On the practice field, you will wear the practice jersey assigned to you that day, and you will wear it tucked in—always! No cutting the sleeves or the bottoms. That is a MICHIGAN uniform!

"In the past," I'd say, "some players would complain. Not you, of course. You're too advanced for that. But lesser men. They'd say, 'Other teams don't do this, why do we have to?'

"Now that question comes up a lot, for all kinds of things we do. And when it does I always have a simple answer: Because you are *better* than they are, and you're going to act like it!

"When we travel, we represent the University of Michigan and Michigan football. That's why all of you have been issued a tailored blue suitcoat with a Michigan patch on the breast pocket and a maize-and-blue tie, with dark pants." I didn't tell them that this also ensured no one stood out because they didn't have enough money for a good suit.

"One player asked me, 'Why do we need to wear a coat and a tie just to get on a bus?'

"I'll tell you why. For one thing, you're going to act better, and you're going to feel better about yourself, when you're dressed properly. You have less chance of acting like a fool, and doing something you'll regret later, when you dress properly. If you're a sloppy-looking guy, then you're probably going to act that way, too. But if you're a class act, then you've got to *dress* like one and you've got to *act* like one. That's just part of the discipline of a good program."

To break things up, I always inserted a story or a joke here or there.

"In my twenty-one years at Michigan, the only managerial mistake I ever made was putting Dick Hunter, one of our assistant coaches, in charge of our attire for our trip to the 1972 Rose Bowl. I'm telling you, he got the most god-awful stuff you've ever seen. We're talking a horrible powder blue, double-breasted polyester leisure suit, dark blue double-knit pants *with white pinstripes,* a royal blue shirt, and a yellow-, blue- and gray-striped tie. It was so bad, when we got back to Ann Arbor the guys got the scissors out and hacked the pants into cutoffs! Frank Gusich, who played on that team, still brings that getup back to our reunions to this day, just for a laugh. That necessitated me firing Hunter from dress duty for life. I remain confident to this day that was exactly the right thing to do. The man gave me no choice.

"Now, I don't want us looking sloppy, but I don't want us trying to look too flashy, either, on or off the field. Everybody makes fun of Penn State's basic uniforms, but I don't. Those uniforms look right to me. When you dress with flamboyance, you're trying to draw attention to your attire and not to your performance.

I'd rather have them judge us by what we do on the field than by how we look.

"Back when we started here in 1969, I was the guy who demanded our players wear black cleats. Our guys were *begging* me to get white cleats, but even if you had to tape up your shoes and ankles, we'd paint the tape black! I was not going to be fooled by their tricks.

"'Oh, Coach, everybody's wearing white shoes. Look at Billy "White Shoes" Johnson!'

"I was not moved. 'Gentlemen,' I told them, 'we are wearing black shoes.'

"'But we look faster in white!'

"'Maybe,' I said. 'But you don't *run* any faster!'

"And what is everybody wearing today? Black shoes, that's what! You see, it just took the rest of the country a little while longer to come around to my way of thinking, but they did. So, thanks to your old-fashioned head coach, Michigan football players have been way ahead of the fashion trend for years!" They always laughed at that.

One player once showed up for our first full team meeting wearing a Notre Dame T-shirt—and we were going to open against Notre Dame in three weeks. I mean, holy smokes! Are you kidding me? So when I got to the part about dressing properly at all times, I paused, pointed to this guy in the second row, and said, "Stand up. Now, turn around, and show your teammates what you're wearing." They read his shirt and cracked up! They were hooting and hollering, because they knew he was going to get it. I went over to him, reached over and grabbed that shirt by the collar and ripped it off his back.

"Son, it's better to die as a young boy than to show up for a Michigan team meeting wearing a Notre Dame T-shirt. Now, you go follow Jon Falk, and he'll get you a good Michigan T-shirt—the best in the land. Not that you deserve it!"

They were howling—and even my victim was laughing. I can tell you this: He was the last guy to wear a Notre Dame T-shirt to a Michigan meeting!

This meeting usually took about two hours, but we don't have two hours! So, I'm going to break down the rest of the meeting into a few general categories.

1. RESPECT FOR OTHERS.

"I expect every one of you to treat everyone you encounter with respect. Period. You do not *demand* anything. You don't have any *right* to demand anything! Whatever you need, you ask for it, and you ask politely. If you need it, we'll get it for you.

"You don't treat the so-called little people poorly, because we don't have any little people here! The trainers, the managers, the secretaries, the people who work in the dorms and cafeterias and classroom buildings are all professionals, and they're all important or they wouldn't be working for Michigan football. So you will treat them all accordingly. They owe you nothing. You owe them your gratitude."

To underscore this, I had just about everyone who was going to come into contact with these guys there in that room to explain what they did and how the players could help them do it better. It also showed the players that I knew these people and they had my support.

I also made it clear that all the professors, all the landlords and all the police in town had my number at work and at home, and they were free to use those numbers at any time. So if these guys sitting in front of me did anything stupid, I was certain to hear about it, and usually within *minutes* of it happening. I always sought to create the illusion that my eyes and ears were everywhere—and I guess I must have done pretty well with that, because my players used to call this town "Bo Arbor."

"Respect must be shown for your immediate supervisor," I explained. "If you have a problem, you go to your position coach. If, after that, the issue warrants coming to me, I might handle it in conjunction with your coach, but I can tell you right now if there is a conflict between a player and an assistant coach, I will be taking your coach's side. Every time. I have confidence in your coaches, and they're going to be here long after you're gone."

At the same time, I promised them that we would always be available to them, and the seniors would nod at that, because they knew it was true. Anytime, anywhere, they could call us, and we'd be ready to help with whatever was on their mind. Because that was the deal.

2. HONESTY.

"Honesty has got to be the hallmark of everything we do, or nothing we do here is going to mean a thing. You know your coaches will always be honest with you—just ask the seniors." That usually got a laugh. "Honesty is the most important attribute of any coach—and for any player, too.

"Almost any mistake you make, if you accept responsibility and come clean and take your punishment like a man, you can overcome it—EXCEPT DISHONESTY. If I can prove someone stole money, for example—well, I don't care who you are. It's over. You're gone!

"If you lie to us, you're gone.

"If you lie to anyone else connected to the program—professors, landlords, trainers—you're gone. No player or coach is indispensable—and if you lie to me, we will prove it!

"ANY DISHONEST PLAYER WILL BE DROPPED FROM THE PROGRAM. DROPPED MEANS DROPPED, BECAUSE WE WILL NOT TOLERATE DISHONESTY IN ANY PART OF THIS PROGRAM!

"I don't have to elaborate on that for you any more, men, do I?"

Why so tough? Because if you catch a guy lying, what are you going to do? Sit down and have a nice chat with him? He'll just lie to you again! It's the one problem that I just can't work with.

One day, when I was coaching Miami of Ohio in the 1960s, I was driving down Main Street at 6 A.M., and who do I see but old Tom Reed, our wingback, sneaking out of an apartment house, dashing across the street right in front of my car. I'm looking *right at him,* and he's looking right back at me—but he tries to act like I hadn't seen him. Well, that was going to be a mistake, because I had!

But it wasn't more than a half-hour after I got to work, when it was still dark out, that he was in my office. First thing he said was, "Bo, I'm not going to lie to you, I was with her all night."

Well, at least he was telling me the truth!

Then I said to him, "Do you know what would happen to that girl if they knew she was out all night? She'd broken curfew. She'd be in big trouble, and it'd be your fault."

Well, I grilled him, but the fact is, he'd come clean. I'd punish him, he'd get through it, and he'd be fine. But if he'd lied to me, he'd be gone. That's why I'll never forget him coming in to say, "Bo, I'm not going to lie to you."

Boy, there's great power in that! THAT is a guy I can work with!

In fact, I hired Tom as a graduate assistant the next year at Miami. I hired him as a paid assistant at Michigan, and he did such a good job, Miami of Ohio hired him to be head coach—where he did an even better job. Then he was on to North Carolina State three years later. And when he left North Carolina State, I hired him right back at Michigan.

But I'm telling you right now: Tom's football career would have ended that day, before the sun even rose, if he had lied to me forty years ago. That is how important honesty is to me.

3. YOU ARE RESPONSIBLE FOR YOUR GRADES.

It's important that you, as the leader, take nothing for granted. That's why I explained everything to these guys—what plagiarism is, how to study for a test, how to calculate your grade point average. Then I introduced Dean Eugene Nissen, our academic advisor, and added that the ultimate academic advisor was Bo Schembechler—and he was the toughest!

Like every other aspect of their lives, I was aware of everything about their academics—their attendance, their classes, their credits and their grades—because I had it all right there in my files. Coaches can't do that anymore, due to privacy laws, so I was lucky to be working in an era when they still believed a coach could contribute to the academic success of a student. Dean Nissen said he couldn't recall a time he came down to give me a report on a player when I didn't already know what had happened. Bang, bang—I already had read the files!

"I've got your files, and I can tell if you're trying or not. The NCAA and the Big Ten require a 1.0 GPA to stay eligible. But *Dean Schembechler* requires a 2.0, so you'd better get your act together.

"That means you better attend class. We'll help you in any way we can, but I'm not going to look out for anyone who does not attend classes. If you're really trying, we'll get you everything you need, including a desk down here, study table and tutoring, too. But we're not going to lower the bar for anyone. We're just going to help you get over it!"

Every business has got numbers, and we did, too. And that's how you do it: You explain everything, you monitor everything, you never lower the bar, but you do everything you can to help them get over it. Then, it's up to them.

4. KEEP OUTSIDERS ON THE OUTSIDE.

"When you're part of a top-flight program—and you are—you're going to attract a lot of attention you don't need. *Ignore it.* Ignore the press, ignore the alumni, ignore the 'instant friends' who will come around looking to gamble or be your agent or be your drinking buddy.

"Ignore what you read in the paper, because I do. I may call you every name in the book in my office, I might scream and holler at you in practice, but I will NEVER say a negative word about you in public—because it's none of their business. We know what's happening, and it's our job to fix it. No one else's opinion matters around here.

"That goes double for alumni. That's why, unlike some programs, you will never see boosters in our locker room or on our team bus or on our team plane. Never! The only guys allowed in those places are coaches and trainers and players—you! That's it. Because *you* earned it!"

Once the players saw that I didn't care about outsiders, they didn't, either.

5. THE TEAM, THE TEAM, THE TEAM.

"At the end of the day, all we have is each other, so you need to get to know your teammates. That's why we decide who rooms with whom, in the dorms and on the road."

This was by design. I didn't see any point having two seniors room together on the road, because they already knew each other. No, you split them up and put each of them with a freshman who could benefit from a little guidance.

Same thing with the dorm assignments. Two guys from the same neighborhood? That's too easy. So you pair up the kid from downtown Detroit with the kid from rural Ohio. They get to know each other. Four years later, you've got one helluva senior class, and they get a friend for life.

I just didn't go in for cliques, but there are lots of ways to break them up. When we mixed guys up, they almost always got along, because we weren't recruiting jerks. Might have taken some of them a little adjusting, but what's wrong with that? Come back to one of our reunions, and you'll see how many long-term friendships started in South Quad or the Campus Inn or at dinner on the way home from a road trip.

So I told them: "We can play individually like a bunch of fools and lose, or we can come together as a team and win. Take your pick. But if you're going to play on this team, I'm going to make your decision for you, and that decision has already been made. YOU WILL LOOK LIKE A TEAM, ACT LIKE A TEAM, AND PLAY LIKE A TEAM!"

If the people in this country got along as well as the people we had on those teams—man, I'm telling you, we wouldn't have half the problems we do. And the only reason we don't get along is because we don't know each other. You may *think* you hate someone, but once you find out what they're really about, you realize they're okay. They're like me.

And that's the most important thing a team can do for anyone.

But it only works if you lay out your expectations on Day One. In that first meeting, we defined who we were, where we were going, and how we were going to get there—and that's exactly what happened.

8

Set Goals That Get Results

I've made thousands of speeches for all kinds of organizations, and at a lot of these meetings, after I'm done the CEO will get up to the podium to give a little pep talk to his people. At some point in his chat, the guy will put some slide up there showing everyone what their goals are supposed to be for the coming year.

"Now I want everyone to look at this slide up there," he'll say. "We need to increase our total revenue by this much, we need to increase profits by this much, and we need to increase customer satisfaction by that much."

Everyone nods—and then they go home and forget the whole thing.

Now, I believe in goals—big time!—but the goals these CEOs put up on the screen almost never work, and I'm going to tell you why. First, the people staring at that slide didn't have a single thing to do with establishing those goals. That list is just the *boss's idea* of what he thinks they should be doing. The employees have never seen those goals before, and after that meeting, they're never going to see them again. How important can those goals be when the employees never even write them down? The slide goes off, the lights come on, and the whole idea disappears that instant.

That's almost the *exact opposite* of the way we made our goals at Michigan.

As soon as I had finished my annual first meeting with all the players, the seniors would get up in front of the room, address the team, and then *they* would establish the goals for that season.

That's right! *I didn't set any goals for the team!* NONE! The *seniors* set the goals for the team—because it's *their* team. And the funny thing is, they almost always set their goals higher than I would have. It's pretty damn hard for them to claim I set the bar too high for the team, when *they're* the ones who set it!

Here's how we did it: After I called the seniors up to the front of the room, it was their show, and they started asking their teammates what their goals were going to be for that season. Then they wrote them on the chalkboard, and I wrote them down, too.

Their goals could be anything, but they'd *always* say, "We're going to beat Ohio State," "We're going to win the Big Ten title," and "We're going to go to the Rose Bowl." Why? Because we're Michigan football, and those are our expectations.

Sometimes they might add they're going to *win* the Rose Bowl—which was always tough for us—and maybe even win a national title. If they got carried away, I might say, "Hey, that sounds great, but do you have any idea what it takes to win a national championship? You have to bust your butt constantly, you have to be perfect in *every* practice, and *every one of you* has to have your greatest year of practice. If you understand this, you go right ahead and put it up there, but if you don't, then don't just put it up there for the hell of it. Don't put any goal on that board you aren't willing to sacrifice everything to achieve."

Now, I never had a single team that backed down after I said that, but I wanted them to know that they'd better mean it—and they did.

That's what I call setting your goals. And you do that immediately, the moment you get your group together.

Once the seniors set up their main goals for that season, it was my job to tell them how we were going to achieve their goals. And that's why, in sports and in business, you keep score. I don't care what field you're in, there's always a score at the end of the day. It might not be fair, it might not be right, but when your day is done, there's going to be a number next to your name. That's just life. For us, the numbers we cared about weren't just total points, but first downs and rushing yards and passing yards and tackles and sacks and turnovers and penalties. You name it, we measured it, and we had *goals* for everything we measured, *every* game.

We kept track of so many stats it'd make your head spin, and we recorded all those results on a big board everybody walked past to get to the practice field. Why did we do it? If you study your football—or whatever industry you're in—you know what it takes to succeed, what the little things are you need to do right that add up to the big things.

For example, we always set the goal for our offense to score 24 points. We told our squad, the way we play football, no one will beat us if we score 24 points. Get 24, and we'll win. We'll worry about the defense. You get the points. And that's how we broke down the big goals into smaller goals, for every game.

*   *   *

Once the seniors established what we were shooting for that year, we wrote down all of their goals, and we posted that list in our locker room. Then I made every one of them write down all the team's goals on a three-by-five card.

Next, on the back of that card, I told them to write down what their *personal* goals were for the season. What are *your* goals? They might write down that they wanted to start in every game, to make so many tackles, to get named to the All-America team—or even just get in a game for the first time in their careers. Didn't matter what it was, so long as they meant it. I didn't want them to be embarrassed, either, about aiming too high, so I'd tell them that only one other person is going to see your goals, and that's me. I kept one copy of everyone's goals in my cabinet with each file, and they kept the other copy.

If your name was Anthony Carter, your job was to catch a lot of passes, score a bunch of touchdowns and be an All-American. But if you're a walk-on, your job might be to show up every day ready to work, be the best demo team player on the squad, and push the guy you're going against every day to become All-Big Ten. Doesn't matter. You have to have individual goals.

Then we slipped all of these cards into little blue plastic sleeves with a nice maize M on the front, and each player was *instructed* to carry that card with him wherever he went throughout the season. I did that for a few reasons. First, whenever a player came to see me, for any reason—it could be for their scheduled appointments every spring and every fall, or because they'd screwed up or even if they just had something on their minds they needed to talk about—I pulled that card out to see if they were making progress toward their goals. It gave us a framework to start our discussion. You've got to realize: If those are *your* goals on the back of *your* card, and you're not cutting it, you don't have much basis to complain to *me* that it's unfair or unrealistic. Well, hell, if it's too hard, why'd you say you were going to do it?

Those cards are a hell of a tool. If we're having a god-awful practice, and I'm getting madder and madder at what I'm seeing out there, all I had to do was blow my whistle, and tell them: "You guys are going inside that locker room, and before you take a shower or take your shoulder pads off or do *anything* else, you're going to pull out your goals and you're going to look at them, and then you're going to remember what we're trying to do out here and why your current effort just isn't going to cut it, if we're going to achieve YOUR goals, for YOUR team and YOUR self. Wake up! And *show* me you meant everything you said you were going to do when you wrote those goals down in our first meeting!"

The thing is, I wanted *everyone* in our organization to have their team goals and their individual goals on their minds when they woke up each morning, and when they went to bed each night. *This is what we're doing here, and this is what I'm doing today!* There's no other way to get there.

This worked. They learned how to set goals, and how to *achieve* those goals. And every year, the new class of seniors would pick up where the class before them had left off. Some years they might add a revenge game against a team that had upset us the previous year—*that* was always good motivation—or try to solve some internal problem we had the season before.

Do you know what the number one goal of the last two teams

I coached was? Number one, right at the top of the list—and it was unanimous!—"NO COMPLAINTS." *No complaints!*

Because we had harped so long and so hard on the importance of attitude for two decades—and we had great captains in 1988 and 1989—that was their number one goal. It came from *them*! And that's no BS. You ask those guys, they'll tell you: No complaints.

"No complaints" didn't mean you couldn't make a suggestion or ask me a question. That's still fair game. But what those seniors were saying is, No one on this team is coming into the locker room bitching and crying.

That, to me, was astounding. That was impressive. *That* is how leaders lead! There isn't anyone alive who wouldn't love to lead a group like that—and I did! I tell you this: It was no accident those were two of my best teams. They both won Big Ten titles and finished in the top ten—and the three teams after that did the same thing. Five straight Big Ten titles, five straight top ten finishes! Those were *leaders*!

And it started with "No Complaints!"

If you're going to lead, you need to make goals. And those goals can't come from the top down, they've got to come from the people who are responsible for achieving them. *Your* job is to help them get there, and remind them every day what *their* goals are, and what they have to do to make their dreams come true. Sorry, but showing them a slide once a year about what you think their goals *should* be just doesn't cut it, and it never will. Their goals have to come from *them,* and those goals have got to be in their *bones.*

Trust your people with that crucial responsibility, and they will never disappoint you. Far from it, they will almost always set the goals higher than you would have ever dared—and then *they* are the ones who are accountable for *their* goals!

When they show you what they are capable of conceiving, and accomplishing, they're going to knock your socks off. You just have to give 'em the chance to lead.

III

Build Your Team

9

Hire People Who Want to Work for You

This is really a key chapter, because it is absolutely *critical* that you surround yourself with people who understand your program and what you stand for. If you don't have that, you're in trouble, because no one—*but no one*—is good enough to succeed without great people.

Fine. So how do you put a great staff together?

Let's start with what you DON'T do: hire people who are begging to leave their current jobs!

The one surefire way to get me *not* to hire you is to send me your résumé, especially if you've already got a good job. I won't be interested, because in a couple years, you'll be doing the same thing to me that you're doing to your current boss: looking for a better deal. Nothing irritates me more than that. Then I'll be stuck training someone new, trying to get him to figure out me and our system all over again. And now I'm wasting a lot of time and energy I should be spending on bigger things. Like our goals, and our people!

Like I said earlier, when you're the subordinate, don't spend your time looking for your next job. Work hard at your current job, and they'll find you.

Now, when you're on the other side of the equation, the opposite applies: Don't hire people looking to jump somewhere else. Hire the ones looking to *work harder where they are*!

It's easy to avoid job jumpers: Hire people you already know. I know this is a pretty simple concept, but how many companies ignore it? If you have to rely solely on a résumé and an interview, you're headed for trouble.

I'd see the people I hired coming up through the ranks, working at a good high school we recruited, or coaching for people I trusted. I knew what their bosses and players were saying about them. Sometimes they'd start working at our camps, so I could watch them work up close for years before I made them an offer to join us.

I spent more time critiquing a potential assistant than I did a recruit—and for good reason. That coach is going to be around a lot longer than that player is! That's why, before I hired someone, I'd go to his house and meet his family, just like I would with a recruit. But in the case of a coach, instead of getting to know his parents, I wanted to meet his spouse, because you can ruin a good person real fast with a bad spouse. But if you have an enthusiastic man with a strong wife who supports him, that's someone you can count on. I even got to know their kids, and if their mother and father were close by, why not visit with them, too?

All right, you say that's fine for a football program with 150 people involved, but it takes too long for a business with thousands. Let me ask you this: If you don't take the time to do this, and you hire the wrong guy, how long does it take you to hire and train his replacement when he leaves you in two years? How long does it take you to clean up the mess the guy left behind because he didn't know what he was doing, or he was dishonest or lazy? It's a classic "pay me now, or pay me later" scenario. Your time is better spent up front. If you have the time and money to clean up after them, you have the time and money to avoid the mess in the first place.

I never, ever hired someone just based on some piece of paper and an interview. By the time I offered them a job, I knew they were my kind of guys, hardworking and loyal. I was only surprised once—but that's for a later chapter.

The easiest way to avoid all these problems is to hire from *within your organization.* For me, that meant hiring former players to become graduate assistants, and graduate assistants to become position coaches, and position coaches to become offensive or defensive coordinators. And when it was time for me to step down, I hired my coordinator to replace me!

Heck, when I came to Michigan from Miami, I brought my whole staff with me. Look at the guys I hired. Gary Moeller was a captain at Ohio State when I was working for Woody there, back in 1962. You think I didn't know that guy? He was a great captain, a great assistant coach at Miami of Ohio and Michigan, and of course he became a great head coach here, too, after I stepped down. You never had to worry about that guy.

I hired guys like Jerry Hanlon and Tirrell Burton. I met Jerry when he was coaching high school football in Ohio and I was recruiting his players for Miami. Tirrell was the best tailback Miami of Ohio ever had—and I know this because I was coaching at Bowling Green when Tirrell was terrorizing our defense!

I once told Tirrell's wife, Sue—a great woman—that we just couldn't catch her husband, but then no one could. And she said, "I did!" Unfortunately, we didn't have Sue Burton on scholarship at Bowling Green when we needed her.

Those guys got calls all the time but they stayed with me at Michigan, and don't think I don't appreciate that. If you want to have long-term success, you need some long-term lieutenants, and you simply will not find two better ones anywhere than Jerry Hanlon and Tirrell Burton. Just don't tell them I said that, because it'll go to their heads. And we can't have that.

When you promote from within, you motivate everyone else in your organization, too. When they see other guys at their level getting picked for bigger things, with a little hard work they know they can do it, too. And I want that!

You put all that together, and you see why we never had a problem here with guys spending all their time trying to jump to the next job. Since 1929, we've had seven head coaches, and since I came here in 1969, just three, and we never should have lost that second one, Gary Moeller. Lloyd Carr's been here eleven years already, and there are a lot of people—a *lot* of people—in these hallways who've been here ten, twenty, even thirty years. Coaches, trainers, secretaries, you name it. And this is a tough business.

So what does that say? It says we hired the right people.

Well, you live by the sword, you die by the sword, and that's fair, too. Our guys were not résumé writers. They focused on the job they were doing for Michigan, and they did it damn well. Naturally enough, other schools came calling for them. NFL teams, too.

When this happened, they would come in and ask me, Should I apply for this one or not? I'd ask them about it, and tell them what I knew about the people there, and give them my advice. If it was a bad situation, I'd tell them not every promotion is a step up. But if it was a good opportunity, I'd tell them "I'll make the call for you." I couldn't be a hypocrite, because that's how I got every job I've had in coaching—and that's how we got them to come here, too. That's the kind of turnover you're going to have if you're successful.

I had thirty-six assistant coaches at Michigan, and eleven of them became head coaches elsewhere, and I'm sure many more could have done it if they'd wanted to. Look at the list. Larry Smith won three consecutive Pac-10 titles at USC—and beat me in my last game at the Rose Bowl, the bum! Don Nehlen had a great run at West Virginia, and I think Les Miles will win one at LSU. No ham-and-eggers in there. For three years the head coaches of Army and Navy were both former assistants of mine. And they all went with my blessing.

Now, when they take a job at another school, and I need to replace a position coach here at Michigan, I might call them to see if they know someone good. They might even have someone in their ranks ready to take the next step. The key is, they know exactly the kind of guy I want working for me at Michigan. So we hire their guy, and everyone's happy. And that's how it's *supposed* to work!

Let's talk about Bill McCartney. You might recall him as the former Colorado coach who won a national title, then became a leader in Promise Keepers. But when I met him he was a completely different guy!

When I arrived in Ann Arbor, Bill was the head football and basketball coach at Dearborn Divine Child, a Catholic high school about thirty minutes from Ann Arbor. I'd recruited his players, we'd talked a lot, and I had watched him win state titles in football *and* basketball. Now, you just knew, *this* was a guy who could coach!

But because I was around a lot—talking to his players, talking to other coaches, and sometimes just watching him—I knew what was going on. After games, Bill would head for the bar, have a few beers, light up a smoke, and the first guy who said something he didn't like, he'd take him out back! Obviously, that wasn't something I needed at Michigan.

So one day in 1974 I went down to see him. I sat across from him and laid it on the line. "Bill, you're obviously one helluva coach, and I'd like to hire you at Michigan. But I'm going to tell you something right now: You're going to quit smoking and going to bars—and without an ironclad guarantee from you about all of that, I'm not going to take you on."

He looked me in the eye, he gave me his word, and because I knew him, I felt I could trust him. I also knew his wife, and she was rock-solid. So I hired him on the spot.

Well, Bill came up here to Ann Arbor and not only did he quit smoking and drinking, before you knew it, he was born again. He started coaching the outside linebackers, then I promoted him to defensive coordinator, and I wasn't surprised when Colorado came calling for him in 1982. I encouraged him to take the job, and he had the best run of any football coach in Colorado history.

But think about it. If I'd just taken Bill because he won some state titles, I wouldn't have known what I was getting into, and it would have been a disaster for both of us. Can you imagine having a guy like that in Ann Arbor, when everyone here watches everything we do? Ho, man!

But if I had ignored him because of a few things I'd heard, I would have missed out on one of the best coaches we've ever had here, and he might never have made it to the national stage. But because I knew him, *really* knew him, I believed he could change, and he did. That was a great decision.

Bill still calls me every once in a while, and the first thing he says is, "Bo, I'm praying for you." And that's a good thing, because I'm sure I could use it! He's a helluva coach and a unique guy, and I love him.

Every coach I hired—hell, every trainer and manager and secretary, too, for that matter—I hired exactly this way.

Take Lloyd Carr. When he was a high school coach in Downriver Detroit, he came to our camps, he watched our practices, and we recruited his players. After he was named the state's high school Coach of the Year in 1975, he became an assistant at Eastern Michigan for about a third the money he was already making. Like I said, you've got to put mentors before money, and Lloyd did that. That impressed me.

When we had an opening here, Gary Moeller and Bill McCartney told me we've just got to get Carr. Right there, they had my attention.

Well, Lloyd comes in for the interview on the same day my decision to suspend five players for smoking pot hits the Detroit papers, so I'm already in a great mood. After we talk for a while, I ask Lloyd if he's hungry. Knowing Lloyd's interest in Michigan, he could have eaten a porterhouse steak an hour earlier, and he'd still say he was famished. So I grabbed Bill and Gary and we all went to the old Pretzel Bell here in town. After dinner I'm backing out of my parking spot in the structure and some guy behind me just *leans* on the horn. I mean, really lays into it.

Well, if you know me, you know that's just an invitation. I just hold my position right there, until the guy stops honking his damn horn, then I shift into forward to make room for him to pass. But at the same instant I'm about to do it, this SOB leans on the damn horn again! That did it. I throw it back into reverse, and this guy doesn't think I'll do it, but I don't care and I back into his bumper. He clearly doesn't know who he's dealing with! He finally figures I'm crazy and backs way the hell up, and we get out of there.

By now Lloyd is probably wondering if he really wants to work for me, but when we go back to my office to settle things up, he's still very interested. Before we can finalize the deal, though, my phone rings, and I've got to take this call, so Lloyd excuses himself to give me some privacy. I'm yakking on the phone, and Lloyd's in the hallway, talking to McCartney.

Bill asks him, "Did you get the job?"

Lloyd pauses. "To be honest, I don't know."

After I'm done barking on the phone and hang it up—bang!— Bill knocks on the door. "What is it?"

"Bo, did you offer Lloyd the job?"

I gave that a second. "If he's too dumb to realize he's been hired to coach football at the University of Michigan, then he's certainly too dumb to *work* for the University of Michigan!"

Too harsh? Maybe to an outsider. But you got to figure, if he can't take *that*, he's not going to like our coaches meetings! Better to find out now.

And that's how we hired one of the greatest coaches in Michigan history. I know Lloyd could coach elsewhere for a lot more money—but he's loyal to Michigan. Guess that one worked out pretty well.

And you know why? *Because we knew him!*

10

Get the Most Out of Your Staff

After you hire good people, it's your job to get the most out of them.

Don't surround yourself with a bunch of yes-men. Heck no! Guys like that just don't do you any good. I wanted their honest opinions—and I got 'em. But after you hear what they have to say, you've got to make the final call. No one else.

Now, I know I've got a reputation as some kind of control freak. And yeah, there's probably some truth to it. I paid attention to all kinds of details, from the distance between my tackles' feet when they lined up in their stances—which I measured with a yardstick I carried around during practice—to the exact minute the bus left the parking lot. But when it came to my assistants, I didn't want to control the conversation. I wanted to hear what they had to say.

If you walked by one of our staff meetings, with everyone shouting and pounding their fists, you'd probably think we hated each other. But the fact is, we loved it! In those staff meetings, I *wanted* a debate—even an argument, if it got things out in the open.

We'd have these great, knock-down, drag-out coaches meetings where we'd argue about *everything,* from which guy to start to what plays to run to how to block a basic goal line off-tackle run. That's why I never wanted an assistant coach who couldn't contribute anything to our meeting. Because if he can't, why do I need him? By the same token, I didn't want an assistant who's just going to spew out a lot of BS that isn't going to work. We don't have time for that!

What I *did* have was a lot of smart, strong-willed guys who knew what they were doing, and weren't afraid to speak up. And I was NOT intimidated by that. No! Because why should I be? I wanted the best ideas on the table. Hell, you don't want to hear on *Sunday* that someone in that room had a better idea for stopping that play. That's too late. Game's over! Your idea is no good to us then.

Let's say it's a typical Tuesday morning meeting, and I lay out my plan for how to run some play that Saturday. Jerry Hanlon might come back with, "Dammit Bo, you can't block it that way!"

"Like hell we can't! We can, and we will—and that's the way it's going to be!"

Then Jerry, who set up the practice schedule every day, would just growl, making me think he'd surrendered. Then he'd quietly go off and set up the list of offensive plays I wanted to run—but Hanlon would pit my plays against certain defensive schemes that our offense couldn't block the way I wanted to.

I wouldn't realize this until the middle of practice, when it was too late. I'd just glare at Jerry and say, "Why you little sonuvabitch!" But we'd end up blocking it his way—for that practice, at least. And a lot of times, I've got to admit, Hanlon was right. Just not nearly as often as he claims.

That's all right. If you didn't want their opinions, you shouldn't have hired them. And if all their opinions are the same as yours, you don't need them! It's good for morale, too—because they know their opinions are important to you, that they're valued.

A few years ago, Lloyd Carr and I were just sitting around, talking about the old days, when he said, "You know, sometimes, when things were going just a little too smoothly in one of our staff meetings for your taste, I think you'd throw a wrench in things, just to see what would happen.

"We always loved it when you were mad—so long as it wasn't at us! You'd pick on an assistant, just to see what he'd stand up for and what he wouldn't. You might say, 'I don't think so-and-so is practicing worth a damn. In fact, I think the second-stringer's better. I say we move him up!' Then you'd sit back and see if the coach defended the starter or not. If he did, you figured the starter's job was safe. But if he didn't, you might wonder if you were right about the second-stringer after all.

"And sometimes you'd get two of us arguing over this play or that blocking scheme, just to see the fur fly—then you'd just sit back and watch us go at it! I can see why you did it, now, though—to make sure all our ideas were tested, and the best ones rose to the top."

Well, damn you, Lloyd! And here I thought I was so clever.

But I tell you this: We never, *ever* took the field on game day when we didn't agree on what we were going to do and how we

were going to do it. On Saturdays, make no mistake, we were on
the same page.

Lynn Koch served twenty years as my secretary here. She's a
very together woman, very sweet, very traditional. But trust me,
we don't have any shrinking violets around here. She had some
moxie!

In our tenth year at Michigan, 1979, we hired a new assistant
for Lynn named Mary Passink—another sharp one. It was near
the end of Mary's very first week, I can't find my plane ticket
for some recruiting trip, and that just drives me crazy. I turn
my office upside down, files flying everywhere. I storm up to
Lynn's desk, and I'm going on and on while she's trying to get
my attention. Finally she reaches across the desk, grabs my lapels
and says, "Dammit, Bo! Would you shut the hell up and listen
to me!"

Now, Mary's standing right there, completely stunned. I
mean, she's frozen! She'd probably heard plenty about my famous temper, and she's figuring Lynn's about to get fired—or
worse—and then Mary would be forced into the top job on her
fourth day, working for a tyrant.

But that's not what happened. I finally snapped out of it, shut
up and looked at Lynn. "Bo," she said, *"the ticket is in your
briefcase."*

And it was. Problem solved!

If there's yelling back and forth, but the right people are doing the yelling—well, hell, you forget about that. And you get
your plane ticket out of your briefcase, and get going, so you
don't miss your flight!

*   *   *

Here's another pitfall: The leader who runs his regular staff meetings just by going point by point, without ever bringing anything in from the outside world, every day. Man, that gets to be pretty dull pretty fast. You're not going to last a month doing it that way.

Sometimes our coaches meetings weren't tense or technical at all. Sometimes I'd just be opening my mail, Hanlon would be doing a crossword puzzle, and Burton would be talking about some movie he and his wife had seen the night before. That was all right, because I always believed there's a time to BS a little.

If there was something going on in the world that I felt required discussion, we'd discuss it! We'd talk about anything and everything, whatever was on our minds. Current events, campus stuff, politics. THAT was always interesting—oh yeah!—especially when you've filled your staff with a bunch of *Democrats,* for crying out loud.

One night we're sitting here in a meeting, and it gets to be nine o'clock, when someone says, "Wait a minute! Muhammad Ali is fighting Joe Frazier tonight, and it's on closed circuit TV at Crisler. Let's go!" So we take off, right then and there, racing to get there before the fight starts. I'm tailing Elliot Uzelac, an assistant coach, when he slams on his brakes, and I rear-end him. He starts giving me some crap about a bunch of cars stopping in front of him at a red light, but I'm not buying it. He got an earful.

All this stuff may seem like a waste of time to you—and sometimes it is. There always comes a point in any meeting when you want to get to the bottom line and get it done, because you only have so much time. In the same way you have to read your players, you have to read your staff, to see what they need.

But when you have the time to knock a few random topics

around, I think it humanizes your staff. True, we're football first, last and always, but we're human beings, too. That's how you get to know your people, and how they get to know you.

Once you become the top guy, you've also got to accept the fact that, from now on, you're the bad cop, and your lieutenants are the good cops. It just can't be any other way, because it's the difference between your uncle telling you to straighten up, and your dad.

This is exactly how Doyt and Ara and Woody all operated— because it's the right thing to do. When I was Woody's assistant, I was the youngest guy on the staff, and probably closer to the players than anyone else he had. I could go into any fraternity house on campus and find anyone we needed in a minute. I knew *perfectly well* what was going on with those guys, what they were up to. When Paul Martin, a kid from Canton McKinley, was still on campus when school let out, I was the guy who took him out to the movies that weekend—and he remembers that to this day.

Because I was in touch with the players, I could play the middle man sometimes, and try to cool things down between Woody and a player before everything blew up. I know damn well I saved Woody a lot of grief—just as my assistants saved me a lot of grief.

I first hired Gary Moeller when I was at Miami. All the Miami players were asking Mo what this new guy Schembechler was like. "Oh, you're gonna love him!" he said. "Great guy. A players' coach. Woody was the bear, not Bo!"

Boy, were they in for a surprise!

When you become the top guy, you simply cannot act like an assistant—because you're not one anymore. It's like Harry Truman said: If you're the top guy, and you want to be loved every minute of every day, get a dog.

Before I go on, let me be clear: Your assistants can't be buddy-buddy with the players, either, because once they go that route, they've lost their authority. And they can't undermine your decisions, either, by telling the players they don't agree with you. All the players I coached at Ohio State knew I adhered to all the rules and regulations of Woody Hayes, and I did not waver. My players at Michigan knew the same thing about my assistants. If you have any assistants who try to elevate themselves at the expense of the head coach, they HAVE to be gone—because there's a difference between being a good cop with the players, and being a traitor to the head coach.

There's a flip side to this, too, of course. If there was ever a dispute between an assistant and a player, it was a simple solution: The assistant reigns, just like I told them in the first meeting. If you're consistent on this, the players will quit trying to go over the assistant's head to you, because they know it won't do them any good.

If you let the subordinates go over your assistant's head, pretty soon you won't have any assistants worth a damn. Why would they want to work for a guy who doesn't back them up? I remember one time Anthony Carter, our famous wide receiver, wasn't getting along with Don Nehlen. As great as Anthony was, that was easily resolved: The assistant coach reigns!

I liked my coaches—a lot—but I wasn't always exactly warm and fuzzy to work with. I'd listen to the assistants as long as they wanted to talk—unless I decided I really didn't like what they were saying, in which case I'd say "Well, that's just plain horse crap, and this meeting is over!"

When people ask Jerry Hanlon what it was like to coach for me, he always says two things: "One, I'm going to heaven. And two: If you're working for Bo, all you've got to do is be hired one more time than you've been fired."

He was fired many a time. He'd be out the building, and already home. "How'd your day go, honey?" "Well, Bo fired me again. Otherwise, it was okay."

But before long, I would look around and say, "Who's gonna do the practice schedule?"

"Hanlon does it, Bo. You know that."

"Aw, dammit. Well then get him back here!" And I'd send someone to get him. Jerry's always said, "I was hired one more time than I was fired. And around here, that's called job security."

Like I said, we were a *very* organized outfit, and the secretaries had a lot to do with that. One day I'm in our coaches meeting, and I can't find the damn itinerary. So I storm out of the room and bark at Lynn. "Where the hell is the return trip on the itinerary? How the hell could you forget that? Now get your head out of your ass, and get some work done around here!"

Not more than a minute later she barges into the coaches meeting with the itinerary file and says, calm as can be, in front of everyone, "The reason there is no return trip on the itinerary, Coach Schembechler, is because you didn't fill it out. Now get your head out of your ass, and get some work done around here!"

You could have heard a pin drop!

But as soon as I burst out laughing, everyone else did, too.

*   *   *

So we argued and battled plenty, but the key was, I never felt that after all the dust had settled, and it was time to make a decision, that I wasn't still the head man—just like I learned from Doyt. My assistants never confused the fact that just because we'd argued back and forth in those meetings that, in the end, it didn't mean I wasn't still the head coach when we walked out of that room.

Here's why: In the long run, you cannot win consistently *in any field* if you let someone else make the important decisions for you. You cannot delegate important decisions. You've just got to make them yourself. If you mess them up, then it's your fault. But that's the price of leadership.

That's why for twenty-one years, Michigan had just one guy giving the scouting report, one offensive coordinator, and one guy breaking down the quarterback's performance on film on Sunday—and his name was Bo Schembechler. Yes, I had very talented assistant coaches who gave me a lot of good information—they were the best in the nation, bar none—but when the play went into the huddle, it was me who sent it in—and it was me who answered for it if it failed.

We debated almost everything, but I don't recall any debates about that.

You can't throw your assistants under the bus, either, whether that's in front of your stockholders or your board or the media. If you set up the deal I'm talking about here—where you get all their opinions but everyone agrees the top guy makes all final decisions, and everyone supports those decisions—well then, you sure as heck better take responsibility for those decisions afterward, no matter how they turn out.

September 16, 1989. It's my last year, and we're playing Notre Dame at home. We've got a good team—with Leroy Hoard, Greg McMurtry and Greg Skrepenak—but they do, too, with Tony Rice and Ricky Watters and Rocket Ismail. Good? Hell, we were ranked number two, and they were ranked number one. That's pretty good!

We start the second half down just 7-6. We kick the ball to Rocket, and he runs the damn thing all the way back for a touchdown—the first kickoff returned for a touchdown since I had arrived at Michigan twenty years earlier! That makes me mad.

Early in the fourth we cut their lead to 17-12 and we've got to kick off again. Now I'm on the headset, telling the coaches I want to squib it, kick it out of bounds, eat it—anything but kick it to Rocket Ismail. But they're unified. "No, Bo, we can stop him. Last time was a fluke. Let's send a message!"

I agree. We kick it to Rocket—and I'll be damned if he doesn't run it all the way back again for another touchdown! We lose, 24-19, with Rocket scoring 14 of their points on two kick returns.

Afterward the know-it-all writers are asking how I could be so stupid to kick the ball to Rocket twice. Whose brilliant idea was that?

I did not think twice before answering: "It was my decision, it's my responsibility, and if you don't like it, you can blame me." I wasn't being noble here, folks—I was just telling the truth. Because if everyone on my staff knows I always make the final decision, and they're sworn to support it even if they disagree, then it's also true that I could have overruled them and said, "No! We are NOT kicking the ball to Rocket again! Squib it!" And we would have done just that. But that's not what I decided to do.

Why did I take the blame? Because I deserved it—that's why!

11

Recruit for Character

I don't need to tell you talent is important—anyone knows that—but it's easy to get blinded by it. And it's a big mistake, too. Character counts for more. Much more.

I can't tell you how many times we passed up hotshots for guys we thought were better *people,* and watched our guys do a lot better than the big names, not just in the classroom, but *on the field*—and naturally, after they graduated, too. Again and again, the blue chips faded out, and our little up-and-comers clawed their way to all-conference and All-America teams. And even when some bad-acting blue-chipper did the job on the field for some other school, I never felt any remorse over not taking him. We didn't want him, anyway!

When you recruit for character, you sleep a lot better, too.

I remember this great prospect we were trying to get. This guy was a serious player—the real deal. So we sent Denny Brown to recruit this kid.

By this time, almost everyone out there knows we don't pay players to come here. Heck, we don't even promise them playing time, no matter how good they are. And there's no discussion about it, either.

When Denny comes back, he says, "Bo, you're not going to believe it, but the kid's coach said his player wants to go to Michigan, but it will cost us several thousand dollars."

"Denny, he didn't say THAT, did he?"

"Oh yeah, Bo, he did. I swear it."

As usual, I didn't spend a minute mulling it over. "Denny, you get me that coach on the line, and get me a tape recorder, because I'm recording every single word that SOB says."

A few minutes later, we're all set up, and I get on the line. "Jeez, Coach, I haven't seen many high school players like the guy you've got."

And this coach got right to the point. "You can have him, Bo, for $5,000."

"You're talking $5,000 for the kid to come here?"

"Yeah."

"Now where do you think I'm going to get money like that?"

"Come on, Bo—you can get it from your alums."

"How in hell could I ask my alums for that kind of money without raising eyebrows?"

"You guys got your ways," he said. I couldn't believe the nerve of this guy! I knew I had to end this thing fast—before I threw up.

"Coach, you're making a big mistake," I said. "You're not doing the right thing for this kid. You shouldn't be doing this."

I hung up, and played the tape for the assistant coaches, and we all had a good laugh. Then I sent it off to the hardworking folks at the NCAA—and they promptly did nothing, which is the case far too often.

Could I have gotten away with paying that high school coach off? Probably. But every time I'd look at that player, knowing how we'd gotten him, I'd get sick to my stomach. Wouldn't you?

Would that kid have helped us? Who knows? A few years later he made it to the NFL, so he could play. But he would have ruined the chemistry of our team—and if you lose that, no star can save you. Besides, the guys I already had playing that position were darn good anyway, so what's the difference? But I was certain of this: Whoever I had in that position *wanted* to play for Michigan, and he didn't need $5,000 to convince him.

Things like that I didn't even think about, because there was just nothing to debate.

Do you know what I did that night? I slept like a baby. Just like always.

In the recruiting process, home visits are critical. You can win or lose a prospect right there, and sometimes it can be pretty dramatic—or downright funny.

It's 1977, I'm recruiting a kid from Michigan, and it's colder than hell. As I'm leaving their home, John Robinson is walking in. Now, he's just finished his first season as Southern Cal's head coach—which he capped by beating us in the Rose Bowl, the devil—and he can offer the kid California weather.

John walks up wearing this snazzy suit—but it was designed for California in July, not Michigan in January. He's freezing his tail off. And to top it off he's wearing these fancy Italian loafers, with no socks! That guy wasn't from around these parts.

Now, John and I were already becoming close friends—to this day he stays at my home here in Ann Arbor a few times a year—so I put my arm around him and told the family, "This man is a fine coach, a fine person, and USC is a really good school. But I'm sorry, you just can't trust a man who wears shoes like this!"

Johnny told me later that after I left, he thought he was making a pretty good pitch—but they sat there the whole time staring at his shoes! Needless to say, that kid went to Michigan.

Just a few years ago, Robinson was over at my house, and he looks down at my shoes.

"You dog! You're wearing the same damn shoes you made fun of twenty years ago!"

"Why, yes, I am," I said. "But John, they're *in style* now!"

Just like any stage of recruiting, in any field, the home visit can cut both ways. If we lost a few in the home, I'll bet twice that many prospects lost *us* during our visit. Some guys probably didn't realize it, but we were checking them out, too.

When we left a prospect's home, I'd always discuss the visit with whoever was traveling with me. "You see that living room, Tirrell? That's a nice home." I didn't care if they were rich or poor; I just liked to see a neat, orderly, comfortable place to live. That told me something about the prospect's family.

One time we were gunning for the best quarterback in the Midwest—and everyone else was, too. We thought we might have a shot at him, but when we got there, this kid was slumped in his chair, he didn't bother to get up to shake our hands, and he started barking at his mom to get him a pop or something—and she ran to the kitchen to get it for him! Boy, that wasn't the way *my* mom did it!

It didn't take long for me to realize this boy might have been blessed with a golden arm, but he was also cursed with a nickel head. After just thirty minutes or so, I gave my assistant the nod, thanked the family for their time, then got the hell out of there.

Now if that guy had really wanted to come to Michigan, it'd be a tougher call, but I'd only consider taking him if I thought we could change him. And that seems not to have been possible. He went to a rival school, and he really was great—but he really was a jerk, too. He set records, ticked off his teammates, transferred to another school, and did the same thing. He bounced around the NFL for a long time, but after a couple years with one franchise, he'd tick off his teammates again and they'd have to trade him. He finished his career with great numbers, but he never won a Super Bowl like Tom Brady, or a Big Ten ring like—well, like every quarterback we've ever had here at Michigan.

That long list includes Jimmy Harbaugh. His dad, Jack, was an assistant coach here until Stanford hired him in 1980, so Jim played his last two years of high school football in Palo Alto—but Stanford didn't even recruit him. Wisconsin showed some interest, and we scooped him up at the last minute.

Jim ended up being twice as good, in my book, as the Golden Arm—Harbaugh was the Big Ten MVP his senior year, beating the other guy by a mile—and Jim's teammates *liked* him. Maybe Harbaugh didn't have half the arm of the Golden Boy, but he had twice the brains and ten times the heart. Give me those specs, anyday.

Sometimes the make-or-break moment didn't happen until the final minutes of the process, when the recruits visited my office in Ann Arbor. We typically had about twenty in town each weekend, and we'd schedule all of them for back-to-back meetings with me in my office.

On a Saturday in 1984, we had Chris Spielman come in for his interview, with little Jamie Morris waiting right behind him.

Now, Spielman was a swashbuckling linebacker whose picture was on the Wheaties box—in high school! Jamie was just a 5-6 kick returner who had dreams of being a tailback.

Well, Spielman walks in wearing a T-shirt, torn jeans and a five-day shadow with some dip in his lip. I could only conclude he had not been fully briefed as to how we generally conducted business in my office. He's leaning back in his chair—and hell, those are *my* chairs!—and he starts telling me that Ohio State has promised him he'd start immediately, something we never do.

So I respond in my typically cool manner. "I'll tell you what, Spielman. With your torn T-shirt and your ripped jeans, you *go back* to Ohio State, you start for Earle Bruce, and we're going to *kick your butt*—each and every year!"

Now, Jamie claims he could hear me yelling outside the door—but I doubt it. The interview did end abruptly, however, when I stormed out the door and told Jamie all remaining interviews were canceled.

Sunday morning I came to my senses, and called Jamie at Campus Inn—at 6 A.M.

"Morris? Schembechler here! Let's talk!"

Jamie got down to my office just like that, and we had a nice chat. I liked him immediately. He was well dressed, polite and respectful. Jamie's dad was a Green Beret, who made his kids keep their rooms up to military standards, so I guess I shouldn't have been too surprised by that.

But none of that changed the fact that Jamie was five-foot-six. I honestly wasn't going to offer him anything, but Bob Thornbladh, the assistant coach who recruited him, really pushed for Jamie, and everyone else liked him so much, I had to consider it.

"Son, I don't know if you're big enough to handle a Big Ten season. Look at you! But I hear you can stop on a dime, and all the guys like you. I'll tell you what—if I've got a scholarship left over in a few weeks, I'll give it to you."

Then, dammit, I saw Jamie's eyes. Aw, fer cryin' out loud! You've never seen such a puppy-dog look. This was a kid from Boston whose brother Joe was a star at Syracuse—he went on to win a couple Super Bowls with the Giants—but Jamie somehow got his heart set on Michigan's winged helmet. You had to love that. So I backed down in a way I never would have the day before.

"All right," I said. "You just may be Michigan material after all." I offered him a full scholarship right then and there, and Jamie took it.

Of course—and I'll say more about this later—Jamie didn't just return kicks for us, he became our all-time leading rusher. Boy, can I judge talent! And, okay, we didn't beat Ohio State every year Spielman played, but two out of four ain't bad. Spielman ended up being even better than everyone had projected, he became a fine NFL linebacker, and is now one of the best analysts on TV—almost as good as Dierdorf. I like and respect that guy, so maybe I guessed wrong about him, too.

But in 1986, Jamie Morris ran wild over Spielman's defense for 210 yards—and nobody would have guessed that.

So you can give me the guy who *wants* to join us, every time. And you should take that guy, too.

12

Develop Leaders Underneath You

If you want to be a truly great leader, you'll develop other great leaders below you. And if you don't, you'll have to do everything yourself.

For most organizations, that means developing the people a tier or two below you, so they can lead the tier below *them*. I firmly believe this applies to just about every organization out there—and if you don't establish this, then the top managers get tired out by trying to supervise too many people, and the lower tiers get neglected and go wild. You can't have that, and succeed.

For Michigan football, the solution is senior leadership. We establish that every year, right up front in our first team meeting, and we reinforce that every single day. I simply could not manage a dozen coaches, three dozen staff members and 125 players without a lot of help at every level of our organization, and I know Lloyd Carr feels the same way.

If it was only Bo yelling all day, before long it becomes me against them, and they'll tune me out. And hey, they had me outnumbered! You really can't afford a mutiny. So senior leadership is essential.

Players listen to each other differently than they listen to me. It's one thing if I chew you out. Hell, they expect that! But it's another thing entirely when one of your teammates, a senior you look up to, tells you you're not cutting it, that you're not acting like a Michigan man. Sometimes that hits home a little harder.

Our seniors were more than just policemen, though. They were guides. If I had a freshman who was a little confused, I could tell him, Just follow a senior, and you'll be all right.

I expected an awful lot from my seniors, and I made no apologies for it. If you were a senior on my team, I didn't care if you were a preseason All-American or a four-year demo team player, you better be playing the best football of your career—and you better be ready to *lead*! Otherwise, I'm not going to have any use for you.

Now, in exchange, the seniors got a lot of things from me the younger guys didn't. If you ask my players, they'll tell you I didn't treat anyone differently on the team—didn't matter if you were offense or defense, were All-Americans or walk-ons, black or white, whatever—with ONE exception: seniors.

There's just no denying that I treated seniors differently than the rest of the team. NOT in terms of discipline, or punctuality, or effort or the rules. No one got a break on those things, *ever*. I'm talking about little perks, so everyone knew the seniors held a special position on the team. And the other guys knew that one day, they'd be seniors, too. That gave them something to look forward to.

What did I do for the seniors? Let's say we're playing Stanford in Palo Alto, California, and we're going to fly across the US of A.

I'm going to guess that there were maybe fifteen or twenty first-class seats. And in those seats, every time, you will NEVER find a coach, or an athletic director, or some VIP. Not even the head coach. ONLY SENIORS. If you're a senior third-stringer, you've got a seat waiting for you in first class, and if you're a freshman all-everything, you're sitting in the back next to the bathrooms.

Seniors also had greater access to me. They had a bigger say in team decisions. *They* decided, not me, what the team's goals were going to be. Whenever one of their teammates got in trouble with me, on campus or with the police, those were the only players I consulted. And they were even tougher than I was!

I can think of no better example than the case of Mike Gillette, one of the best kickers Michigan's ever had. He could punt, he could kick, he could nail field goals from halfway down the field.

This was not a player I had trouble with. I also liked him because, unlike some kickers, he was a stone-cold athlete, and mentally tough. We had recruited him as a quarterback. I wanted him to redshirt his freshman year, back up Harbaugh in Jim's senior year, then quarterback the team for the next three years, but Mike also played catcher on the baseball team, and he wanted to play right away. I could understand that.

In 1985, as a freshman, Mike took the starting kicker's job and he held it all season. We were on a great run, with just one loss to top-ranked Iowa, 12–10, and a 3–3 tie against Illinois, heading into Ohio State week. The Thursday before the big game Mike was back in South Quad studying, like he was supposed to be, until he let a few other freshmen talk him into going down to a local college bar and shooting some pool.

Now, I don't need to tell you I didn't spend my evenings going from bar to bar trying to find my players, so I didn't catch him. One of the *seniors* did—and boy was he mad!

At 7 A.M. the next morning, the day before the Ohio State game, a few of the seniors walked into my office to see me. They laid out the situation for me, just the facts. They didn't say anything else. They didn't tell me what to do. They had no say in the punishment. But they didn't walk all the way down to my office that morning for the hell of it, either.

Their actions alone let me know they felt it was time for Michael to be held accountable for his actions. The seniors were counting on me to be consistent and fair, and not influenced by Michael's vital role on the team or the enormity of the game ahead of us—because they all knew how badly I wanted to beat the Bucks, too.

Now, think about this for a minute. For these seniors, this was going to be their last Ohio State game—the biggest game of the year for us. Heck, it's probably the biggest game in the country. Our guys only get four chances to beat Ohio State their entire career, and they might get to play in only two or three of those games, if they're lucky. And it didn't take a genius to figure out that benching Gillette risked sacrificing the biggest game of their lives.

So the stakes were huge for those guys—and yet, they were not going to compromise the values of *their* team just to win. And by God, that impressed me. *Those guys were leaders.*

When they finished saying what they had to say, I thanked them for coming down, because I knew that couldn't have been easy for them. I told them I'd take care of it—and I did.

The second they left my office, I had our assistant coach, Alex Agase—my old friend from Ara's staff—call Gillette, pronto.

Of course, he tells Gillette to get his butt down to my door immediately, and Gillette runs, gets here in about three minutes. He shows up at my door right as Brent Musburger and Ara Parseghian—who are doing the game for ABC the next day—are leaving.

Gillette's not stupid. He knows I know, and he knows he's in big trouble, so I don't waste any time. "How the hell am I going to tell the national TV commentators that my starting kicker is not going to start for the Ohio State game?"

Now, Mike is tough. He doesn't cry. He doesn't make any excuses, but he explains that he and his buddies went to the back of the bar, they weren't drinking, and they were there for only ten or fifteen minutes when one of our senior captains, Brad Cochran, came in with a teammate to see if any of our guys were out. Of course Cochran sees these freshmen playing pool, and when he tells them to get the hell out of there, they do.

It turned out Mike's story checked out, but I didn't care. I did not hesitate. Not a bit. Because Mike knew the rules, and he violated them. How the hell could such a smart kid be so damn careless during Ohio State week, of all weeks? Maybe he figured, I'm just a kicker, it doesn't apply to me. To be honest, I don't know what he was thinking. But the rules applied to everybody—and I never did it by position. So, nothing personal—but you just don't go out playing pool on Thursday night.

The upshot was pretty simple: I felt I had no choice but to bench Mike, so I put Pat Moons in to do all the kicking that day—and he did the job. We won, 27–17, with Moons knocking in three extra points and two field goals.

On that basis, we didn't lose much. But that had nothing to do with my decision. Moons could have blown every kick he had that day, we could have lost a heartbreaking game to the Buckeyes by two points, and I still would tell you right now that benching Mike was the right decision. Because it was! Gillette violated the rules, the seniors turned him in, and I benched him. What credibility would I have with the seniors if I didn't? They would have no reason to believe a thing I said after that, and no reason to think their opinions mattered.

A month later I was still so mad at Mike, I didn't let him kick in the Fiesta Bowl either. Moons kept the top job for the first five games of the next season, too.

What happened next? Mike grew up, just like he was supposed to. I respected the fact that he took his punishment like a man, and we became pretty close after that.

By midseason of Mike's sophomore year, 1986, he hammered a record-breaking 53-yard field goal against Iowa, and later won the game with a last-second field goal. Mike still ranks third in scoring among all players at Michigan, just 29 points from first. If he hadn't missed those seven games, he'd probably own every Michigan scoring record there is, for anybody at any position.

Mike went back to baseball in 1990, just as I became president of the Detroit Tigers. He was going to sign with the Milwaukee Brewers when I called him up. "Now why the hell would you sign a contract with the Brewers when you can sign with the Detroit Tigers? I'm going to mail you a contract today, and you're going to sign it and get it back to me and get down to Lakeland next month for spring training."

Mike moved up to our AAA team in just a year and a half, but we had Mickey Tettleton up there, so Mike's career stalled again. I still think he could have made it to the NFL or the major leagues if he was more patient, but he was twenty-seven years old by then and wanted to get on with his life. I'm sorry, but you can't argue with that.

Mike's done well in finance, he's got a wife and four kids, and he's a helluva dad. And if his four-year-old boy keeps growing, he might break all his dad's records at Michigan, too—though I might advise him to stay in the dorm on Thursday night.

If you think back to that Friday morning, when the seniors came into my office, that's what the seniors wanted to see happen, that's exactly what *did* happen, and that's how senior leadership works. If you stand behind your seniors, they'll stand behind you.

Only a weak leader is threatened by strong leaders underneath him. If you don't have leadership *inside* the ranks, you're not going to be successful, because you will spend too much time policing the small things yourself, and create an "us against them" environment. It's far better to develop leaders underneath you, and trust them to do the right thing. They will.

13

Scuttle the Star System

All right. We've covered how you become a leader, how you hire your staff, how you recruit your people, and how you entrust your lieutenants to lead the rookies. All of it is essential to building a first-rate organization.

But none of it will count for much unless you know how to *manage* your people. You've got to keep your stars in line, the guys in the middle motivated, and the people at the bottom contributing to the success of the team.

Let's start with the stars. If you've recruited some hotshots, the easiest thing to do is let the stars run the show—and let me tell you, THAT is a big mistake! Because if they think they come before the team, you will simply not be successful in the long run. I know, it happens all the time—and I guess that was a good thing for us, because we loved beating those teams!

*   *   *

Like everyone else in coaching, I have a lot of respect for John Wooden, but I just can't abide by one of the principles he talks about in his latest book. He says his policy was not to be *equal,* but *fair.* Not equal, but fair? What the hell is that? I guess that means that if you're Bill Walton, you can break all the rules you want because you're a big star, but if you're some backup forward, you'd better be on time, or you're going to be in trouble.

I'm sorry, but that's just bull. How can your rules be fair, if they're not equal? I've got news for you: If it's not equal, it's not fair, and *everyone on your team already knows it*! The fastest way to demoralize your entire team is to make exceptions for the stars. Everyone sees it, and everyone resents it. You'll lose your troops—and it doesn't even help the stars either.

I've heard a lot of leaders—from coaches to corporate heads—give lip service to "No double standards" and the like, but you're not going to fool your people. They know if you're willing to make the sacrifice to enforce your rules or not.

If you're going to build a team, a *real* team, you simply *cannot* have one standard for the stars and another standard for everyone else—no matter what it costs you, or them. And that's a crucial point: As competitive as I am—and trust me, the legends about that are true—I *will not* compromise my values or the team's values to win a game. I refuse!

That means I have to be willing to lose. And that's not easy.

When we hammered home our famous mantra, "The Team, The Team, The Team," that didn't leave a lot of room for interpretation. When I came up with that, I wasn't trying to be clever. It means if you're late for the team bus, I don't care if you're Jim Mandich, Anthony Carter and Desmond Howard rolled into one.

That bus is leaving, it's leaving on time—and it's leaving without you!

Look, they *know* Bo is always sitting up at the front of the bus, and when pullout time comes, he just checks his watch and says, "Driver, it's time to go." We don't have anyone checking who's here and who isn't. We don't check! I never took roll. If you're on the bus, you must be on time, and if you're not on the bus, you must be late, and it's your fault. Driver, it's time to go!

We've had guys running up to the bus as we were pulling out—starters, even—and the guys on the bus always started yelling, "Coach! So-and-so's running up to the bus!" I didn't care who it was. I guarantee you right now I never even turned around to look, because the answer was always the same: Driver, it's time to go!

Everyone knew Bo's not mad at you, he's just leaving you. And I'll tell you why: Because it's just not fair to the other guys who took the trouble to get there on time. The bus waits for no man!

Driver, it's time to go!

And as your big All-American grows smaller in the bus's rearview mirror, he'll have time to consider if you really meant what you said about The Team, The Team, The Team. Leave a guy standing in the parking lot just once, and you better believe he'll be a half-hour early next time. Once everyone knows I'm not holding the bus for anyone, trust me, they get there. They always do.

That bus symbolized the foundation of our values: simple, straightforward, no exceptions. You start cutting corners for this guy or that situation, and before you know it, you're spending all your time playing judge and jury, deliberating over every little incident, when you should be leading your team. It's painful sometimes, but you create a lot fewer headaches for everyone, including the players, when you simply stick to your guns.

I always told Will Perry and Bruce Madej, our sports information directors, "Don't you *ever* promote any single player above the others, because we're not doing that here." It's not that I didn't want our guys to become All-Americans or win the Heisman, but if they won those things I wanted it to be solely because they earned it on the field, not in the PR department.

We're not giving a tailback more carries in the fourth quarter of some blowout so he can win a trophy, we're not going to change the way we pronounce the guy's name—like Notre Dame tried to do with their "Theismann as in Heisman" campaign—and we're sure as heck not paying good money to paint Joey Harrington's face on the side of some building in Manhattan. I'm sorry, that's not how a Michigan man earns his hardware.

We had some great players at Michigan, and a lot of them earned national honors. Nine times when I was coaching, one of our guys finished in the top ten in voting for the Heisman—Carter did it three times—and Rob Lytle, Rick Leach and Jimmy Harbaugh all finished third. With another coach, I've got to be honest, maybe they would have won it. They were good enough, I know that.

But I wasn't going to ruin the chemistry of our team—with 125 players on it, working every bit as hard as those stars—just so one guy could win some damn trophy. That wasn't the deal here at Michigan, and the stars knew it. Our sign didn't promise, "Those Who Stay Will Get Their Faces Painted On Manhattan Skyscrapers." No. Those guys didn't win the Heisman, but *every single one of our players* won a Big Ten title ring. THAT was the deal! "Those Who Stay Will Be *Champions*." And they were!

That's why Rob Lytle didn't flinch when I asked him—right before his senior year, when he was a strong candidate to win the Heisman—to move from tailback to fullback, so Gordie Bell could carry the ball. "Whatever's best for the team," he said, just like that. He finished third that year—as a fullback. But you should have seen Rob Lytle's face after we whipped the Buckeyes, 22–0, at their place. God, that was great! And Lytle loved it.

If you stick to your standards, don't worry about your all-star—because if your star is really an all-star, he'll like it that way. And that's what all those guys were about. They were beautiful.

After I stepped down in 1989, we had two Heisman Trophy winners here at Michigan—Desmond Howard and Charles Woodson—and maybe that's no accident. But I guarantee you, neither Moeller nor Carr altered their game plans for those guys to win that trophy. No, those guys came from out of *nowhere* entering their senior seasons, on championship teams, to win the Heisman *based solely on their performance that season*! That's how it's supposed to work.

And Theismann and Harrington? They didn't win the trophy anyway.

Some of our best players have argued that I was actually tougher on them than I was on the walk-ons, and maybe there's some truth to that—though I doubt it.

But Dan Dierdorf might have a case. After my first season at Michigan, 1969, Dierdorf entered his senior year as a consensus All-American. Fair enough. But that meant he was in all the magazines, on the Bob Hope show, and even got invited to the Playboy Mansion for making their preseason All-America team. The less I knew about that, the better.

When Dan came back that August, I pulled him into my office. "Dierdorf, you're the best tackle in the NFL right now."

"But I'm still in college."

"I know, but that's how good you are. And that's why everyone on this team is going to be watching how I treat you. They're wondering if I'm going to show you any favoritism, maybe let you cut some corners, or be afraid to criticize you.

"Well, I'm not going to do any of those things. In fact, I'm going to go *out of my way* to treat you *worse* than everybody else on this team. I swear to you right now, Dierdorf, that you will not be able to do a single thing right in my eyes this entire month! And you will hear about it, and you will have to take it."

I can assure you, I kept my end of the deal! Dan didn't like it, not one bit, and you can't blame him. But he put up with it, even if he didn't understand it. Not for years.

Not until he earned All-American at the end of that season.

And played thirteen years in the NFL.

And earned six Pro Bowl invitations.

And was named to the NFL's All-Decade Team.

And was inducted into the College Football Hall of Fame.

And the NFL Hall of Fame.

And raised his daughter to become a star on the University of Michigan women's basketball team.

Only *then* did Dierdorf understand why I had to do what I did. Because nothing, not even your greatest star, can ever come before The Team, The Team, The Team. Because when you've got that, you've got something special.

It just takes some guys a little longer to figure it out.

14

Motivate the Middle Men

I know there are times you've got to bring the ax down, but these days if you want to fire someone, you've got to consult with lawyers and unions and the National Labor Relations Board and God knows who else. I'm on a few corporate boards, and I know it's just not that simple anymore.

But even without all those obstacles, I think letting people go is usually a bad idea. It eats up too much time, energy and morale. That's why I'd much rather *teach* them than *fire* them.

You have to do everything you possibly can to develop your middle tier of talent. It's your job, as the leader, to make those people do more than they thought they could—maybe more than *you* thought they could—and put them in the best possible position to help the team.

We have always played in the upper echelon of college football here at Michigan, but I never thought we were the most dominant team, year in and year out, in terms of raw talent. We brought some of that on ourselves by passing up on the Golden Arm types, but I still thought we could compete better than anyone else, on any given day, with the people we had.

When we went down to play Auburn in the 1984 Sugar Bowl, those Auburn guys were giving my guys a hard time at every official function, saying how small they were, how they didn't have a chance, and how'd they like playing on the junior varsity? Stuff like that. In fact, in Bo Jackson's autobiography, Jackson says he started giggling during warm-ups because our guys weren't nearly as big as the SEC players he'd been facing all year. So he's thinking, *Hey, I'm going to have a day at the beach!* But Bo wasn't giggling at the end of the game—which we lost 9-7, on three field goals, the last one coming with no time left—because he'd taken a pounding all night from a swarm of Michigan defenders who "stung like bees," as he put it. What our guys lacked in size they more than made up for in technique and hustle. You can teach those things.

Everyone thinks talent is fixed—that this guy's got it and that guy doesn't—but it's just not true. Talent is elastic, and particularly so in team sports. A team of athletes that are well coached, well disciplined and play hard together can beat a team with more talent, if that team lacks character, or proper attitudes or cohesiveness. You can beat a team like that—and it's satisfying when you do!

Everyone knows this. But how do you do it? I'll tell you how: *You coach them all*—and let the cream rise to the top, as Caldo once told me. But for that to work, you have to set up a strict meritocracy, so the cream really *can* rise to the top, and everyone is motivated to do their best. Otherwise, you're stuck with a lot of unmotivated guys who just aren't going to help you—or worse, they're going to become cancers and poison the rest.

*   *   *

I didn't think my philosophy was any philosophy at all until I started working for the Detroit Tigers. In my stint as club president, from 1990 to 1992, I was stunned to see how baseball clubs work. They figure they only have one or two guys on their lowest minor league team who've got a shot, so they concentrate all their attention on them—and forget the rest.

Now, to me, that's crazy. For one thing, it's more cost-effective to pick good prospects through the draft, and develop them in your minor league system. And that's true in business, too. It's much cheaper—and much better—to develop your own people from the ground floor up than to steal stars from other organizations at top dollar. Even if the hired guns do perform, they'll have no loyalty to you, and they'll go for the next big contract first chance they get. And you're going to miss out on a lot of young talent.

Like most major league organizations, Detroit had a hitting coach, a pitching coach and a weight coach for their major league team. That's good. But for their four or five minor league teams—over a hundred players—they had only *one* hitting coach, *one* pitching coach and *one* conditioning coach traveling around the country—what they call roving coaches. Come on! What the hell is that? There's simply no way you can develop a hundred players with three part-time coaches.

So I set out to give every team in the organization the same resources the big club had, including three full-time coaches, videotape systems, weight rooms and batting cages. It didn't fix everything overnight, but it helped. Okay, so getting fired after just a couple years on the job *didn't* help—but that was *not* my fault!

*   *   *

Here's the point: *You're not going to yell your way to the top of your profession.* If your people are going to perform their absolute best, you need to give them the tools to do so.

If you're mining gold, you better give your miners the best shovels and picks out there—or you won't get much gold out of them. If you're running a newspaper, you better make sure everyone has a top-of-the-line computer. And if you're coaching a football team, you better have the best weight rooms, coaches, trainers and helmets money can buy.

That's why we always insisted on the best of everything, for every player, regardless of his rank on the team. And it sent a message to our people, too: We take you seriously, and if you need it, we'll get it for you.

But that comes with an expectation, too: We've given you everything you need to succeed. Now you've got to keep up your end of the bargain.

Why coach everybody? Because no one is so smart they can tell you *which* young prospects are going to develop, *when* they're going to develop, or *how far* they'll go. And while you're spending all your time with the Next Big Star who might end up being a big bust anyway, you could be overlooking a diamond in the rough sitting right next to him—a guy who, with a little attention, might become a Hall of Famer. Heck, we've had dozens of those guys here at Michigan.

You look at Curtis Greer, a defensive tackle in the late 1970s. Like everyone else, we were after his high school teammates, Harlan Huckleby and Tom Sebron, who both made it to the NFL, and have done well in business since. But Curtis Greer, the tack-on, *he's* the one who made All-American here, and *he's* the one who played nine years for the St. Louis Cardinals.

The Cardinals were owned by Anheuser-Busch back then, so Curt—being no dummy—asked them for a job in the off-season. The brass at Anheuser-Busch weren't stupid, either, and they hired Curt in a flash. He's done extremely well, he's put three kids through Michigan, and he even moved his mom next door to me. I know whenever Curt's been in town, because when I come home there's a case of Budweiser on my front step.

Now, how many recruiters predicted Curtis would accomplish all that? I know *we* didn't—and we were the guys who got him!

I already told you how we recruited Jamie Morris—or more accurately, how he recruited us. But you haven't heard the rest of the story. I planned on having him just return kicks, until I got so sick of him asking every damn day to try tailback, I finally let him carry the ball in practice—and wow! First down. And another. And another. After he tore through our defense four times in a row, I decided maybe he was right.

The truth is, I really had no idea what we had in Jamie Morris, until we gave him a chance. Just think how many games we would have lost if we hadn't let him show us what he could do? I don't even want to think about that.

Not everyone who wore Maize and Blue was an All-American, but that didn't mean they couldn't help the team. Andy Moeller, Gary's kid, had the slowest feet and the worst body you've ever seen. But man, he'd hit you—and he'd keep hitting you, until *you* gave up! It was the same thing with Coach Bill Mallory's son, Mike. No feet, no body. Didn't matter. By their senior years, both Moeller and Mallory were starters, and team captains. God hadn't given them much. They were just determined to be good.

I'm not putting them down by saying that. I respect the hell out of those guys, *because* they didn't have all that natural talent. They never saw the inside of a pro camp. Heck, they wouldn't even know where it was located. But that didn't stop them from leading our team—and winning Big Ten titles.

And both are now great coaches. Now that did NOT surprise me!

Here's another reason you should coach them all, instead of just the hotshots: because you recruited them! And if you picked them, you should help them. If he's no good—well hell, who's fault is that? Yours! So you'd better do your best to make them better.

When I recruit someone I've got him for four years whether he's any good or not. If he doesn't develop, I can't just run him off. So I've got to make him as good as he can be, because he ain't leaving anytime soon. And that's why I like college football better than pro football. Coaching everybody makes the whole team better, more unified and more fun to be around.

If they can't make it at their first position, you need to find them another position where they can help the team more. We've had a hundred of those guys.

Rich Hewlett started his first game at quarterback against Ohio State—*as a freshman.* The problem was, the next year we had John Wangler return as the heir apparent, with Anthony

Carter at receiver, and Hewlett was an option guy. So I sat Rich down, looked him in the eye, and told him he could either be a second-string quarterback, or try to become a starter at defensive back. I've done this dozens of times, and I never had a guy say no. Sure enough, Rich became a solid starter for us, and a great leader.

Because Rich stayed five years, he had to endure four years of spring football. Back then, we were allowed to have twenty spring practices—it's fifteen now—spread out over five weeks so we could hit more. I make no apologies for that. We weren't running an arts-and-crafts camp. But this kid, Hewlett, he did not miss a single day of spring ball for four years. Eighty practices, almost all of them hitting. Now *that* is a record that will never be broken!

Changing positions was usually our idea, but sometimes the players came to us. Jim Betts was a talented quarterback from Cleveland, but he needed a knee operation his freshman year. When Betts returned to the lineup a year later, he was behind Don Moorhead at quarterback, so Bump Elliott—who coached Jim his first two years at Michigan—moved him to tailback. But that put him behind Ron Johnson, one of the best there ever was.

Now it's 1970, Jim's about to begin his senior year, and despite all his potential, he still hasn't started for the Wolverines. One day he comes barging into my office like only Betts could.

"Bo," he tells me, "I'm moving to safety."

"Now who the hell do you think you are to come in here and tell me where you're going to play?"

"Coach," he said, holding his ground, "we just graduated Barry Pierson, Brian Healy and Tommy Curtis from the defensive backfield. Unless you plan on moving Moorhead over for me to start at quarterback, D-back is where I'm going to go."

"Who the hell are you?" I said, clearly not getting to him. He didn't flinch. "Well, I'll tell you what you're going to do: You're going to play *both* positions, practice on *both* sides of the ball, and go to *both* meetings. Got it?"

"Got it, Coach."

Even though he was still backing up Moorhead, Betts did such a great job at safety the New York Jets drafted him.

Thank God I thought of moving Betts to safety.

For big-time moves, no one beats what Paul Seymour pulled off. His brother starred at Notre Dame, but Paul came to Michigan in 1968, God bless him. Bump Elliott started him as a freshman at wide receiver, where he caught 19 passes for 257 yards, but then Paul got a bone spur as soon as I showed up.

This was one of the nastiest spurs I've seen. Paul couldn't even get his football spikes over that foot, so he cut the back of the shoe, wedged it on like a slipper and taped the damn thing closed every day. Nice try, but you just can't play like that. It got so tender, he couldn't even put a *bedsheet* over it at night. He clearly needed surgery. While everyone else was out celebrating our big Ohio State upset in 1969, Paul was in the hospital, watching on TV.

When Seymour came back in 1970, as a redshirt sophomore, we moved him against his wishes to tight end for two years. His future looked pretty bright, but by his fifth year, 1972, we had Paul Seal coming in at tight end, so I called Seymour into my office and told him I was going to move him to offensive tackle. Switching a kid from wide receiver to tight end to tackle is a lot to ask of anyone, but it's what the team needed.

Some of my players would do whatever I asked without questioning it. Others liked to question everything I said. Paul was squarely in the second camp—and to be honest, I liked that sometimes. Sometimes!

"I'm playing great at tight end," Paul said. "Why do you want to move me?"

"Because I don't need two future pros at tight end. Besides, you'll have a better shot at making the NFL playing tackle."

"But you just told me you don't need two *pros* at tight end."

"Why you little—!" Seymour was an academic All-American. He was *irritating,* but he wasn't dumb! "Look, it would be more beneficial to the team if we moved you to tackle. Trust me."

That's all he needed to hear—and, with a guy like Seymour, that's all I should have said in the first place.

That spring, Seymour grew a mustache just to tick me off—and it worked great. I'd relaxed my policy a little, but still hated them. Every single day of spring ball I told him, "Seymour, with that stupid mustache, you look like a damn walrus."

When it was time for our annual spring meeting, I was ready for Seymour. I was going to tell him what a great student he was, what a great job he'd done at tackle that spring—and how he still looked like a damn walrus with that mustache!

So Seymour walks into my office . . . clean-shaven!

"Why you *sonuvabitch*!" I said. "You shaved it off just to spite me!"

"Coach," he said. "You are one hundred percent, absolutely right."

Well, what are you gonna do? We both started laughing. He had me.

The guy earned All-American status as a fifth-year senior—his first season at strong tackle. The Buffalo Bills drafted him in the *first round,* and he played five years for them. They had O. J.

Simpson, so they were paying Seymour to block. And he did it right alongside our own Reggie McKenzie, whom we had moved from tackle to guard his sophomore year.

They might have grumbled at the time, but they weren't complaining when they were cashing their NFL paychecks.

When Paul came to visit me, he said, "Thanks to you, Bo, I made it in the NFL—as a tight end. Boy, you sure do know talent."

Some guys, you just gotta let have the last word. Seymour was one of the few who got it.

15

Give 'Em a Chance

Now, what about the lower tier? And don't tell me you don't have one, because if you have more than two people in your organization, you're going to have an upper, middle and lower level of talent. That's just the way it is. So you'd better find some way to get the most out of *all* of them.

For us, the lower tier was the walk-ons. This might surprise you, but we never had tryouts, no cuts. We took in anyone who was willing to do the work, and as you'll see, we were right to do so. You take a guy who has that much desire to be a Michigan Wolverine—who's willing to go through all those two-a-days, without any guarantee of even getting in a game—well, we'll find a place for a guy like that. And we'll treat that guy *exactly the same* way we treat Dan Dierdorf or Jim Harbaugh or Jamie Morris. Like dogs, of course!

I've always thought you can get more out of every player, even the stars, if you coached them as a team. If you try to win championships, instead of individual awards, *everyone* will get better.

When you do things the Michigan way, no one resents the stars like Dierdorf, because everyone knows they're not getting any special treatment. And everyone respects the walk-ons, because everyone knows they're going through the exact same hell as the All-Americans. That's why, if you came to one of our reunions, you couldn't tell who walked on and who won a Super Bowl ring. They all get along. They're equals. They're *teammates,* even twenty years later.

But for that to happen, you've got to give them all a fair shot, every one of them.

My coaching philosophy has been shaped by a lot of good men and some tough times. During 1948, my sophomore year at Miami of Ohio, we had a lot of guys still coming back from the service. As a result, we had some players on our team who were twenty-seven years old, and thanks to the GI Bill, the school didn't have enough room to house everyone. So they put twenty-four football players in the temporary Army barracks down on South Campus—including me—because we were the only guys too dumb to forget to make arrangements for housing that fall.

The second game of that season we were going to play Virginia in Charlottesville, the biggest trip of the year, and we were going to go by train. That was a big deal back then, because a lot of us had never been on a train. Hell, a lot of us had never even stayed in a hotel—including me—if you can believe that.

But when the coaches posted the travel list on the locker room door that week, twenty-three of the twenty-four guys living in the temporary Army barracks on South Campus saw their names on that list, telling them they had a seat saved for them on the train the next day. There was only one name missing: Bo Schembechler. The coaches probably didn't realize that everyone else in that barracks had their name on that list but me, but imagine what it felt like to be the one guy—the *one guy*—who didn't make that trip.

I was embarrassed, even a little ashamed. Hell, who am I kidding? I was flat-out *pissed*. I didn't leave the barracks all weekend. I didn't go into town. I didn't visit anybody. I didn't even go to the library, because on a small campus like that, everyone knew me, and they were bound to ask, "What the hell are you doing here? Shouldn't you be in Virginia?" I just stayed in my room all weekend, and studied, and waited for the team to return. That just might have been the longest weekend of my life.

The hell of it is, if the coaches had just told me, "Hey, we're taking these two guys instead of you and here's why," I wouldn't have said a word. I might not have liked it, but I would have understood. But they didn't explain anything to me. They just posted that damn list.

People not involved in sports probably don't realize what a crushing blow that is, to be left behind like that. That was more than five decades ago, and I can remember it like it was yesterday.

And that's why I never wanted a player of mine sitting there and stewing, wondering why he's out of the lineup. If you have to make a decision they're not going to like, it's better to tell them why you're doing what you're doing. They *still* won't like it but they'll usually understand, and they'll *always* appreciate being told instead of being left in the dark. And if you *don't* tell them why, they'll feel abandoned, and start coming up with all kinds of crazy conspiracy theories.

Man, just tell them the truth. They can handle it.

Another lesson I learned that weekend, brooding in my dorm room: If you tell everyone they're an integral part of that team—well dammit, then you'd better back it up. You've got to show 'em. Players aren't stupid. I sure didn't feel like a part of the team that weekend.

By that Monday, I decided to make my discontent known. I was determined to do something, *anything,* to get back on that travel list and make sure I never got left behind again. I went to our captain, a big defensive tackle named Ernie Plank, and said, "Ernie, that little SOB Joe Madro"—our line coach, and frankly a pretty good one, even though he didn't like me—"he won't take a look at me. Can you get him to give me a chance?"

Ernie was a good captain. He granted my request that same day. "Okay, Bo. Madro said he'll work with you an hour before practice. I'll go with you, so we can work one-on-one."

The next day Madro gets Ernie and me down in our stances. He tells us he's going to call the count and then we'll go at it. I'm jacked, I'm angry, and I'm going to show what I've got! So the instant Madro blows that whistle, I fire off that line as hard and fast as I can, like a *wild man,* and I'm up in Ernie's face before he knows what hit him.

We didn't wear any facemasks back then, so when I put my forearm right on Ernie's nose, I flattened his face. He fell back on his ass, and blood started shooting out his nose all over the place.

Boy, was Ernie mad! "Goddamn you sonuvabitch! I bring you out here, give you a chance, and you bust my freakin' nose!"

Now, I must admit, it's just possible I might have jumped the count a fraction of a second early. Wasn't intentional, I was just excited to get off that line. Ernie might have been hotter than hell, but Madro was impressed! I got back in the lineup, and amazingly, Ernie and I are still good friends.

When I was coaching I spent as much time with our fourth-stringers as I did with everyone else. Why? Because I know what it's like to be a nineteen-year-old college kid, staring at that travel list, and seeing everyone's name on it but yours.

Nothing I know demonstrates the value of giving a guy a chance more powerfully than the story of Donnie Warner.

It was the summer of nineteen hundred and seventy, and we were getting ready for my second season at Michigan. We had stunned the Buckeyes the year before, and we were preparing to defend our Big Ten title.

It was a quiet day, with the players and most of the staff on vacation, but I was still working down at my old office at State and Hoover. My secretary, Lynn Koch, knocked on my door to tell me there was some kid outside on his bike by the name of Donnie Warner, and he wanted to talk to the head coach.

"How big is he?" I asked her.

"He's just a little devil."

Now, I've always been known as a pretty hardworking coach, but in my first years at Michigan, I was even more . . . *intense,* shall we say. Every minute was precious to me. Still, if some kid had the steel to come down and ask to talk to the head coach, I was willing to give him a few minutes.

"All right," I said, looking up from my paperwork. "Show him in." This kid walks in, and he's 5-9, *maybe,* and 170 pounds, tops. Smaller than Caldarazzo! So, I decided to keep this brief—thank him for coming down, tell him good luck, send him on his way—and get back to work.

He told me he was in town for freshman orientation for the engineering school. I said congratulations—that's an impressive achievement—but I suspected that's not why he came down to talk to me. He was too nervous just for that. And he kept calling me "Coach," never Schembechler, because it turned out he didn't know how to pronounce my last name! Can you imagine?

"What can I do for you, son?"

"Coach, I want to come out for football."

"Well, what do you play, halfback?"

"No, Coach, I'm a lineman. I want to play offensive guard."

I about fell out of my seat right there. Good Lord, most of our *punters* were bigger than this guy!

"Young man, do you know who the offensive guards are here at Michigan?" I had Tom Coyle, who went 6-3, 255, and I had Reggie McKenzie, who went 6-5, 250 pounds, and would go on to have a great career for the Buffalo Bills. I'm telling you, we had a couple of big boys up front.

I always hated to burst some kid's bubble, but you've got to level with them. "Look, I like your attitude, but you're just not big enough. How the hell are you going to play against guys like that?"

He wasn't giving up that easily. "All right," he said. "If I'm too small to play on the offensive line, then I'll play on the defensive line. Middle guard."

I let a little chuckle slip. "That doesn't exactly solve your problem, son, because then Coyle and McKenzie will be the guys knocking you from one end of the field to the other. That's even worse!"

This little son of a gun *still* wouldn't give up. He was starting to get irritating! "Coach, I went to Dearborn Divine Child High School. Do you remember speaking at our team banquet?"

"Yes, I do," I said, not sure where he was going with this.

"Coach, do you remember when you got up there, you told us if you've got your mind set on doing something, you *do it,* and you don't let *anyone* talk you out of it?"

"Why you little smart-aleck," I said.

"I had planned to go to college out East, until my sister dragged me to the Michigan–Ohio State game last fall. When I saw that great upset, I decided right then and there I was going to play for Michigan!"

He had me, and he knew it.

"All right," I said. "You can come out for our team. But if you decide it's too much for you, I'll understand. I won't think any less of you, because you've already shown me a lot of guts just by trying out."

So little Donnie Warner comes out for the team that fall, and I'm worried sick about him getting killed. His first year, we only put him in on the demo team for the last few plays of each practice—and even *those guys* sent him flying like a volleyball. But he survived, he didn't give up, and when he came in for his scheduled meeting at the end of the season, I congratulated him.

"I admit it, Donnie: I wouldn't have bet on it, but you made it. You came to every practice, and you never quit. But I'm sure you recognize now that this is a big man's game, and you're just too small to play here."

The little bugger didn't blink!

"No, Coach. *Now* I realize I can do this, so I'm going to lift weights, get bigger and stronger and see you in the spring."

Some guys you just can't get rid of.

The next year Donnie earned a regular spot on the demo team. When I met with him after spring ball his sophomore year, I had to admit he'd proven he belonged on the team.

After he sat down in my office—same place I'd told him to get lost just a couple years earlier—I said, "Now, Donnie, I want you to know that I'm going to help pay some of your expenses for your junior year here at Michigan, but this is going to be the first and only time. I GUARANTEE you won't get a dime from me your senior year."

He just smiled at me and said "Bo"—he's calling me Bo now!—"that doesn't make any sense."

"What do you mean?"

And he said, in total seriousness, "Bo, what if I'm first-string? You'd cut my stipend?"

Ha! I threw him out of my office.

By his junior year, Donnie was number three or four at middle guard on our depth chart, and he was starting to become a pain in the neck because he kept disrupting my offense's plays by getting into the backfield and tackling the ball carriers. And whenever he did it, he'd jump up and down and carry on with his teammates like he'd just sacked Joe Willie Namath.

I'd complain to my coaches, "For cryin' out loud, if we can't keep little Donnie Warner from breaking up our plays, how in hell are we going to stop Purdue?" After a while, instead of watching the offense, you'd catch yourself watching little Donnie Warner, just to see what he'd do next.

Well, Donnie got his break the spring before his senior season, when both middle guards in front of him graduated. I told my assistants, "Go ahead and write Warner in there as our number one middle guard. He's earned that much. But as soon as you can find someone bigger and better than Warner, you put him in there. One of our young guys has *got* to beat him out."

I'm sure when Donnie came down to the football building at the beginning of spring ball and saw his name at the top of the list of middle guards, he thought the coaches finally figured out he was the man for the job. He didn't know I had no intention of keeping him there.

But I'll be damned if that kid didn't play *inspired* ball that spring. Warner was *everywhere,* always getting his nose in the middle of things and driving the offense crazy. He was as irritating on the field as he was in my office! By the time we closed down spring practice, we still hadn't found anyone better than he was.

Well, when little Donnie Warner walked in for his annual meeting after his junior year, I sat him down and said, "Warner, as of right now, you are still our starting middle guard. But I have to tell you the truth: I'd still like to replace you with someone bigger, someone faster. But until that happens, you're it. On that basis, I'm going to have *all* your expenses paid your senior year by the University of Michigan athletic department."

"A full scholarship?"

"A full scholarship."

Now, here he is, this little guy, busting his butt for three years, and he's finally gotten a full scholarship for his senior year. You'd think he'd be ready to kiss my ring, but that wasn't Donnie. You see, I'd forgotten the guarantee I'd made in our meeting the previous year, when I told him there was absolutely no chance he'd get a cent out of me his senior season.

Donnie just leaned back in his chair, snickered and said, "You know, Bo, I knew I'd eventually get a full ride out of you."

You just gotta love a kid like that.

When the 1973 season started four months later, we *still* hadn't found anyone who could outplay little Donnie Warner—he had just made up his mind that *nobody* was going to take his job—so he was our starter. We burned through the first 10 games undefeated, riding a defense that was just *dominant.* Got it? *Dominant!* I'm talking about giving up just seven points against

Iowa, 10 against Stanford, then *shutting out* Navy, Oregon and Michigan State, three in a row, just like that. After 10 games, our defense had given up 58 points—less than six a game. Over my twenty-one years at Michigan, we had the best-scoring defense in the country, and *that* defense might have been the best of them all. So you'd have to conclude that starting Donnie Warner at middle guard apparently didn't cost us very much.

How did he do it? You had to watch him awhile to figure it out, but when you looked at enough tape, you'd notice two things about him that stood out.

First, Donnie Warner was smart as a whip. He'd watch the offensive huddle, notice who the quarterback was talking to, and try to listen in on the plays. Then he would get down in his crouch, and start looking around to see which way their backs were leaning, even if it was just a little bit left or right, the same way a pitcher tries to figure out if the runner on first is going to try to steal second by watching his feet. Finally, you'd see him read their splits—the gaps between the offensive guards—and watch how their center lined up over the ball. And *solely on that basis, he'd know what they were going to do before they did it!*

He not only knew if they were going to pass or run, he knew who was going to get the ball, and which way their guards were going to block the play. I'm telling you, that guy could read a play like no other. There were times I thought Donnie Warner knew their offense better than their center did.

Second, Warner was quick! That kid could *dance* between the guards on the rush. Didn't matter how big their center was, if Donnie could get around him, the center couldn't catch him—and Donnie was around that center before he could say "Boo!" The kid had taken what God had given him—which frankly wasn't very much—and used it to cover everything He didn't.

* * *

In 1973, Ohio State buzzed through the first 10 games, unbeaten and untied, just like we had, and they came into Ann Arbor ranked number one. We were ranked fourth. This was the game the whole country wanted to see.

Ohio State week is always something special, but particularly when Woody was coaching the Buckeyes. Our players came down to the football building every free hour they had just to watch more tape of Ohio State, trying to pick up another little secret or two.

On Thursday, this boy Warner walks out of the projection room down to my office. "Hey Bo, I've seen every film we've got on those guys, and that's the best line we've seen all year. But their center, Steve Myers"—who was an All-American!—"he'll need help blocking me. That's when you send our linebackers flying in after their ball carrier, because everyone else is going to be busy helping Myers trying to stop *me*. And we will stuff them!"

I just listened to him go on, until he finished. "Thank you, Mr. Warner. I can tell you I feel a whole lot better about Saturday now that I've been privy to your astute observations."

But that little son of a gun was convinced. And I'll tell you something else: *He was right!*

We couldn't score any points in the first half, while the Buckeyes scored 10. In the locker room at halftime, I stood at the chalkboard and said, "Men, we only need to score 11 points, and they are done! DONE! Because I know the Buckeyes are *not going to score another point on our defense all day*!"

Sure enough, our defense stopped the Bucks cold in the second half. They couldn't get another point off of us—and this was a team with Archie Griffin running the ball, the only guy ever to win the Heisman Trophy twice. Their center, Steve Myers, was everything you'd expect from an All-American—but he couldn't contain Warner by himself, forcing Woody to double-team Donnie. Warner would take out two of their linemen, which allowed our linebackers to jump in and attack the ball carrier. Donnie was right!

On the other side of the ball, our offense tied the game at 10–10, and we were driving again late in the game when our quarterback, Dennis Franklin, broke his collarbone. A few plays earlier, unnoticed by most fans, little Donnie Warner went down with a knee injury, and had to be carried off the field.

With Larry Cipa subbing at quarterback, we got the ball to the Ohio State 27-yard line, leaving us just a chip shot to win the game, the Big Ten crown, a Rose Bowl bid and a shot at the national title—everything you work for. But our boy misses the kick, sending it just a little wide to the right. The game ends in a 10–10 tie, and the next day, with the help of the Big Ten commissioner—and I will *never* forgive him for that—the athletic directors vote six to four to send Ohio State to the Rose Bowl. You probably know that part.

But immediately after that game, when we still thought we were going to the Rose Bowl—hell, even Woody wished us luck in Pasadena—our team doctor, Gerald O'Connor, was driving Dennis Franklin and Donnie Warner to the hospital. Denny was sitting in the front seat, his arm in a sling, and Donnie was in the back with an ice pack on his knee.

Donnie says, "When we go to Pasadena, Denny, Larry Cipa will do a great job subbing for you at quarterback. But Denny, who the hell can Bo sub for *me* at middle guard?"

Ha! I loved it. That's Donnie Warner.

To this day, I consider Donnie Warner the greatest player I've ever coached, simply because I've never seen anyone else do anything close to what he did, before or since. He made up his mind that he was going to play for Michigan and he would not let anyone talk him out of it—just like we said at his high school banquet.

Now, you see this movie, *Rudy*, about some little guy at Notre Dame, and he gets in the last game of the year for one play and he makes a sack. But we've got this guy, Donnie Warner, who rose up to be a starting nose guard on an undefeated team. His teammates loved him, and he's now a manager at Ford who has graduated three of his kids from Michigan. I'm sorry, but to me, that's a whole lot more impressive. That's a better story.

If your team is going to reach its potential, you're going to have to give the underdogs in your organization the chance to show you what they can do. No favors, nothing special. Just an honest chance. Do that for them, and you'll be amazed at what they can do for you.

Just ask Donnie's teammates.

16

Give Everyone a Role, and Make It Important

Sometimes the walk-ons of this world can step up and take a starter's place, like Donnie Warner or Henry Hill, one of the quickest defensive linemen Michigan has ever had. The guy was a walk-on with an *academic scholarship,* and became an All-American! Even better, in my book, his teammates elected him captain. I don't need to tell you, that means something around here.

But even if the walk-ons don't become starters—and that's almost always the case, of course—that doesn't mean they can't help your team.

Ultimately, it makes no difference what they accomplish. They're all on your team, and whatever your team achieves, *every one of them* must feel like this is *my* team, and *we* did this *together.* Because you did!

Doesn't matter if we're talking about the people answering the phones, the guys waxing the floors or the big lugs playing third-string tackle. If you don't appreciate the value of these people and the work they do—by recognizing them and reinforcing how important they are to the team's success—you'll never lead a truly great organization.

This means everyone on your team must have a clear, specific role to play, and *they* have to see those roles as being vital to the success of the entire organization. Because if they don't, they're just going to go to work every morning and pick up a paycheck at the end of the week. They will have lousy attitudes, and it will rub off on their customers and co-workers. Those kind of people just bring everyone down.

But if you motivate them, make them feel like they belong— look out! Those people are like booster shots for your entire organization. Everyone sees them working hard, everyone sees how jacked up they are, and that rubs off, too, even on the all-stars.

Nowadays we have a big football banquet at the end of the season, where anyone who wants to buy a ticket can show up, and it's great. We get more than a thousand fans to join us to honor the team, we raise some money and we have a good time.

But in the 1970s, we used to have a private banquet at Weber's in Ann Arbor, with only the football coaches and the players invited—no press, no alumni. We established early in my tenure that the biggest trophy we gave out, bigger than our MVP award, went to the demonstration player who, in the eyes of the coaches and the players, contributed more to the success of our team than anyone else. We called it the Champions Trophy. You win that, brother, and you've got to be special!

The first time we named the winner, when he came on up, everybody spontaneously jumped to their feet—the coaches, the all-stars, the demo team grinders—and they have ever since. The winner of that trophy still gets the loudest, longest ovation every year—and that, to me, shows you how much everybody thinks about our demo team players.

I coached literally hundreds of players at Michigan, and every one of them feels that he was an important part of the team—because he was!

Now, why does everyone feel that way?

Simple: Whatever the All-Americans got, the walk-ons got, too.

We put every player's name on the back of his jersey, no exceptions. If you did the work, you got a varsity letter. That might not sound like a big deal, but when I came here it was the policy of the football program—like most programs—to give varsity letters only to those who logged so much game time. Under that system, most walk-ons would get nothing after four years of hard work. We changed that. So now, when you come to one of our reunions, you'll see those guys wearing their M rings and letter jackets as proudly as any All-American we ever had.

The most important things we gave every player, though, were time and attention.

If one of our players wanted to see me, he got to see me, no questions asked. And whether or not they wanted to see me, I wanted to see *them*! That's why we set up those meetings twice a year, so I could go over their grades, their goals, and let them know what they could do to contribute to the team's success that season.

When they left that meeting, they had no confusion about where they stood on the team, what I expected of them, and why they were important to us.

*   *   *

Same thing goes for the people on our staff. If they're in this building, it doesn't matter if they're stuffing envelopes or taping ankles, they must be important to our success as a team, or we wouldn't have hired them. And they better want to win, as much as everyone else in this building does, or we will not be successful. And they will be gone.

Mary Passink's job is not to answer the phones. Mary's job is to help us win Big Ten titles, and she does that by being the best executive assistant on campus. Jon Falk's job is not to fit a few hundred helmets every season. His job is to help us win Big Ten titles, and he does that by being the best equipment manager in college football. And when we win a Big Ten title, they get rings, too. (Well, actually, the ladies usually choose to get just the face of the ring on one of those thin gold chains—but you get the idea. Whatever they want. They're champions, too!)

Now, if I was running a business I would do these *exact* same things—the meetings, the attention, the recognition—for the *exact* same reasons. Does that create pressure to perform? Sure it does. But that feels a whole lot better than feeling forgotten.

Michigan football has earned a reputation for being one of the cleanest, straightest programs in the nation, and I'm proud of that. But if you want to know if I ever cheated the NCAA, the answer is yes. And now I'm going to tell you how I did it.

When those no-account SOBs passed a rule saying only the guys with football scholarships can eat at the team training table—well, I just didn't think that was right, and I still don't. How can I tell a man who had the guts to walk on—a guy like Donnie Warner or Henry Hill—a guy who worked every bit as hard as the All-Americans he's battling all day, a guy I give *nothing* to except a practice uniform—how can I tell that guy at the end of practice: Go get your own meal. Pay for it out of your own pocket. You're not one of us.

I'll tell you right now: I *can't* do that. And I *won't* do that. Because it's wrong!

I've probably been in more corporate dining halls than most food inspectors. One thing I will never understand is why some companies have an executive dining hall for the bigwigs, and another, lesser one for everyone else. You can't possibly tell me your team is going to feel like a team if the bigwigs get to eat better food in a fancier room while everyone else eats warmed-over fish sticks in a high school cafeteria. Again I tell you: They are not dumb.

Once the average Joe sees the executives walk past them to their separate dining room, you can never again say to him with a straight face, "We're all on the same team." Because you're not!

So this is what we did. Our training table at South Quad made meals for the ninety-five guys on scholarship at that time—it's eighty-five now—plus ten coaches and one trainer, and they weren't going to make any more meals than that. So, after practice, I'd ask who was planning to miss the meal because they had a class, or a study session, or anything else that was going to conflict with the training table. If we were still short seats the first time we went around the room, we'd keep asking until we had scraped up enough dinners to make sure every man who was hungry after busting his butt for me on the practice field could go eat.

Your meal's on us. Enjoy it. You've *earned* it!

This is where the NCAA drives me absolutely crazy. You see, all those wonderful walk-ons who get into school solely on their academic merits, they make every sacrifice the all-stars make, and they certainly don't do it for fame and glory. To me, those guys are the embodiment of everything college sports is supposed to be about—and the NCAA wants me to treat them like *pariahs*? I'm sorry, but I am not going to do that!

I dare those SOBs at the NCAA—I DARE them—to tell me the right thing to do is send those men home without a meal. The statute of limitations has already passed, so if they want to investigate me, tell them to go right ahead!

Okay, the walk-ons get a hot meal, an M ring and a varsity letter. What do you, as the leader, get out of this approach? How does your team benefit?

Let me tell you the story of another walk-on. Brad Bates grew up in Port Huron, Michigan, where both his parents taught school and his dad coached his high school football team. Now, Brad didn't have much size or a ton of natural talent, but coaches' kids are almost always hardworking and highly disciplined, and Brad was no exception.

Brad wanted to be a part of Big Ten football, even if it meant walking on. So his father—his coach—contacted both Michigan State and Michigan. The secretary at State told him that after Brad had enrolled at State—and *only* after—he should come down to talk to a graduate assistant about trying out for the team. Problem was, that would be after their preseason camp was over, so he'd already be behind the rest of the squad—a pretty clear indication they weren't too interested in some skinny walk-on from Port Huron.

After State's response, he didn't think he had much of a chance at Michigan. This was 1977, after all, and we were about to be ranked second in the preseason polls. But when Brad's dad called my secretary, Lynn Koch, she encouraged them to come down and meet with me. When Brad and his dad showed up for their appointment—which happened to be during spring ball—Lynn walked them down the hallway to the coaches room. We were planning that day's practice, but as instructed, Lynn pulled me out to meet Brad Bates and his dad.

We went to my office to sit and chat for a bit. Brad was about six foot, and he looked like a skinny guy, but it was hard to tell because he was wearing one of those poofy down jackets every-one was wearing back then—and the kid kept it on the entire meeting! He told me later he was trying to hide his small frame, and he was so committed to the stunt that I could see sweat run-ning down his face by the end of the conversation. Well, I guess that showed dedication.

We talked for maybe thirty minutes. I told him about our pro-gram, our philosophy, and how walk-ons fit in with the rest of the team, and he said, "Okay. That's for me."

Brad knew the first week of our preseason practices focused on conditioning, not plays, so he was determined to finish first in everything we did so we would remember his name. And I'll be damned if he didn't do exactly that!

When the season started we put Brad at defensive back, where he got in a few plays over the years, but not many. Didn't matter. Brad Bates came out for football all four years—and some of his records on conditioning tests *stand to this day, twenty-five years later*! Nobody ever beat him, ever—because he wouldn't let them!

During Brad's four years on the team, we had eleven All-Americans—including Anthony Carter—and three times that many drafted by the pros. *And they could not touch Brad Bates!*

Man, was that a great motivator! I just *loved* to saunter up to one of our big-name All-Americans, gasping for air after Mike Gittleson, our strength and conditioning coach, had just run him ragged. He'd be bent over, dying a slow death. I'd put my hand on his shoulder. "Son, they say you're the best at your position. Yet I couldn't help but notice *you can't catch Brad Bates*! And look at him over there. He's not even breathing hard. He looks great! But you, son—you are no Brad Bates."

Most of them just glared at me, trying to catch their breath, but one of them straightened up, looked me in the eye and said, "But Coach, *no one* can catch Brad Bates!" And he was right! Those guys had a ton of respect for Brad. I did, too.

It's tempting to think guys like Brad Bates need us more than we need them. But anyone inside our program knows it is just the opposite.

Brad was a bona fide letter winner, just like all our walk-ons who stuck it out for four years. He graduated on time, and got into grad school here at Michigan. When he asked me if he could come back as a volunteer coach, it took me all of two nanoseconds to say, "Absolutely."

Today Brad Bates is the athletic director at Miami of Ohio— and they love him, there, too. They love him! He's done a marvelous job, and I'm sure you'll be hearing his name whenever a big job opens up. I would not be surprised if he becomes Michigan's athletic director down the road. If he doesn't, it'll be our loss.

But that's not what I remember most when I think of Brad Bates.

It's August 1980, and we've got three weeks to prepare for our first game against Northwestern, followed by Notre Dame, so we're deep into two-a-day practices. We meet every night as a team to review the day and set the tone for the next day's work. I also announce the winners of each strength and conditioning test that day—from the 40-yard sprint to the 225-pound bench press—then bring the winners up, shake their hands and let them bask in the applause of their teammates. It not only creates incentive, it's just fun to do. When we concluded the tests at the end of that first week, I announced the winners for the entire week, too.

Needless to say, Brad Bates cleaned up. "Jeez, Bates, I'm getting tired of seeing your face up here!" But the last time I called him up and shook his hand, he was about to walk away when I kind of yanked his hand back toward me, threw my left arm around him, and—like an emcee—asked him a few questions about what it's like being a walk-on. What keeps you working so hard? How much does your family have to pay for tuition, books, room and board? Things like that.

Then I turned to face the entire team, and said, "Gentlemen, these awards are not all Brad Bates has won this year. I'd like to announce that, AS OF THIS DAY, the University of Michigan football program will be paying ALL of Brad Bates's expenses for the coming academic year!"

All the guys in that room leaped to their feet and gave Brad a thunderous ovation. Now, you've got to know, Bates had *no idea* there was even a chance of his getting a dime that year— and here he's getting a full ride, just like the All-Americans. I gave Brad a hug, and once I let him go—this was the best part—he had to work his way through a sea of high-fives and hugs just to get back to his seat.

Once Brad sat down, Mike Trgovac, a two-time All-Big Ten middle guard who's now the defensive coordinator for the NFL's

Carolina Panthers, leaned over and said, "Don't tell your parents about this, and you can pocket their tuition!"

And you tell me Michigan State didn't have five minutes for a guy like that?

Hell's fire!

17

If You Must Fire, Fire Fast

Only a tyrant likes to fire people, but I will do it if I discover dishonesty or disloyalty in my ranks. If you must fire someone, I say: Fire fast, and move on.

Like I said before, if a guy here gets called to interview for a good job, I'll help. But if I ever caught wind of one of our guys trying to work some deal behind my back, that guy would find himself leaving sooner than he might have planned.

And that's exactly what happened when we caught our basketball coach, Bill Frieder, trying to jump to Arizona State under cover of darkness.

It's Sunday afternoon, March 11, 1989, and Michigan just finished the basketball season by getting destroyed by Illinois at home, 89-73—and it wasn't even that close. That same night the NCAA tournament selection committee gave Michigan the third seed in the Southeast Region, so we still had lots of hope, despite the Illinois debacle. I was the athletic director then, so I visited Frieder at practice on Monday, and wished him luck for the tournament. But at midnight Tuesday, I got a call from Mitch Albom at my home.

"Do you know where your basketball coach is?"

"No," I said. "Do I want to?"

"I just saw him at the airport, getting on the red-eye to Phoenix."

It turned out Frieder was in Tempe to finalize the deal that would make him the head coach at ASU. The rascal hadn't even told his assistant coaches!

I got Frieder on the phone as soon as I could. He knew I'd be calling, and he was ready. He said, "Don't worry, Bo, they have a jet waiting for me, so I can meet the team in Atlanta for the first round of the tournament."

I didn't sleep on it. I didn't deliberate over it. And I sure as hell didn't consult some damn committee about it. I made up my mind right then and there.

"No you're not," I told him. "We're going to have a Michigan man coaching Michigan's basketball team. In fact, I don't even want to see your face in Atlanta at all."

I'm telling you, even if I had to coach that team myself, I'd have done it. I'm not kidding you! I might not know a thing about basketball, but I'd have those guys running hard, diving for loose balls, rebounding and playing like a team—all the things they weren't doing all season. But as far as strategy goes, I'd have to tell 'em: "Don't call any timeouts, because I wouldn't know what to tell you!"

I'm pleased to report I wasn't quite that crazy. I appointed Frieder's top assistant, Steve Fisher, to coach the team for the tournament, but I made it clear I was not making any guarantees about who was going to be the head coach after the tournament. There were just too many questionable people hanging around that program for me to feel comfortable with the current regime.

But there we were. Before the team left Ann Arbor for the first round in Atlanta, Fisher asked me to give a talk to the team—but there was a danger in that. The day after I fired Frieder, one of the team's star forwards, Sean Higgins, was blabbing to the papers that he might transfer—and he said this right before the NCAA tournament!

So I asked Fisher, "Are you sure you want me to talk to your team? Because you might be without one or two players in that room when I'm done."

"It's okay," he said. "Do it."

So I gave them a speech. I told them, "We've got Rumeal Robinson, the best point guard in the country. We've got Glen Rice, the sharpest shooter in the land. And we've got two great big men, Mark Hughes and Loy Vaught. Men, I'm telling you: There's absolutely no reason we can't win this regional.

"But Higgins, I've been hearing about you squawking in the paper, wanting to transfer now that Frieder's gone. Well, if you want out, be my guest. You can get out *right now*. I have the transfer papers right upstairs on my desk. We can go up there this minute, you can sign those papers, and we'll have it done by lunch.

"So you've got a choice: We're going to go upstairs and grant your wish, or you're going to get on that plane. But you are *not* going to get on that plane unless you're going to play basketball here at Michigan. If you have any mixed feelings, let's sign those papers."

That guy was stunned! I don't think anyone in his entire life ever talked to him like that.

"No mixed feelings," he said. "I'm getting on that plane."

Well, you know the rest: The whole team played inspired basketball for three weeks—including Higgins—and they shocked the world by winning the NCAA basketball tournament, Michigan's first. After the season, Fisher and I had a long talk, and then I named him our permanent head coach.

It all worked out well enough for Michigan, of course, but when I look back at the whole Frieder thing, I can only say Bill and I could have handled that situation beautifully, a month beforehand, if he'd just been straight with me from the start.

In Frieder's case, Arizona State probably would've been a better fit for him anyway. But I couldn't accept the way he handled that interview. Behind his players' backs. Behind his coaches' backs. Behind *my* back.

He blew it, and I regret that. I felt I had no choice. Still do.

But this whole story just goes to show you, the most important thing you have to do is be up front and honest. There is no substitute, and it means absolutely everything.

And sometimes, when you stick to your guns, you get an NCAA basketball championship in the bargain.

18

Promote the Will to Prepare

Twenty-five seconds.

Everything a football coach works on 365 days a year—hiring staff, recruiting players, developing players, monitoring their studies, practicing plays and executing the game plan—all of that gets boiled down to 25 seconds.

That's all the refs give you to send your play—and your players—into the huddle, line up and hike the ball before they call you for delay of game. Your players do this a hundred times a game, 12 games a year. That means each one of them has got 1,200 chances—or 13,200 total—to screw it all up for everyone!

And you wonder why football coaches have high blood pressure?

The only way to be certain—and I mean *stone-cold certain*—that your people will be ready is to make sure everything they need to know and do in those 25 seconds has been organized, rehearsed and mastered long before they need to do it.

Yes, we lost a few games when I was head coach, but I can honestly say I cannot think of a single game we lost because we were not prepared. And I can *guarantee you* we never lost because we were called for delay of game or too many men on the field. Because you can *control* that—so we did!

Look, I know most people don't have to worry about a 25-second clock. But even if you aren't a college football coach, you probably get only a few minutes to make your presentation at a big conference, to make your pitch in a board meeting, or to make your case in an interview. That's all you get. If you're going to maximize your performance in those pressure situations, you have *got* to be organized long before the moment of truth arrives.

If you're not organized, you're a dead duck. You can't waste an hour, you can't waste a minute. If you're in charge, the time pressure is even greater, because so many people are asking for your attention. If you can't handle that, you're gonna get beat!

If there's one thing that would surprise the average fan about what we coaches do, it's the amount of time we spend organizing a practice, a game plan or even a *meeting*. I've been able to meet a lot of our nation's greatest leaders—CEOs, senators, generals—and I'm convinced the most underestimated skill all effective leaders have is the ability to organize their people and their mission.

The top job is too complicated to rely on instincts and inspiration alone. If you're not organized, you'll end up spending too much time taking care of the small stuff when you should be taking care of your people and their concerns.

That's why we organized everything we could months before our guys got into that huddle. Twenty-five seconds!

*   *   *

Let's start with recruiting. Like most businesses, we had serious time constraints and a limited budget—*very* limited, when we first got here. So we had to maximize every trip we took. I didn't want my coaches bouncing from school to school, trying to grab this kid or talk to that one, all helter-skelter. And I definitely didn't want them to lose touch with the home base when they were traveling.

Our recruiting system was designed to get as much of our work done before we left Ann Arbor as we could, because once you're on the road, you've got to be able to focus on the recruits, their coaches and their parents—not where you're going to stay that night.

So before the season started we created thick, coded files on every potential recruit on our list—and we're talking hundreds of them, every year, just to get the twenty or twenty-five players we really wanted. We had it down so we could find any kid's file in a second, and know ten things about him just by looking at the marks on the label before we even opened it. I honestly believe we had more information on every young man we talked to than just about any other program had, because we talked to more people about each candidate, we wrote more information down, and we organized it more effectively than anyone else out there. Knowledge is power, as they say, and we had it.

Then we sat down with a map, we gave each coach a region, and we started plotting where our top prospects lived and built our travel plans around them, adding as many second-tier candidates as we could. Basic organization, sure, but vital.

I also felt our highly detailed itineraries—down to the minute—gave us an advantage because we knew exactly where every coach was going to be every minute of the day, whether he was in this high school or that guy's home or back in such-and-such hotel. Keep in mind, this is before cell phones, faxes, e-mail or any of that stuff, so we had a landline listed at each and every stop. That takes some doing!

The way we had it set up, we knew our guy was going to be there when he said he was going to be there, and we knew how to get ahold of him if we got some information he might need. Maybe Ohio State just signed someone else at this kid's position, for example, or there was some great kid dying to come to Michigan who lived ten minutes from our coach's hotel. We could get in touch with our guys just like that, in an era when few others could.

In our business, you're simply not going to show up to see the greatest high school tackle in the nation and have a shot at getting him a week before signing day. And some schools tried that. Man, we just laughed. They had no chance. And the reason is, they weren't prepared. They weren't organized. We were.

We were just as organized when it came to our itineraries for road games, and the recruits' visits to our campus. We knew where they were and who they were with every minute they were here. The more we knew, the fewer problems we had—probably because they *knew* we knew!

Why were we so manic about organization? You gotta think of it this way: There are so many things you don't control in a football game—hey, the ball is pointy, it bounces funny, and then you ask some nineteen-year-old kid to kick it at a 30 degree angle through uprights forty yards away into a crosswind—that I wanted to control everything else.

That included team meetings, individual meetings, coaches meetings—and most important of all, practice, down to the *second*!

* * *

If you're a leader, your ultimate responsibility is *the training* of your people, because every job requires training. If you can think of one that doesn't—well, jeez Louise, then why should you hire someone to do it? If it's a job worth paying someone, it's a job worth training. And it's your job to make sure they're trained well.

It all goes back to those 25 seconds.

You need to plan your training with the end product in mind. During the season we spent every Monday devising a game plan for a 60-minute game five days later. Then we'd break that game plan down into all the little pieces we needed to perfect that week in practice to make sure the plan worked on Saturday. We spent twice as much time planning each *practice* every day as we did running it.

We headed to practice with a list of drills we were going to cover that day, and I'd hold that list up when practice started and say, "Gentlemen, this practice is scheduled to go two hours, but this is going to be done right, every single drill. So if it takes you till Wednesday morning to get it all done the right way, that's your fault, not mine." That puts pressure on the guys to do every play right—which is okay with me.

Let's say you're in there at right tackle and you blew your guy clear off the line of scrimmage, just like you're supposed to. That's great. That's what we want. But the tailback fumbled the damn ball or your buddy jumped offsides, so everyone has to run the play again. You did your job, but when it's a team game all eleven guys have to do it right or it doesn't matter—just like in the games.

That teaches accountability to your teammates—and that's okay, too. I don't have to yell at the guy who fumbled the ball, because his teammates will probably make their discontent clear enough—though I might yell at him anyway, just to be sure he got the message. You just can't be too careful.

So we're going to run it again and again until we get it right. Pay attention!

Next, you need to design your training as close to the real thing as possible. Too often I hear employees say they had to learn their job *while on the job.* Well, customers don't like that! Why should I, the customer, be responsible for training *your* employees, and suffer through all their mistakes?

That's why we insisted on covering every possible situation our people might face under pressure. We *never* asked our players to do something on Saturday they hadn't done a hundred times before. And that included hitting!

In the early 1980s, I met with the coaches and said, "Men, we are not simulating what's going to happen on Saturday well enough. We're not tough enough up front, and we're not defending against the run the way a Michigan team should. From this day forward, every Tuesday and Wednesday we'll do something called 'Full Line'—the offensive line against the defensive line—and we're going to run sixteen plays that way, and I better hear pads smacking!"

So that's what we did, every week, every year, right up to the day I retired. Nowadays, with fewer scholarships, coaches are afraid to hit in practice because if anyone gets hurt, they don't have the depth to replace him. Well, hell! *I* was afraid we weren't going to be ready to hit on Saturday!

If you can't simulate on Tuesday what's going to happen on Saturday, they're going to be shocked at how *fast* the other team is coming at them, shocked at how *hard* they're getting hit, and shocked at how *quickly* the whole thing happens. I say, let the *other* team practice soft, and let *them* be shocked on Saturday!

Our players were proud of the fact they knew *no one* was going to practice harder than we were. Nobody. My guys always looked forward to the games, too, because they were *easier* than our practices. Probably more fun, too.

My old friend Bill Gunlock served as an assistant coach at West Point for the legendary Colonel Blaik. Bill was like me, a technique-conscious coach, and Blaik gave him a lot of rope. At just twenty-eight years old, Bill was already the top assistant of one of the nation's top teams, and he's generally credited with creating Army's famous "Lonesome End" formation.

One day during spring practice Bill says, "Coach Blaik, I think we're scrimmaging too much and I need more time to work with them individually so we can perfect our technique."

And Blaik calmly says, "Too much scrimmaging? Bill, can you think of a better way to find out whether our team is ready for the *game*?"

Well, that shut Bill up pretty fast.

The lesson was simple: Make your training as close to the real thing as possible. Sounds easy, but from what I've seen, not many companies do.

Now, if you do all these things right, but you have a slow, sloppy, boring training program, it's still no good. They won't pay attention. They won't be ready!

Well, we had a solution for that, too. *We ran every practice at full speed.* When we did a "Full Team" scrimmage on Tuesdays and Wednesdays, for example, we set up two fields, with the first and second offenses going against the demo defense on one field, and the first and second defenses going against the demo offense on the other field.

This has to be *extremely* well organized, because we're running two plays a minute, every minute, on two fields for twenty minutes. That's forty plays, at thirty seconds each—faster than you run them in a game—times *two* fields.

To pull this off, you've got to be aggressive, sharp and *very* well prepared. It runs like air traffic control at rush hour, with the coaches directing college kids in football gear instead of Boeing jets.

Two plays a minute. My God—we were not screwing around!

When we finished our work on one drill, we ran—RAN!—to get the next one started. "On the hop! On the hop!"

If somebody lost a contact lens—and this happened a lot, especially in the days of the hard lenses—we sure as hell weren't going to stop practice for that. No way! We just put a bunch of orange cones around that area, asked the student managers to help look, and went to work on the other side of the field.

Every summer our incoming freshmen report a few days before the returning players to get a crash course on how Michigan football works. Most of them are from good programs, and they all think they know what a tough practice looks like. Well, they don't.

Our recruiting class of 1988, my next-to-last, was loaded with big linemen like Doug Skene, Steve Everitt and Joe Cocozzo, all future NFLers. During their first practice, their offensive line coaches were drilling them when I blew the whistle, signaling them to move to another station for another drill. But these lumbering linemen just started *jogging*. Big mistake.

I *blasted* on my whistle four or five times—loud enough to

stop traffic on State Street—and started screaming. "When I blow that bleeping whistle that means for you lard-asses to SPRINT to the next bleeping drill! Now dammit, get going, or I'll *run* your bleeping asses until you bleeping *die*!"

You have never seen a group of big boys run like that! It was something to behold.

"On the hop" was about more than just saving time or running fast. "On the hop" breeds focus, especially with those suffering from short attention spans. And we never had to do sprints after practice—because we sprinted everywhere we went!

I loved the speed and intensity of a good practice. And that included the coaches, too. If you or your assistants continually stop your training to talk to this guy or that guy, you start to lose that energy, and that's wrong. You have to have that energy! If you're going to coach for me you're going to coach *on the run*. Don't pull a guy aside and stop practice and slow me down. On the hop!

You're not going to coach someone into *becoming* a Don Dufek or a Jamie Morris. But you can *train* them not to make mistakes, like fumbles, offsides and missed assignments. Because, to me, those are just a lack of discipline. And that's ultimately a lack of coaching.

That's why, if you play for me and you fumble the ball, you could hide behind the other team across the field, and I'll still find you. If you fumble twice, you will get the best seat in the house—right next to me. And you're probably going to be enjoying that seat for a quarter or two, while your replacement enjoys taking your job. I'd say that's pretty strong incentive to hang on to the ball.

If you like to run out of bounds, that's even worse. You like

being out of bounds that much? I'll give you all the time you want
on the sidelines. You'll be in heaven! You run out of bounds
playing for Michigan, you'll never get back in bounds again.

But *nothing* drove me crazier than getting called for too many
men on the field. I cannot think of a dumber penalty than that.
Yes, you've got guys running in and out of the huddle, you're under huge time pressure, and you're probably calling the play at
the last second. But is that any excuse for losing a game like that?
Hell no! When we got called for too many men—and it didn't
happen often—I used to blow my stack. Because we trained not
to do it!

So every Friday before a game, we'd practice something we
called our "sideline discipline." We'd line up all the offensive
starters in their positions: linemen in front, backs right behind
them, wideouts on the sides. Then we put the second-string
player at each position right behind the starters, all up and down
the bench. Everyone had a particular place to sit, so we knew immediately if someone was injured or missing. It was the backup's
job to watch the game and be ready the second the starter came
out, for any reason. And we'd do the same thing with the defense. You have to make sure everyone is indoctrinated.

When it was time to do this in the games, we'd get everyone
together right before the offense or defense took the field. We
could get it all done in *seconds*. I'm sure what we were doing
looked like chaos from the stands, but it wasn't. Everyone knew
what they were doing. Do this correctly, and you will never get
called for too many men on the field.

Some coaches say, "Well, even good teams are going to jump
offsides sometimes," or "Well, there's a lot of pressure, so these

For my money, the most impressive year of Ara Parseghian's career was the season he went 0-9 at Northwestern—and kept the team together. THAT is leadership!
UM ATHLETIC DEPARTMENT

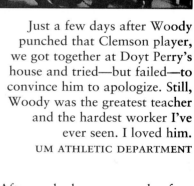

Just a few days after Woody punched that Clemson player, we got together at Doyt Perry's house and tried—but failed—to convince him to apologize. Still, Woody was the greatest teacher and the hardest worker I've ever seen. I loved him.
UM ATHLETIC DEPARTMENT

After we had won a couple of titles at Miami, bigger schools started calling. But I wasn't going to jump for just any job, because I already had a good one at Miami—the cradle of coaches! MIAMI UNIVERSITY ARCHIVES

How many former leaders go out of their way to make sure the next guy succeeds? That was Bump Elliott, on the right, a man of great class. In the middle is Don Canham, simply the best athletic director in the country. Those two set me up for success. UM BENTLEY HISTORICAL LIBRARY

If you're the leader, you need to learn the history of your organization, respect it, and teach it. Of course, it helps if you have legends like this preceding you.
UM ATHLETIC DEPARTMENT

Don't be afraid to surround yourself with the best people you can find—and no one had a better staff than I did.
UM BENTLEY HISTORICAL LIBRARY

Back then, that sign cost $150. Today that phrase is written in letters a foot high, spanning the doorway of our new practice facility. We've kept our promise for 37 years—and counting.
UM BENTLEY HISTORICAL LIBRARY

You can NOT be a leader unless you like people! Here are my two captains from 1970: Henry Hill (left), a walk-on who became an All-American; and Don Moorehead, who played one of the gutsiest games I've ever seen.
UM BENTLEY HISTORICAL LIBRARY

When you're dressed properly, you're going to act better, and you're going to feel better about yourself—even these guys, who lived in a house they called "The Den of the Mellow Men." Can you believe it? And can you believe those pants?
UM BENTLEY HISTORICAL LIBRARY

No one, not even the head coach, is more important than the team, the team, the team!
UM BENTLEY HISTORICAL LIBRARY

I used that yardstick to measure the space between my linemen. If it wasn't exactly 24 inches, they might get a whack on the backside. I used the flimsiest sticks, because when one broke it always got a laugh.
UM ATHLETIC DEPARTMENT / BOB KALMBACH

In the first loss of my career at Michigan, a 40–17 pasting by Missouri, the game turned when the Tigers blocked one of our punts. Guess what we worked on the next week? UM BENTLEY HISTORICAL LIBRARY

My friend Jerry Ford once told me that when you're at the top only the tough calls get to your desk, because people below you have already handled the easy ones. As usual, he was right. He was not quite as helpful on the golf course. UM ATHLETIC DEPARTMENT

How important were the seniors? Let me put it to you this way: It didn't matter if you were on the All-American team or the demo team. If you were a senior, you sat in first class. Everyone else— including me—sat behind you. UM ATHLETIC DEPARTMENT

Don't believe anyone who says you can't coach during games. You have to! If you don't lead them, who's going to? They *want* you to coach them. UM BENTLEY HISTORICAL LIBRARY

This is Cathy's favorite photo of me coaching. She's lucky she met me *after* I retired! UM ATHLETIC DEPARTMENT / BOB KALMBACH

If there's one thing that would surprise the average fan, it's the amount of time coaches spend organizing everything we do, including the game plan I'm holding in my hand here. Because if you're prepared, you're confident. PER KJELDSEN

I always tried to help the refs every chance I could. And they always appreciated it. UM ATHLETIC DEPARTMENT

If you don't care what the press thinks about you, they're a lot more fun to be around! UM BENTLEY HISTORICAL LIBRARY

Ah, finally! A Rose Bowl victory—on my sixth try. Before the 1980 season, we decided to change the attitude of the team, and we did! After a 1-2 start, we *dominated* our remaining opponents. UM ATHLETIC DEPARTMENT

Here I am announcing my retirement in 1989. The *only* condition I had when I left was simple: Only one guy is leaving, and his name is Schembechler! Everyone else stays.
UM BENTLEY HISTORICAL LIBRARY

After you step down, don't look back. It won't do you any good. I have no regrets—none whatsoever. If you gave everything you had, and left the right way, you're going to have a lot of fun in retirement. I know I have! UM ATHLETIC DEPARTMENT

I never had time for vacations when I was coaching. And to have this second chance at life, traveling all over the world with this smart, beautiful woman—it's more than a mortal man could ask for. I'm a lucky man.
SCHEMBECHLER FAMILY PHOTO

things happen," or "I don't want to be so strict about offsides that we're not aggressive."

That's bull. Those are excuses.

In 1961, I coached the offensive line for Woody Hayes at Ohio State. Woody was mad because we had been offsides too often the previous year for his taste, so we were going to fix it. And we did.

We decided to snap the ball on the third count *every time*! We just walked up to the line, said "Hut, hut, *hike*!" and snapped it. We weren't trying to fake anyone out. Hell, after three downs you knew what we were doing the rest of the game. But you still had to stop us. And you knew damn well we weren't going to give you any second chances, because we were not going to be offsides the entire game.

The result: The 1961 Ohio State Buckeyes *were not offsides once,* the entire season! Now, think about that. That means five guys on the line, 50 times a game, 10 games a year, had *2,500 chances* to jump offsides. And not one of them did—ever!

You fell behind that team, you'd better start praying, because we were *not* letting you get back in it. That is discipline. That is training. And that is one big reason why the 1961 Buckeyes were national champions.

What you have to understand is this: *You get what you emphasize.* Plain and simple. If you think staying onsides is important, and you harp on it all the time, that's what you're going to get. Particularly in high-pressure, critical situations, your disciplined teams are not going to make mistakes. And the reason is, they've practiced it a thousand times!

Bill Walsh might be the most famous two-minute drill coach in the history of the game. Everyone thinks it's all because of Joe

Montana or Jerry Rice, but let me tell you: The 49ers were devastating in the two-minute drill *because they practiced it*!

I once flew Bill in to speak to the high school coaches at our summer camp. They probably thought he was going to talk about the West Coast offense, but he surprised them—and me. "Let me ask you coaches a question," he said. "Let's say you get a 15-yard penalty that puts you back on your own five-yard line, and it's fourth down, you're behind by six, and you have 10 seconds left on the clock. What play do you call?"

Well, there was a lot of hemming and hawing, but the fact is, most of them didn't have a plan. The 49ers did.

"I closed every offensive practice with a play I would run under those circumstances: Three wide receivers on the right, with Rice on the left. Montana would look at the defense, and if they sent two defensive backs over to cover Rice, Montana would throw to the other side where they had the defensive backs outnumbered. If they tried to cover Rice man-to-man—usually a big mistake—Montana threw to Rice. We were pretty successful with this."

The 49ers had all those great comebacks because they *practiced it*!

Hail Mary, my ass!

IV

Fix People Problems Fast

19

Listen Before You Lead

Look, I am fully aware that my public image is—how can I put this?—that of a cantankerous guy who rants up and down the sidelines screaming at people and smashing headsets. But that's what you saw on Saturday—although that's also pretty much how I acted at practice during the week, too.

But what you didn't see was how we talked to each other during the week—my coaches, my players, my staff. I'm telling you right now: You can NOT be a leader unless you like people! You've got to spend time with them, so you know them. You've got to be interested in who they are, what they do away from the job, and how they think.

If you do not like people, you will not take the time to get to know them, and if you don't get to know them, you will have no idea what scares them, what inspires them, what motivates them. If you don't listen to what your people have to say, you will not know when they have a problem with you—and you will not know when you have a problem with them, either.

My players listened to me for one very simple reason: *I listened to them!*

Without that, they really have no reason to respect you, and they will not follow you. Because they know you really don't care.

When I was head coach at Miami of Ohio in the 1960s, I went up to see the great Green Bay Packers in summer practice. They had already won five NFL titles, three in a row. They were awesome, and I loved the way they played the game.

I'm standing there in the locker room talking to Coach Lombardi when his quarterback, Bart Starr, walks up to him with his playbook and says, "I've been thinking about this, Coach, and for this reason and that reason, I think this is the way we ought to run this play next time."

Now, I'm just some young college coach, watching this, and I'm leaning in, trying to hear every word, waiting to see what Lombardi's going to do. This is the best coach in the league—maybe the best there ever was—and he was one tough son of a gun, probably the toughest. You did not want to cross Vince Lombardi. So I had to wonder: Is the old man going to blow his stack?

But Lombardi says—and I'll never forget this—"You know what, Bart? I think you're right. Let's do it that way."

I was surprised—but I saw it happen, right before my eyes. There Lombardi was, looking right at Starr—listening, not interrupting—and then agreeing. The great Vince Lombardi telling his quarterback, We're going to do it your way.

Holy smokes!

At the Packers' training table that night, I had to ask Lombardi about that exchange. I think he probably knew I was going to ask, and he was ready. "You want to be stern with your players and make sure they're doing things the way you want them done. But sometimes they have a better idea. And if they have one, you ought to listen. Bart's a smart guy and a great quarterback, so if he has a better way, you don't want him to shut up and keep it to himself, because then he's demoralized—and you're missing out on a great idea."

Lombardi was as gruff and tough as they came. But you can't tell me he didn't care about those guys. It was *obvious*! He clearly had a special relationship with his players, and that's why his methods worked.

Now, I've never seen a great team where the players are running the program, but there are times a player might tell me, "Coach, I could do a better job if we did it this way." And you look at him and say, "You know what? I think you're right." Now when he gets back on the field, *that* is going to be one motivated guy!

Write this down: *You cannot lead if you cannot listen.* Even if you're doing *everything else right,* if one of your people comes to you with a good idea—or a personal problem—and it just goes in one ear and out the other, YOU WILL FAIL.

I spend a lot of my time listening to my coaches, my players, my support staff. And they spend a lot of their day listening to each other, too. If you can't listen—or you won't listen—you can't work for me.

In my twenty-one years at Michigan, I had to let only one assistant coach go. This guy had played for Michigan, and he was a bright, likable fellow, but he just didn't listen—not to me, not to his colleagues, not to his players—and it did him in.

I remember one day one of his players came to me with a

2

football question, and I told him the first person you need to talk to is your position coach, and only after that can you come to me. That was our policy, established on Day One. But I knew right then, as soon as that player left my office to go talk with this particular assistant, that the coach was going to do all of the talking, and the player was going to do all of the listening. And that kid was going to come out of that meeting and say, "He didn't listen to a word I said. He doesn't understand my problem."

And right there, you've lost him. You've lost him! Why is a player going to bust his butt for a coach like that?

After this happened a few more times, I called this assistant coach into my office. I sat him down right in front of my desk, and I told him flat out: "Your problem is you talk, talk, talk—and you don't listen!" And you know what happened? Everything *I* was saying to him was just going in one ear and out the other! He wasn't even listening to *me*!

At that point, I realized this coach had to go, and he did. He hasn't succeeded anywhere else since then, either. And I know why.

If you don't listen to the person talking to you, then you've sent that person a clear message that you don't need him. And they know this. I don't care how tough your people are—and I don't think people come too much tougher than the coaches and players and staffers we had here at Michigan—they need to know you care. You need to show them—because you're not going to fool them.

It's one thing to listen to a good idea from your star quarterback. It's another to listen with just as much interest to the problems of a walk-on. When someone—*anyone*—in our program had a problem, I wanted to know about it. And I wanted to do something about it, too.

So I had a hard-and-fast policy: Any player who needed to see me, *at any time,* could. That simple. If he's wearing Maize and Blue, he's a Wolverine, he's one of mine, and he's welcome to call me or see me anytime he needs to, day or night. To this day.

Is it easy? Not always. We're pretty busy! And these guys know that the most valuable thing I've got is my time, the scarcest resource I have to spend. But if they've got the guts to come down and pull me out of a meeting, it must be pretty important to them. Something must be eating them up. So I owe 'em that much, at least.

If you think that's foolish, then think about what would happen if I *didn't* have that policy. If a guy comes down to see me because he's eating his heart out over something, and my secretary says, "Bo's in a meeting right now. Can you come back tomorrow?"—well, that guy probably ain't coming back. He'll lose his nerve, and then his problem—whatever it is—isn't going to get solved, and it'll start festering inside him. And I'll lose him.

That doesn't mean there aren't limits. If the same guy keeps coming down to see me for every little thing, I might say, "Hey, you've been here five times for the same thing. You're becoming a pain in the neck! What is it *this* time?"

But the policy works. You just can't delegate something like that. If they need to talk to you, they need to talk to YOU, not your assistant or your secretary or anyone else.

I maintained this policy even during the busiest times of the year, which for us were the Tuesday and Wednesday coaches meetings during game weeks. That's when we put the entire game plan together, by going over tape, poring over our stats, our opponents' stats, and debating what we're going to do, who we're going to start, what plays we're going to call. If I was in one of these staff meetings, my secretaries knew, if the president of the university calls, take a message. If the president of the United States calls—I'll call him back. (And I'm not kidding!) But if one of my players comes down to see me, for any reason, I am *always* to be interrupted. I'm sorry, folks, but you just can't build a team if you don't know your people, and when the chips are down for them, that's when they need you most.

It's October 1975. We've got five wins, two ties, and no losses, we're ranked seventh in the nation and we're getting ready to play our seventh game of the year against Minnesota for the Little Brown Jug.

Jimmy Hackett was a junior on that team. His dad, Bill Hackett, was a great All-American guard at Ohio State in the late 1940s. Jimmy's brother played for the Bucks against us in 1969, but Woody didn't want Jimmy. Didn't offer him anything. But I liked his attitude, so we gave him a full scholarship to come to Michigan.

Jimmy wasn't fast enough to play linebacker for us. Who ranked ahead of him? Just about every linebacker on the team, including All-Americans like Calvin O'Neal and John Anderson. We were loaded at linebacker! So Jimmy moved to center, where he wasn't *big* enough. We were loaded there, too, with Jim Czirr and Walt Downing and George Lilja—three All-Big Ten centers, two of them All-Americans.

So where does Jimmy fit in? Hard to say, but Jimmy had the kind of determination we loved, and he never missed a practice. But by his junior year he was getting his doubts. He wasn't sure where he stood on the team, if he was really making a contribution, or even if he was *ever* going to be able to make one someday down the road. This was really getting to him, so he walked down State Street to see me, to make sure that he wasn't wasting his time. Jimmy wanted to play *so* badly, the least you can do with someone like that, someone who's sacrificed so much for the team, is to give him some of your time.

Jimmy came down on a Tuesday morning, when all the coaches were with me in the conference room with the projector running, and all of us talking and arguing and doing all the things we do to make sure we've gone over absolutely everything before Saturday. In the middle of all this, I see Jimmy through the window, talking to my secretary, Lynn Koch. When a player came to see me, all he had to say was, "I am here to see Bo." Lynn was great because she never made them feel bad for asking, and she never asked them why, either. She just said, "Hey, Jimmy. I'll get him for you."

When Lynn stuck her head in the door and told me Hackett's outside, I came right out to see him. Jimmy was no malcontent, so I knew this wasn't easy for him, pulling me out of a meeting like that. I asked him what was on his mind, and Jimmy reminded me that he hadn't missed a practice in three years—something I knew already, because we kept track of those things—and he told me he felt he had improved, and he knew he could be a starter on almost any other Big Ten team that year. All that was true, and I knew it.

Now, when a guy like Hackett screws up his courage like that just to talk to you, you listen intently. You *never* look at your watch, or gaze out the window, or glance back at the meeting room to see what's going on. You listen. You LISTEN!

When I was sure he was done, I looked him straight in the eye and said, "Jimmy, I know how you feel." Because I did. I'd been in his shoes. But that didn't mean I was going to give him a bunch of bull just to make him feel better. I intended to tell him the truth—because you have to. You owe him that, too. So I made it very clear what was keeping him from being a starter—a lack of size and speed, mainly, plus the incredible competition he was facing at his position—but I also told him I knew he hadn't missed a practice, I knew how hard he was working, and that all of his coaches saw it, and all of his teammates saw it, too, and we all respected him for it. And most important, he was the best demo team center in the nation. I wasn't kidding. No one did a better job of getting our defense ready for the next game than Jimmy Hackett did. And that was the truth.

Jimmy listened to me. When I was done, he wasn't despondent. He had some hope in his heart, and the clear impression that he was contributing something important to this team. He needed to see that his value to the team wasn't just about how talented he was, but about how hard he worked. He realized he was playing an important part on a great team, at an outstanding university. Jimmy never missed a practice his entire career, and after that meeting he never felt he had to see me again to have his value confirmed. He knew what he was giving us—and perhaps just as important, that day, was that he knew we knew it, too.

Hackett shook my hand, and he headed back up the hill to class.

I'd like to tell you Jimmy got in the next game, and that we creamed Minnesota like we were supposed to, but none of that happened. Jimmy didn't get in, and we narrowly pulled out a fourth-quarter victory over an unranked Minnesota team, 28–21. Not our best effort.

Did my meeting with Hackett have anything to do with our team not playing our best that day? Hell no! If I can't spend fifteen minutes with one of our hardest-working players and still get the team ready to play on Saturday, then I must not be a very good coach. No, we didn't have a great game, but it wasn't because of Jimmy Hackett, I can tell you that.

Years later, Jimmy told me he learned a lot from that meeting, that you can have a tremendous impact as a leader just by taking a little time. Your people have to know that their value to you and your organization is not determined just by what they *do,* but by who they *are.* I can't make it any clearer than that.

Today, Jimmy Hackett is the CEO of Steelcase Furniture in Grand Rapids, Michigan, number one in its field. Hackett's policy at Steelcase is the same policy I had at Michigan: Anybody who wants to talk with him can do it, from the custodians to the vice presidents. But I told him, "Jimmy, that's impossible. I had 125 players, but you've got 14,000 employees! You can't do that!"

"You're right, Bo. The odds of me seeing everyone in this organization in my lifetime are pretty slim. But Bo, you didn't meet with every one of us every week, either. That wasn't the point. All of us knew that if we felt we had to see you, we could. *That* was the point. My employees don't come to see me that often, but they know they can. So if they feel they have to come talk to me, it's probably pretty important to them, and they know I'll make time."

Then he told me something else that made a lot of sense to me.

"I sit in this office building over here, and they're working in that factory over there. If I wanted to be walled off, it'd be easy to avoid them. But if you want to know what's going on with the rank and file, you better *talk* to the rank and file. I learn more about how to run this company from the people who actually do the work than from all my vice presidents put together. My VPs don't want to tell me bad news, but the guys on the line aren't scared. They want me to know. So you've got to stay in touch."

Now, that's just as true in business—*any* business—as it is in coaching.

Keep in mind, if you're the leader, your supervisors don't want you to worry about their divisions. So, where are you going to get the truth? The guy on the line probably isn't shooting for your job, so he doesn't have much incentive to hide the truth. He'll tell you!

Dave Brandon, who played for me a few years before Hackett did, rose to become the CEO of Domino's Pizza. And he says it's the same thing at his company, even with 145,000 employees. You send him an e-mail at midnight, you're likely to have your answer before you wake up the next morning. I don't know how he does it, but he does.

To this day my former players come back—in their thirties and forties and fifties, now—to see me in my office at the football building, and it's the same thing. They've got a problem, they need some help. Could be their jobs, their wives, their kids, maybe they're going through some tough times of their own— whatever—but if they feel the need to come down here and see me, it must be important.

If you can help someone with a little attention, don't you think you should do that? And the answer is, Yes, of course you should. That's got nothing to do with football. That's just doing what's right. And that's what leaders do.

These days, though, most of the time they're just coming down here to tell me the success stories, how all those things we were yelling at them years ago have finally sunk in—or just to shoot the breeze, and tell some old stories.

If you listen long enough, you get to hear the good news, too.

20

Know Your People

A few years ago I read a story in *Sports Illustrated* about a big-time college coach who didn't know the names of all his players. "I don't coach players," he said. "I coach coaches."

That just doesn't fly. You've got to lead your people, *all* your people, not just your top managers. Hey, if you're the top guy, it all comes back to you. And if they have to answer to *you,* you have to know *them.*

I've seen some absolutely outstanding assistant coaches who, the day they become head coach somewhere, absolutely laid an egg. If I had to tell you one reason why some excellent assistant coaches failed as head coaches, I'd say it wasn't a lack of football knowledge or energy or intelligence. It's because they had no relationship with their players. They lost touch with the grass-roots of their organization, thinking they could delegate personal connections. And when that happens, they start getting paranoid.

I know people in football and in business whose relationship with their people is so weak, who so lack confidence in their own leadership abilities, that they will not walk through their own locker room or their own factory floor. They don't want to go in and face those guys, because they don't know them, or they haven't been truthful with them, and they have no idea what their people are thinking. They're scared—and maybe they should be!

Now that is a guy who will not be successful, in coaching or in business or anywhere else. I don't know how you can lead a team if you're afraid to walk through the locker room, just like you can't be a CEO if you can't walk through your factory floor or a principal if you can't walk through the cafeteria. I don't know how you can lead anybody you don't like. I think that's pretty basic.

Keep in mind, they don't have to like *you*. And if you're doing a good job leading your team and sticking to your principles, on any given day there will probably be someone in the locker room who'd rather not see you. Well, so what? It's my locker room, and I'm going to like that guy anyway. You've got to walk in there, and have no fear.

I was never afraid to go in our locker room and face my men, because I knew them. I knew I had been honest with them whether they liked it or not, and I knew what they were thinking, because I talked to them.

The most important thing any leader can do is not draw up some organizational chart or give a fire-and-brimstone halftime speech.

No. The most important thing you can do is *know your people*. Know them inside out. Know where they're from, what their goals are, what their strengths and weaknesses are. Know what their buttons are.

When I was coaching at Miami, I had a defensive tackle by the name of Kenny Root. He was a big guy, not tightly muscled, but heavy, thick. And great feet. I mean, he could dance! But in his first two years with me I couldn't get anything out of him. I wasn't doing anything special with him, just the normal yelling at him, pushing him, trying to get him to do things the way we wanted them done—but I had no success.

Now, you've got to understand, this is a nice jovial kid, a gentle giant. Kenny wanted to be everybody's buddy. I'm not dealing with a malcontent here. I'm just not getting any football out of him!

After a while I realized I'd done everything I could do, and I just got sick of doing it. So I finally resorted to my last option.

At the end of Kenny Root's sophomore year, I sat him down, and I looked him in the eye and said, "Root, I've had all of you I can take. I've tried to make a football player out of you, and you've not responded, and the only reason you've not responded is because you're a big lazy guy with a bad attitude and I'm sick of coaching you. You are the biggest underachiever I have ever run into, and as long as you're here and you continue to perform the way you are, I will not speak to you. I'm not going to talk to you again."

I didn't pull his scholarship. I didn't kick him off the team. I just didn't talk to him his entire junior year! I walked right past him every day, morning, noon and night. On the practice field, on the bus, in the hallway. Didn't matter where I saw him, I'd walk right past him and wouldn't even give him the time of day, all season. And I'm sure there were times he was about to burst. This guy wanted to be my buddy, and I wouldn't even look at him! It was probably the only thing I could have done that was going to make him mad.

But I'll be damned, by his senior year he must have gotten the message, because he really began to play. He even became a starter, and a good one. He actually stayed for a fifth year—rare, back then—and by then he was great!

Now he calls me all the time. All the time. When he gets me on the phone, I know it's going to be a good half-hour, and that's fine with me. I like the guy. He became a highly successful insurance salesman, he has a wife and three sons, and everyone's doing well.

Now, would Kenny Root have been better off today if I'd just said, forty years ago, "Kenny, that's all you've got. I understand. That's fine."

Of course not! It wasn't any fun for either one of us, but it's what he needed. And it worked because I *knew* him.

21

Don't Sleep on It, and Don't Hold Grudges

When you're faced with some personnel problem, conventional wisdom says you've got to sleep on it before you do anything rash. But I say that's pointless, because if it really is a problem you're not going to sleep anyway. So you might as well face the damn thing and get it over with. If you're wrong, you can always apologize later. Either way, after it's all said and done, you just forget about it, and move on.

I've coached lots of players who have never been in my doghouse. As a matter of fact, *most* of them have never been there, though it probably depends on what you mean by the doghouse. Did you have a bad game? That's not going to put you in the doghouse with me. I'm just upset with your performance. We'll go back to work the next day, we'll get better, and I'll get over it.

But if you get in trouble with a landlord or a professor or you were picked up drunk at one o'clock in the morning by the *police,* you're going to be in my doghouse, for sure. It's not hard to get in my doghouse—once—and we'll handle that, but if you do it consistently, you're going to have a hard time with me, and I'll make sure it's not any fun for you, either.

You can bet my players always knew when I was upset with them. You just can't be afraid to tell them what you think about their behavior. You cannot hold things back. Sometimes I hear coaches say, "You know, I always wanted to tell him he did this or that, but now he's gone." And I say, "Well, why didn't you tell him? He might not have liked it, but it would have helped him—and he probably wouldn't still be doing it now!"

I do not believe in sitting on a problem. Because the longer you sit on that thing, the longer it'll irritate you. If you're keeping it to yourself, there's nothing the guy you're mad at can do to fix it, either, because you haven't told him why you're mad. I simply could not *stand* to keep worrying about a problem if I could correct it now.

NOW!

I simply refused to sit around and stew about it. Get this damn thing out of here!

So I say, *act* on the problem, and get it behind you. And if you have to apologize later, they'll usually say that was class.

Okay. There are those who will tell you apologies do not come as easily to me as I'm claiming here. Jim Brandstatter played offensive tackle here in the early 1970s. He's now a famous TV personality—whatever that is—who does Michigan football and basketball games and *Michigan Replay* on Sunday mornings. He's also become a close friend of mine. He and his wife, Robbie

Timmons, have traveled with Cathy and me all over the world. We have a ton of fun together.

But on this occasion, during practice years ago, Brandy was off-sides, as usual, but the play goes for 30 or 40 yards, so Jim's running downfield—or trying to, anyway. He wasn't exactly the fleetest of foot. I see he's offsides, so I start chasing him down the field, running at full fury, yelling the whole time until I catch up to him.

Now, according to Brandy, I smacked his shoulder pads, slapped his chest and was generally carrying on, when Jerry Hanlon ran up behind me and started yelling, "Bo, it wasn't Brandstatter! It wasn't Brandstatter!"

Finally I hear Hanlon. I stop smacking Brandstatter. And then I say, "Well, he needed it anyway!"

But, that's Jim's story. Of course, he's gotten it all wrong, as usual. And so he became a journalist. I guess it's just as well.

Brandstatter's slander aside, the principle still holds. If you are direct with everyone you deal with, they'll be direct with you. That's my belief. That's my experience.

Hell, they already know when you're mad at them, anyway. At least, they always did with me! So if you've got some guy you're mad at, you tell him why. Then you also make it clear what he has to do if he wants to get out of the doghouse. We're not putting someone in the doghouse and leaving him there without telling him how to get out. And he'd better know that I *want* him out of that doghouse. You're not doing us any good in there!

After that, it's up to him. But you'll feel better. I guarantee it.

You might already know the story about the time I chewed out our captain, Andy Cannavino, in 1980. We started out 1-2 that year—*not* a typical Michigan opening—and Andy had been bitching and moaning that our practices were too long, we were hitting too much, we watched too much film. Of course, I heard about this from one of our assistants, Bob Thornbladh, and I got Cannavino in my office about five minutes later. Let's just say the conversation was brief, one-sided and ended with me yelling at Cannavino to grow up and be a man, and Cannavino leaving in tears.

That's been covered. But here's the part you haven't heard. My assistant coaches were in the next room, and they could hear me blasting away at Andy through the wall. When they saw Cannavino crawl out of my office, visibly shaken, they came running in to see me.

"Wow, Bo, that was something!"

"Yes it was," I said.

"What's he going to do?"

"To be honest, I have absolutely no idea," I told them. "But I can tell you this: *I* feel a whole lot better about it!"

The fact that Cannavino went on to become probably the greatest captain I ever had, leading a defense that did not give up a touchdown for *twenty-four consecutive quarters,* including my first Rose Bowl victory that January, was simply a bonus.

I didn't pull Cannavino into my office because I thought it would help us win a Big Ten title or a Rose Bowl. I did it simply because he needed to hear it, and I needed to say it. I wasn't playing some mind game. I was addressing an urgent problem.

Everything that happened after that was Andy's doing, not mine.

I've got hundreds of examples like that—and I'm sure my players can give you thousands more, because those guys never forget it when they get chewed out. But here's a good one, about Dave Brandon, back in 1972.

Dave was a former All-State quarterback from South Lyon, not far from Ann Arbor, a guy I recruited when I was recovering from my heart attack right after the 1970 Rose Bowl. I first met him when I was still in my bed at 870 Arlington Road, doing my best to recruit guys while still in my pajamas and a robe.

Dave's problem was, we had Denny Franklin and Larry Cipa and Tom Slade at quarterback—all *three* of those guys started at one point, and all of them did a good job—so Dave moved to the defensive backfield to try to get some playing time. Well, jeez, who do we have there but Thom Darden, Randy Logan, Dave Brown and Don Dufek—every one of them an All-American. Hell, Dave could have been the fifth-best defensive back in the country and not gotten any playing time on that team. So, after a couple years, he's still third-string, and he's getting frustrated.

Dave was a junior on our 1972 team, a team that went undefeated until we were upset by Ohio State, 14–11, in Columbus. That team was one of my best, but it was still a challenge keeping everyone happy and involved, even when you're winning big every Saturday.

At a Monday practice in the middle of the season we had a lot of guys who hadn't gotten in the game that Saturday. So we coaches decided to work with all those guys by making up a scrimmage we called the Toilet Bowl. We were just getting started when one of our assistant coaches tells Brandon where he was going to be playing in this little scrimmage. Well, Brandon apparently responded with something less than complete enthusiasm.

This happened on the opposite sideline from me, but the coach told me about this situation right away, because he knew I'd want to know. The second I hear this, I'm rushing across the field and in Brandon's face, yelling and screaming, probably less than a minute after he mumbled his protest to the assistant. Boy, was Brandon surprised!

"I hear you'd rather not partake in our little scrimmage," I said. He was too stunned to respond. "Well, I can solve your problem. Son, you're going straight into that locker room, you're cleaning your locker out, and you're going home. You're done playing football for Michigan. This is an honor you clearly don't deserve."

Whenever I did this, I'd call out for Jon Falk, our equipment manager, and I'd tell him, in front of everyone, to go clean out the guy's locker that instant, so there wouldn't be a lot of lapse between my decision and the consequences. Falk knows what he's doing, and that locker was always cleaned out by the time the guy got back to see it, which is just how I wanted it because when you're the head coach, everything you do is being monitored by 124 other guys. There can't be any wishy-washiness. I don't want to have those guys get back to the locker room and see their buddy's uniform still hanging there and wonder if the coach meant what he said or not. When you see a locker cleaned out, it's pretty obvious to everyone what the consequences were. It kind of proves your point. He's gone!

Now, I've gotta tell you: In my mind, Brandon was only suspended. I knew he'd be back, because there was just too much character in that guy to end his career like that. That man was not a quitter. And I knew that because I knew Brandon.

But in his mind, he's been kicked off. He's done. And he's got to drag his sorry butt back into that locker room, and think about what he just did. Dave sits there in his empty stall for what he's convinced is the last time, completely crushed. He's got to think about what he's going to tell his girlfriend, his dad and his kids someday: that he had a chance to play for the greatest university in the country and he blew it simply because he didn't appreciate it. If you ask him about this today, he'll tell you he was about to cry at that moment—and this is a tough guy!—and I guarantee you, he didn't get a second of sleep that night.

The next day, Brandon calls to make an appointment to see me first thing in the morning, just like I knew he would. He's scared, he's nervous, he's troubled—and he looks like hell. He apologizes for his conduct, and promises he'll never be so stupid again. Of course, I take him back. I *wanted* him on that team. But you can bet we never heard Dave Brandon complain about any scrimmages after that!

What happened to Dave? As I've said, he's now the CEO of Domino's Pizza, as well as a regent of the University of Michigan. They say he might someday be governor, and you can bet he's got my vote.

But even after he became a famous executive, that incident still bothered him. It was embarrassing, it was humiliating, it was something he had a hard time forgiving himself for. He's even asked me, "How could I be so selfish, so negative, so weak?" Long after he'd become a millionaire, he still had never told anyone he'd been kicked off the team. It's just not something you brag about.

Finally, at the first reunion we had for all the guys who'd played and coached for me, in 1989, Dave was sitting with his classmates around a table, and he figured he was a safe enough distance away from the incident to confess his sins. And you know what happened? After Dave spilled his guts, one by one, they went around the table, and everyone else had the same story. They'd *all* been kicked off the team at one time or another! They howled!

That same night, when it was time for introductions, Brandon gets up—and I've quoted this statement a hundred times—and he tells his old teammates: "I didn't get in many games. I wasn't an All-American like a lot of you guys, or even an All-Big Ten player. Hell, some weeks I wasn't even on the All-Scout Team! But in the long run, I became an All-American in business."

They all cheered. People, believe me when I tell you, *that* is what we were trying to teach when I was head coach.

If there's a problem with the people in your ranks, you'd better know about it, and you'd better do something about it— fast!—or else it's just going to get worse. And that's just what Dave Brandon does at Domino's today. He makes sure everyone at Domino's realizes how special it is to work for the top pizza maker in the world, that they never take it for granted.

And that's something everyone in every organization *must* do if they're going to be successful.

One more thing: Once you've said your piece, and they've either straightened out or shipped out, you can't hold any grudges. Okay, that might sound a little hypocritical from a guy who can remember every Big Ten athletic director by name who voted for Ohio State to go to Pasadena instead of Michigan after that infamous 10–10 tie thirty-four years ago. But trust me, I'm pretty good at not holding grudges. Because I don't keep it all bottled up, after I've vented I've got nothing left to be angry about.

Take Bill Frieder. Was I ticked off when I fired him? Hell yes! But once he was gone, he's gone. I didn't see him again until the spring of 2005, at Don Canham's memorial service at Crisler Arena, and it got back to me that he wasn't sure if he should approach me or not. Well, hell, this was sixteen years after he left! If I was still the athletic director, would I hire him? No. But if you ask me if I hate the guy, or even dislike him, the answer is no. If Frieder walked into this room right now and he wasn't representing Michigan, we'd sit down and have a good chat and all would be fine.

And that's exactly what we did that day. We just had a good chat, a few laughs, and caught up with each other. And that was that. Why should I carry around some stupid grudge for sixteen years that won't do me a damn bit of good anyway? There's no point.

Late December 1989. It's our last day of hard-hitting practice before the 1990 Rose Bowl. I announced my retirement a few weeks earlier, and in a few days, I'd be coaching my last game. Well, I'll be damned, but two of our seniors, Marc Spencer and Scott Smykowski, go out and break curfew. I like these guys, no problem there. They weren't troublemakers—except for the time Smykowski got some idiotic haircut like Brian Bosworth's, which I felt compelled to mention in front of the entire team. But that was fun, and Smykowski took it well.

But when they were caught breaking curfew, I didn't flinch. I couldn't. I had to send them home. Didn't matter to me if it *was* my last game. Should I check in my values, the very same values we built the program on for over two decades, because it's my last game? Man, that would have been the *worst* way to leave!

And you know, that was probably a crushing blow to those kids. They probably wish they hadn't done that. They get to go to the Rose Bowl and all of a sudden they're sent home. That's a terrible thing, a real shame. But I can't worry about how hard it is on them—or on me—because they knew the rules. And so did their teammates, who were watching, I'm sure, to see what I'd do. That's why you just can't make exceptions.

Could they have helped me win my last game? Who knows?

I didn't think of that. Absolutely not. Our conversation was brief and to the point. You knew the rules, you broke them, you're going home. They put on their coats and ties and Bob Chmiel drove them to the airport. They were gone within an hour.

I'm the kind of a guy who might get so mad at you I'll want to kill you—but I won't let it linger. I'll speak my mind, and get over it. I refuse to let it eat me up.

So I don't hold grudges. Know how I can tell? I couldn't recall who the two guys were who broke curfew at that Rose Bowl until Bacon reminded me. I recall *them,* but I couldn't recall what they'd done. I never can recall who got in trouble.

But I *can* recall visiting Smykowski in the hospital six months later when he got a blood disease and needed a bone marrow transplant.

I asked him how much he needed to get one. A hundred thousand? A million? We'll get it. Turns out $150,000 was the target, so we sent out letters to every member of the Michigan football family, and we raised the money just like that. We got donations from every class I coached, from NFL stars, from walk-ons, you name it. A lot of them—probably *most* of them—had never met Smykowski. Didn't matter. They understood he was one of us, and he needed our help. So he got it.

Scott's bone marrow transplant was a success, and he's in perfect health today. He's a husband and a father now, and he still comes back to see me, just like he should. That's what we do here.

Here's something else I've noticed: The guys you butt heads with are often the most loyal. They call and visit the most. Maybe it's because they know you really care about them. Maybe it's because you've been through something together. I don't know.

But I do know, if you coached them just to get them to play for you on Saturdays, that's what you're going to get: a former player, not a friend.

If you hold a grudge, all it does is bring you down, and cost you friends. So get it off your chest, and be done with it. And when you're done, you'll never be lonely, because you'll have hundreds of friends who come back to see you—including my old buddy Scott Smykowski.

V

Meet the Moment of Truth

22

Break 'Em Down and Build 'Em Up

If I wasn't a football coach, one thing I know I could never have tolerated was showing up for work and going through the same motions every day. No goals, no deadlines, nothing to shoot for. God, that would be horrible. But I think that's the reality for too many American workers. I'd hate it!

I don't care what your business is—whether you're running a company or a classroom or a Boy Scout troop: You need to find a way to instill *game day urgency* in everything you do. Because without it, every day is just like every other day, everyone loses interest and then they lose focus. It kills morale, productivity, quality—you name it, boredom kills it. And then they're not getting anything worthwhile done.

Let's look at the big picture first. In the off-season we laid out our entire year, with our eleven games as the focal point. We structured our entire program—everything we did, every single day—around those eleven game days. We blew that schedule up and plastered it on every wall we could find—all the meeting rooms, the weight room, all over the football building—and we did it for a reason: *This is why we're doing what we're doing. This is the point!*

When you were lifting weights, you weren't just lifting weights—you were getting ready for our opening game against Notre Dame on September 16. When you were in a meeting, you weren't just in a meeting, you were getting ready for Michigan State on October 14. And trust me, brother, when you were practicing, you weren't just pushing sleds—no. You were getting ready for the Buckeyes of Ohio State on November 25.

Because otherwise, why are we working like dogs in the middle of February? How do you stay motivated to run sprints all spring? I'll tell you why: Because we had Notre Dame on September 16! We had Michigan State on October 14! We had Ohio State on November 25!

Am I beating those dates into your head? Good! Because that's what we did with our players, too.

We reminded them *constantly* why we were asking them to do what they were doing: to win those games! Nothing kept us more focused than knowing game day was coming up.

We tested our players on paper after meetings, we tested them on the ground in practice, and then we gave them the most difficult test they'd ever take, called Saturday afternoons in Michigan Stadium, on the turf on game days. I tell you, knowing there was going to be a number next to our name, displayed for the whole world to see—it focused the mind in March.

Look. I have no illusions. I was a football coach, not a CEO or a senator or a substitute teacher. But I guarantee you this: If I *were* a CEO, I'd turn product launches into a Michigan State game, quarterly results into an Ohio State game, and annual reports into the Rose Bowl. Whatever I had to work with, I'd turn it into something to shoot for, into something for the entire organization to focus on, to create that upcoming *game day urgency*. No matter what field you're in, you can do it—and you need to.

The season had a cycle to it, and every week did, too. That kept the players intense, engaged, and peaking at the right time.

As soon as we finished singing "Hail to the Victors" in our locker room after a win, we started getting ready for the next game. When the players went out Saturday night, we went to the office to break down the film from that game, so we'd be ready on Sunday to analyze everything with the offense, defense and special teams when the players came back that afternoon for our first meeting of the week. What kind of mood I was in for Sunday films depended entirely on how the game went the day before.

Every organization, and every employee, needs the occasional kick in the pants to give their absolute best. But when do you deliver it, and how? Contrary to what you might think, I never kicked my players when they were down. After a loss—which our guys took as hard as the coaches did—they were already down enough, so piling on just risked demoralizing them. If we had put it all on the line and lost to, say, Notre Dame or Ohio State, I wouldn't lay into them. They were hard enough on themselves, so they didn't need me yelling at them.

The *only* time you come down on your people after a setback is if you didn't get maximum effort. But honestly, as long as I coached here, I cannot think of a single game when I really felt we lost due to a lack of effort.

If we lost, my goal on Sunday was to show them what we

needed to do better, but I also wanted to get their confidence back up—and maybe get them just a little ticked off to redeem themselves next Saturday. I always felt that after a defeat I was going to get maximum effort on Monday. I didn't worry about their intensity then.

No, I didn't kick them when they were down. *I kicked 'em when they were up!* It was after a sloppy victory, some 17–10 season-opening mess against Northwestern, when they knew Sunday films weren't going to be any fun. Or even when we blew 'em out, 69–0, in 1975. When you win, you get giddy and loose and you start thinking you're something special. *That's* the time to get on them! You can't let them think what they're doing is good enough, or you're going to get whacked the next week.

When you're winning, don't worry about their feelings. When they're riding high, they're feeling good, they can handle it, and a few knocks help sharpen their focus. "That was a great game," I'd tell them when we started our Sunday film session at the old football building. "But you know what you did? You missed three assignments in a row. Three! Can you believe it? I don't know how the hell we beat those guys with mistakes like that!"

Man, if you just beat Illinois, 70–21, which we did in 1981, I guarantee you, in our film session the next day, you wouldn't hear anything about the 70 points we scored—only the 21 we gave up! "That's the most points we've EVER given up against Illinois since I've been here! How do you expect to beat Ohio State if we give up three touchdowns to Illinois?"

We won't find a single thing you did right. Nothing! We'd look for the *littlest* possible mistake—anything—and we'd find something, every time. Brother, you miss one block or turn the wrong way or make just one mistake—*one mistake!*—in a game like that and we'll play that thing back and forth a dozen times, in front of all your teammates. You'll be the star of the show.

I loved that Sunday film meeting, because it let me get every-thing off my chest that was driving me crazy the day before—and I mean *everything*. "How the hell do you expect us to win the Big Ten title when our offense has three straight three-and-outs? Our offense can't do that to our defense! You're keeping them out on the field too long!"

We ran some plays back and forth so many times that some of those players would start to nod off. Remember, these were college kids, fresh from a Saturday night victory party. When that happened, I'd take the eraser and whip it just above the guilty guy's head. The nice thing about the old erasers in those days—before they invented these damn dry erase boards—is how they would *explode* with a big cloud of white dust when they hit the wall. The guys seemed to wake up pretty fast when I did that!

The fact is, you've got to be a little bit of an actor, and that's never more important than when you're trying to convince your guys they aren't as good as everyone says they are. That's why we wanted you to go away thinking you were *lucky* to squeak that one out, even if we won 70–21!

It's easy to pat them on the back after a victory, but if they're not playing their best, no matter what the score, you've got to get on 'em. When they're fat and happy, you've gotta make 'em mean and hungry.

The Sunday film sessions set up their mind-set for the rest of the week. Once we had them convinced they couldn't do anything right, we'd start to build them back up during the week—but slowly.

Monday was scout day, when we'd go over everything we knew about our upcoming opponent, and then have the demo team imitate what we thought our opponent was going to do that Saturday. If it was Ohio State—well hell, the coaches didn't need to do a heck of a lot to get you to take them seriously. If you play football for the Michigan Wolverines and you can't get up to play the Ohio State Buckeyes—the greatest rivalry in college football—then you probably won't last until November anyway.

But when we were playing one of the lesser teams—let's say an Indiana or a Northwestern or a Navy—then we had to do some coaching. In the same way we broke our guys down after a big win—and for the same reason—we built our lesser opponents up. You put together your scouting film the right way, any team can look like a world-beater. But the fact was, almost every team we played did have *something* going for them, or they wouldn't be on our schedule. And I will *always* believe anyone can lose to anybody on any given Saturday.

That's why we always said: THE UPSET IS IN THE MIND OF THE FAVORITE. Because most upsets can never happen *unless the favorite lets his guard down,* starts getting cocky and believing his press clippings. Coca-Cola could have bought Pepsi a hundred years ago, but didn't think they had to. *Sports Illustrated* could have bought ESPN twenty years ago, but figured it was a waste of money. And the Soviet hockey team could have easily crushed the Americans at Lake Placid in 1980, but they didn't take them seriously—and every one of those giants paid for it.

Well, I was going to be damned if that was going to happen to us. So the weaker our foes, the meaner I was, all week. Any guy on our team will tell you I was a *bear* before we played Northwestern!

We took every opponent seriously, and even if we were heavy favorites—and we usually were—our goal was to *get better every game.* That meant if the spread was 20, we wanted to win by 25. If we beat them by 30 last time, we wanted to beat them by 35 this time. We didn't run up the score at Michigan—that was not our way, and it still isn't—but I sure as hell wanted to see some progress out there, no matter who we were playing, in terms of rushing yards, turnovers, penalties—whatever we were focusing on. Like I always said, "Every day we get better, or we get worse." Well, dammit, I wanted to get better—every day!

Okay, my bowl record stinks, and I was just a little better than .500 against Ohio State. But you look at the record, and we almost *never* got upset along the way. Certainly much less than most big powers. And the reason is that we constantly guarded against it.

On Tuesday and Wednesday, we hit—live! Full Line! Full Line! Hell yes! And we're going to be on you, making sure you're physically and mentally ready.

But we didn't want to burn them out, either, so assuming we got what we wanted from the guys on Tuesday and Wednesday, we started tapering off. Thursday was a thinking practice, where we started taking care of the so-called little things. We didn't want guys jumping offsides, missing assignments or dropping the ball. We may not hit on Thursdays, but I sure as heck wanted you to be mentally sharp.

Friday afternoon was just a walk-through—no pads, just sweats and helmets. If we were playing on the road, we'd do the walk-through at their stadium, get a feel for it. By now the coaches are getting positive, and the players should be, too.

Friday night we ate the same big team meal we always ate—salad, clam chowder, steak and lasagna, baked potato and a chocolate sundae for dessert. No one went hungry on my watch!

After dinner we watched a movie. One night we watched

The Ballad of Cable Hogue, which featured a girl running from an outdoor bathtub up the hill when some strangers came calling. I want my guys motivated—but not in that way! Nineteen-year-old men need no encouragement along those lines. "Who the hell ordered this film?" When I found out it was Dick Hunter, I had no choice but to fire him from that job, too, just like I had to fire him from picking our bowl game attire. All that was left for Hunter to do was coach the defensive secondary. We settled on Clint Eastwood's spaghetti westerns and Dirty Harry movies, and those were great. The guys loved them. I did, too.

When the players were safe and sound in their hotel rooms, the coaches would knock on each door for bed check, make sure everyone was where they were supposed to be, and talk to them a bit, see how they're doing, get an update. As often as not, we didn't talk about football. That's one of those things I really miss about coaching. Then we'd have a cart full of warm chocolate chip cookies and mugs of hot chocolate come down the hallway, so everyone got a little bedtime snack, just like your mama gave you.

For some players, seeing my change in demeanor from Sunday films to Friday bed check gave them whiplash. When we were delivering the hot chocolate and cookies one night, one player I'd been riding all week looked at me sidelong, pointed to the hot chocolate in my hand, and said, "You try it first." Another wise guy asked me to pull off the mask to see who the guy really was who was being so nice.

That's fine. Friday night is a good time for a laugh, and I didn't need them to be scared of me then, because as you approach your moment of truth—and for us it was Saturday at 1 P.M.—you and your people have to lock arms to attack your common enemy, and your people have to feel that.

By Saturday—boy, we were something to see! I'm telling you, we were sharp as a drawerful of steak knives! During warm-ups, when both teams were on the field, I'd meet with my guys near our end zone, and tell them to get in formation, then walk down that line just like a general inspecting his troops. And then I'd point over their shoulders and say, "Look down there at those guys. Their jerseys aren't tucked in, their stretching is sloppy, they're wearing *white shoes,* for crying out loud—and they look like they've seen a ghost, gazing around this big stadium of yours. They're scared of you—because you're Michigan!"

I've always maintained people secretly want to be disciplined, even young people. They *want* strict limits, they want to be sharp, and they want to feel like they're special. Well, when I performed that little line inspection, that's just how they felt. They were *proud* to know they were more disciplined than our opponents were.

After warm-ups we'd return to our locker room for about twenty minutes while the band played. The players would adjust their equipment, retape their ankles, whatever needed tweaking, and we'd go over a few final points before sending them back out. Then we'd gather in our tunnel—surrounded by the biggest crowd anywhere in the country—and get ready to *explode* onto the field, jump up and touch that banner, and huddle together at the far end—with the crowd going crazy and the band blasting "The Victors."

Not too many guys have been lucky enough to do all that, but you ask them what it's like, and they'll just shake their heads. "I couldn't explain it to you," they say—and they're right. But trust me: It got us pumped up like nothing else!

And let me tell you, brother, by the time we were flying onto the field, we had a swagger, even a little cockiness. We'd been through another hellacious week, and we were ready! Hell, *you're* not going to beat us! Not today! *Why did you think you might?*

It was funny: The exact same bunch of guys who couldn't do a damn thing right in the previous Sunday's film session was suddenly the greatest football team ever assembled.

It was amazing how much they'd improved in just six days.

23

Emphasize Execution, Not Innovation

In the spring of 2005, the University of Michigan conferred upon yours truly an honorary doctorate—in law! Can you imagine—a football coach?

It was quite an honor, but I'm pretty sure our president, Mary Sue Coleman, wasn't giving me the doctorate for our razzle-dazzle trick plays.

That's all right. I've always believed eye-popping innovation is not as important as perfect execution. And perfection's a lot harder to achieve.

Look at our technology. Americans invented the TV, the VCR, the CD player, the computer and the cell phone—all these great things—but it's almost impossible to find an American company that makes those things here in the U.S. anymore, even TVs!

Even when you come up with some great new idea, it'll be copied so fast, you can't believe it. And then it comes down to execution, which is why mastering basic fundamentals applies to any field you're in, whether it's manufacturing, medicine or retail.

I've often fantasized about managing a baseball team for one season. I tell you my guys would run out every ground ball, and I'd never have some guy standing there in the batter's box watching a fly ball. When one of our players hit a home run, by the time the ball went over the fence, he'd be on his way to third base!

Everyone says, Oh, you can't do that nowadays. That's bull! Once they know you're not going to let them do it any other way, they'll drop their bats and run to first. Trust me.

If you trained your people correctly, when it comes time for your game day, all you need to do is stick to your guns and make sure everyone's doing everything you taught them to do, the way you taught them to do it. You'll be very hard to beat.

In football, I'd much rather face an explosive but sloppy team than a hard-core, simple squad that does all the little things right. And no one did that better than Wayne Woodrow Hayes. That, to me, was what made our games against Woody so great. They say it was dull, unimaginative football. Fine. But if you get out an old film from one of those ten games—doesn't matter which—you will see two teams that set up so perfectly at the line of scrimmage, with flawless stances and airtight tackling—there were *zero* missed tackles on either side, all day—that it looks like a completely different kind of football from what you see today. And you'll understand the magnificence of that rivalry.

The modern wide-open style is all well and good, but what happened to that kind of tackling? You don't see that anymore. It's gone. But in the Ten Year War, when the guys from either team tackled you—man, they *tackled* you! You were going to feel it, because both teams had been trained to do it right, every time.

I'd love to coach another one of those games. God, they were beautiful! I do *not* believe that brand of football is old-fashioned. To me, it's just *real* football.

Believe it or not, I don't have anything against passing the ball or even calling the occasional reverse or flea-flicker. But there's no point working on the fancy stuff until you've got the fundamentals down first.

We were playing the Buckeyes at Ohio State in 1976. Now at that time, we hadn't beaten them in five years, and we'd never beaten them in Columbus since I'd taken over at Michigan. THAT is pressure. After a scoreless first half, we go up, 13–0, on our second touchdown. Instead of kicking the extra point, though, we call for our fake kick play, which sends our holder, Jerry Zuver, around the right side, where he's looking at a wide-open lane straight to the end zone. It works! Our guys on the sideline go crazy! What a backbreaker for the Buckeyes!

After that, there's no looking back, and we win, 22–0—the first time the Buckeyes were shut out in 122 games. That was something to savor.

But if you think we just called that fake kick out of the blue, you've got another think coming. We'd worked on that play every day in practice all week. And we worked on all those blocking and tackling drills, every day, every week, *all season,* to put us in position to use that trick play. Because, brother, there's no point worrying about faking the extra point until you can get the ball in the end zone. Execution before innovation.

*   *   *

When I go out for a meal, I like to ask the waiter or waitress a few questions. Where are you from? Where are you going to school? And if I like them, they're going to get a good tip. But if they see me as a nuisance, they're going to get the standard rate, nothing more. That tip I leave has *nothing* to do with the food and *everything* to do with the waiter. That's basic execution.

At least once a week I walk to a drugstore a block from my home here in Ann Arbor. They have this fancy computer system that allows them to look up your prescription in a second, so long as you can remember your name. It's done through satellites, and it's pretty sharp.

But their aisles are sloppy, they always run out of the product I want, and almost no one ever says hello to me. They have no reason to be scared of me. Hey, I'm sure as heck not going to yell at a drugstore clerk! They usually don't know who I am anyway.

If I were the CEO of that chain, I'd make sure every store manager always did three things:

1. Walk up and down every aisle every day, to make sure all their products are presented properly. People pick something up and put it somewhere else, and you can't find the doggone thing. You just can't let that happen in your store.

2. Make sure you don't run out of a popular product. If everyone is buying Crest toothpaste and Dial soap, I'd make sure we always had plenty of Crest toothpaste and Dial soap—because that's what they're buying!

3. This is the REALLY important thing—teach everyone in that store how to say "Hello" and "Thank you"—and look me right in the eye when they say it. I don't think they take

enough time to teach those people common courtesy. It's the simplest thing to teach—and the most important, for my money.

Now look. I obviously don't know much about the drugstore business, but I know if they did those three things right every time, it'd be a much better store. It's blocking and tackling, all over again. And people would notice.

If you screw up those three simple tasks, don't worry about your fancy computers, because I'm never going to stick around long enough for you to use them!

Now I have to admit—since I'm being as honest as I can be here—there was a time when I doubted if fundamentals were still enough to produce top-notch football teams. I even wondered if the game had passed me by.

This crisis of confidence occurred after our infamous 1984 season, when we finished 6-6. In the off-season I went to one of these national coaching conferences with a few hundred other coaches, and they had some hotshot young high school coach from California explain his new whiz-bang system of defense.

He had zones two deep, three deep, man-to-man, and combinations of the two. That really caught my eye. I'm thinking, Maybe you've got to do all those things to win these days. Maybe our approach at Michigan is just too simple to succeed in the modern era. Boy, that was an awful feeling.

But after this guy finishes his slide show, someone in the audience raises his hand and asks, "If your defensive schemes are so great, then why did your team give up 400 yards a game last season?"

Well, I wanted to hear this! The hotshot replied—and I will *never* forget this—"We were just a poor tackling team."

Well, hell! That tells you all you need to know! You throw out 50 percent of that fancy stuff, and spend fifteen more minutes every day practicing the most basic thing in football: TACKLING. That's all!

After another coach asked the same whippersnapper why one of his plays failed in a big game, he said, "That play would've worked if the damn guard had pulled." Then don't *run* that play unless the guard is so *indoctrinated* that he will pull every time—and do it in his sleep. That's called *coaching*!

I walked out of that auditorium, and I knew what we were going to do: Get back to basics! Get back to Michigan football! And I was determined that we were going to do it better than anyone else.

Blocking and tackling! Blocking and tackling! Blocking and tackling! Every business has its blocking and tackling, and if you can't do those basics well then nothing else matters.

Want the whole thing in a nutshell? Just talk to Bubba Paris.

It's midseason, 1981, we're ranked sixth in the nation, and we're playing an unranked Michigan State squad. We're ahead maybe 14–0, and we drive down the field again—bang, bang, bang—until we're looking at first-and-goal on their three-yard line.

We get in the huddle and call our play—but Smiley Creswell, State's defensive tackle, thinks he's got our signals figured out, so he starts yelling to his teammates: "Off-tackle right! Off-tackle right!"

Now, on this 1981 team we have a front line of Ed Muransky, Kurt Becker, George Lilja and Bubba Paris—every one of them an All-American. This is not a line you want to be messing with. Bubba hears all this commotion coming from the Spartans, but he just saunters up to the line, as only Bubba could do—he was 6-5, 310—and calmly gets down in his stance. Then he looks across the line at Smiley Creswell and says, "That's right. It's an off-tackle play. It's coming right over you. *And there's not a thing you can do about it.*"

Three seconds later Bubba flattens Creswell. Our tailback just *walks* through the hole Bubba made, and he's in the Spartan end zone, untouched, handing the ball to the referee, Michigan-style. Touchdown!

We didn't fool 'em. We just beat 'em!

Now *that* is execution! *That* is confidence! THAT IS MICHIGAN FOOTBALL.

24

Scrap Your Script

The worst grade I received as a student at Miami of Ohio was a D-minus . . . in public speaking. When I tell people that, they can hardly believe it. That's what I'm doing for a living these days!

But looking back on it, I can tell you exactly why I got such an awful mark. The professor had us write down all our speeches beforehand, and talk about things we didn't care about, to people we hardly knew.

So my advice about giving a good speech is simple: Do just the opposite!

If you want to give a great speech, talk about something you're passionate about. Know your audience, or else you won't know what motivates them. And if you have a script, scrap it. Far better to speak from your heart than from your notes.

As you've seen, we followed a pretty strict routine every season, and every week. But believe it or not, I delivered the big speech, the most important one, not in the locker room right before kickoff on Saturday, but in our football building right after practice on Thursday. That's when the players were most receptive, and that's when we still had time to influence their thinking about the game ahead. It gave them two nights to sleep on it.

The guys would come in after Thursday practice, get showered and changed and return to our main meeting room. They'd sit down in their chairs—hats off, no gum or chew, feet flat on the floor and leaning forward, just like always—and I'd frame the game for them, tell them what we were focusing on this week, and why this *particular* game was important for us.

It was never a prepared speech. My objective was to see how close I could get to the pulse of the team—where their hearts and minds were at that moment—and then bump their heart rate up a bit. I'd think of maybe two or three points I wanted to make, but I never gave a canned speech, because I knew it wasn't going to be worth a damn. By speaking off-the-cuff, I could go in any direction I felt like at that moment, and get *myself* pumped up. It was contagious. If you're not excited by what you're saying, don't expect your audience to be.

To be honest, I'm not sure how my speeches would look in print, because I don't think I said anything that would mean all that much to someone outside our program. And maybe that's the point: Everything I said was for a very specific audience of 125 men, men I knew well, men I'd been working alongside for months, even years. And it wasn't really *what* I said that packed the punch, but *how* I said it—with pure, white-hot intensity! I started out slowly, softly—but when I finished, I was JACKED, man—and that came through loud and clear!

If we were playing Northwestern, I might start by saying our mission for that game is to ignore the scoreboard and work on our blocking, for example, to become the best-blocking team in the Big Ten. Frame it that way, and we're not playing against the Wildcats, but against the very high standards of Michigan football. "If you play for Michigan," I might say, "the goal is not merely victory—but perfection! And in thirty-six hours we will be on a mission to achieve that."

If we were playing Ohio State in Columbus in 1976, for example, I might start by pointing out that none of my teams had beaten them since 1971, and never in Columbus. Demoralizing? No. If you have an elephant in the room, call it out—and turn it into a motivator. "Gentlemen, I've been lucky enough to coach some great teams here. Four Big Ten champions. And some fantastic players. Thom Darden. Dan Dierdorf. Dennis Franklin. But as great as they all were, none of them, not one, ever beat the Buckeyes in Columbus. Someone will do it, of course. But why not you? Why not NOW? CAN YOU GIVE ME ONE GOOD REASON WHY WE WILL NOT BEAT THE BUCKEYES IN COLUMBUS ON SATURDAY? ONE! ONE GOOD REASON! Because if you believe it, we will do it. IF YOU BELIEVE IT, I PROMISE YOU: WE WILL DO IT!"

If I hit the right notes in the right way on Thursday night they'd be thinking of the upcoming game the way I was thinking about it for the next two days, right up to kickoff. It framed everything else we were doing—the technical stuff, the motivational stuff—and we'd build it up each day until game time.

I'd advance the argument a bit more after our Friday night movie. During bed check, I'd put a bug or two in a few ears to make sure we got their best performance the next day. Before the 1986 Ohio State game, for example, I chatted with our great receivers Greg McMurtry and John Kolesar. "Hey, we're going to need some great plays out of you guys tomorrow, so you need to visualize." I never had to tell those guys much.

I was a little more direct with our quarterback, Jim Harbaugh. Just a week earlier, minutes after Minnesota had ruined our perfect season by beating us—at home, on senior day—Jim had *guaranteed* a victory over Ohio State the next week. "Hey, buddy," I told him, poking him in the chest. "You better be ready to back that up!" Harbaugh ate it up. We won, 27–17, thanks to a crucial pass from Harbaugh to Kolesar late in the game.

On Saturday morning, before leaving the hotel for the stadium, I would bring the entire team together in one big meeting room, and *that* is when I put the icing on the cake. I'd get a little intense. I'd underscore a few of the points I made Thursday night to bring all that back to them, to remind them why this was an important game for us, and to hammer home what we needed to do to accomplish our mission that day. Then we'd get on the bus and head to the Horseshoe.

In the locker room, we were all business. I would talk to them again, right before we went out for the opening kickoff, about whatever had come to mind when I was riding on the bus to the stadium. But all I'm doing then is lighting the fuse on that big bomb we'd been building all week—and in the case of Ohio State, all season.

It was particularly important to get the players in the right mind-set when we were playing the Buckeyes in Columbus. When you're out of your natural environment, when you're working in a place you're not used to, and all of the enthusiasm and electricity you get playing in front of your fans is now on their side—no matter how you add it up, there is a certain amount of intimidation you have to overcome when you take the field at Ohio State. Say what you want, but when the crowd gets on you like those crowds do, you have to be ready for it. Again, everyone knows it's there—so say it! And make it positive.

So my final locker room speech in 1976 went something like this. "You are now *inside* the Horseshoe—the toughest place to play in college football, or anywhere else in the world, for that matter. Man, it's loud! It's hostile! AND THEY DO NOT LIKE US!

"You felt it the second you got on the bus this morning. Buckeye fans pounding their fists on our bus, giving us the finger, screaming the worst possible things at us. Then we got escorted by the cops to our locker room, and even now, you can hear the fans shouting and stomping their feet above you. Good!

"This ain't the Big House, boys! We're not at home anymore! Well, hell—I love it! THIS is why you came to Michigan!"

Then I stood up on a box, and gazed out on my players. The freshmen looked terrified, but the seniors looked determined. This was their last chance. And I told them:

"Gentlemen, imagine this: Sixty guys—just sixty guys!—enter the loudest stadium in the entire nation, filled with 87,000 screaming fans who hate us—but we take it over. The whole place. Just sixty guys. Because *not one* of those crazy fans yelling in the stands can touch the ball. *Not one* of them can make a single block, *not one* of them can make a single tackle! Only we can. That's us!

"And that is why you are about to hear the best sound in the world: Ohio Stadium, filled to the brim—and dead silent. Dead silent. That's exactly what we're going to do: Make 'em all shut up!

"YOU OWE IT TO EVERY MAN, WOMAN AND CHILD IN THE STATE OF MICHIGAN TO BEAT THE BUCKEYES AND SILENCE THEIR FANS!

"NOW GO OUT THERE AND MAKE IT HAPPEN!"

They did, 22–0, in one of the most rewarding games of my life. THAT was fun!

25

Make Adjustments on Facts, Not Pride

They say the first casualty of war is the war plan, and I'd have to agree with that.

I knew more about Woody Hayes than any coach I ever went against, hands down. I played for him, I coached for him, I studied him. I knew that guy cold! And every time we played each other, he still did something I didn't expect—ten straight years! Hot damn! *I didn't know he was going to do that!*

So that goes to show you, as much time as we spent scouting and preparing and planning—and I don't think any team in America prepared better for anyone than we did for Ohio State—the game never went exactly as we thought it would. It just never does.

That's all right. If things aren't going your way, you adjust. Forget your game plan, forget your ego. Get the best information you can, and give your team the best chance to succeed *from that point forward.* To do anything less is to let your people down when they need you most. And that's just inexcusable.

The best time to do this, if you're a football coach, is halftime. When you leave your locker room for the second half, you're not going to be the same team. You're either going to be better informed, or you're going to fall behind because the guys in the other locker room are making better adjustments than you are.

We almost never spent that time on inspirational talks, but on technical adjustments. To make the most of that time, we followed a strict routine. As soon as we got into the locker room, I'd bring all the coaches together and get everything I could out of them, then put it all together to revise the game plan for the second half. I'd then pass on a few points for the players to focus on, finish with a quick pump-up, then send them out to play the second half.

And I have to say, our teams almost *always* played better in the second half than they did in the first. Because we weren't afraid to adjust. Sometimes we weren't as talented as the other team, but we were always in better shape, so we knew if we could just stick around long enough, sooner or later we would get a chance to take the game over and run with it.

Some coaches—and some leaders—are reluctant to change their game plan because they're afraid they're going to look stupid. Or they're afraid they're going to look weak by listening to their subordinates, who might have better ideas. That, to me, is just ridiculous. Heck, that's just a weak leader.

Of *course* things on the ground are going to look different than they looked in your war room. They *always* do. And if you don't want to hear your assistants' opinions, then why in the world did you hire them in the first place?

I never felt the slightest bit embarrassed about changing

course at halftime, or taking an assistant's idea over mine. If you're in command, you can do anything—anything!—except be wishy-washy when it's time to admit that someone's idea is better than yours. And you will lose because of it.

If you listen and you adjust and it works, then you have nothing to apologize for. You won! And if you don't do those things and you lose, it's your fault for not listening to the guy who had a better idea. Your assistants will know it, and they'll resent it. You will not only lose the game, you'll lose your lieutenants.

This may seem pretty basic—heck, I think just about every idea in this book is pretty basic!—but how many wars have been lost because the commander didn't listen to his lieutenants or was too stubborn to change his strategy? How many great companies have gone bankrupt because the CEO didn't adapt to a changing economy, and the people below him were too scared to tell him the ship was sinking?

Look at the *Titanic*. I've read a fair amount about this—I love history—and when you take a closer look at the events of that day, you'll see the captain was so paralyzed with his boat going down, he failed to do the things he *could* have done to save hundreds of lives. The seas were calm that night, help was on the way, and they had plenty of things on board they could have thrown in the water to keep people out of the freezing ocean for a few hours. Instead, the captain left the entire rescue mission to his underlings, who let the lifeboats go out with half their seats empty. That's just a lack of leadership.

It's the simplest stuff that often seems to be the hardest for leaders to do. Swallow your pride and adapt to the reality in front of you!

*   *   *

Probably the best halftime adjustment we ever made when I was Michigan's head coach took place during the 1986 Fiesta Bowl against Nebraska. After stumbling through that infamous 6-6 season in 1984, we were 9-1-1 in 1985, ranked fifth in the country, with the best scoring defense in the nation. And we had something to prove.

Well, the only thing we proved in the first half is that we didn't belong on the same field with Nebraska. They just kicked our butts up and down that field. In my twenty-one years at Michigan, no one had ever taken us apart in a half of football like Nebraska did that day. No one. And believe me, at halftime, there was uncertainty running throughout our locker room because we had been so completely dominated. The only silver lining was, despite getting beaten so badly in every phase of the game, we were behind only 14–3.

Now, I know I just got through saying that halftime is a time for engaging in cool-headed analysis based on the facts at hand, and calmly charting a new course for the second half. And it usually is.

But there are times when there are no tactics to discuss, because tactics aren't the problem. For me to go up to the chalkboard and start making some fine-tuned adjustments—hell, I'd just be whistling Dixie. This wasn't a technical problem. This was just an old-fashioned butt-kicking!

You've got to remember, too, that at this time, I'm 2-10 in bowl games, and I'm frankly getting pretty sick of it.

I never threw chairs during halftime—but I threw one that day. I was just that ticked off. Then I told them: "You're in this hole because you did not play with the toughness that you've played with all year long. Keep this up, and it's going to get ugly out there. Very ugly. We will go home not just defeated, but embarrassed.

"But you are a much better football team than what I saw out there. If you remember *who* you are and *how* you played all year and why you *deserve* to be here in the first place—and get back to MICHIGAN FOOTBALL—then we'll get right back in this game. NOW!"

Let me tell you: I have never seen a Michigan team play a more inspired half. On just the third play, our defense forces their tailback, Doug DuBose, to fumble the ball, and we scoop it up. We smell blood! We take it right down and score, 14–10.

On the very next possession, our defense—still on the attack—forces *another* Nebraska fumble, and Mark Messner grabs it. We take *that* one down and Jim Harbaugh plunges it into the end zone: 17–14, Michigan!

Our defense has got its swagger back now, and they shut down the Huskers' offense on their next possession, forcing them to punt. Well, Dave Arnold charges in toward their kicker *untouched* and he blocks his third punt of the year. We turn that one into a short field goal to go up, 20-14.

A few minutes later Jamie Morris takes off on a 14-yard scamper, setting up another Harbaugh touchdown. We've just scored *24 unanswered points in one quarter.* Folks, THAT is a COMEBACK!

We gained 171 yards rushing that day, almost all of it in the second half, and Jamie Morris got 156 yards of it. The little guy was *possessed.*

And our defense—hell, by the fourth quarter our guys were *breathing fire*! They shut Nebraska down one more time on their last possession, and we win the thing, 27–23. You can imagine how good that locker room felt. We'd just won our third bowl game in six years, we were now 10-1-1, and we were about to finish second in the nation.

I didn't recognize the team I saw that first half, but the team I saw in the second half was the team I saw all year—tough, smart, disciplined.

And what did it take? A halftime wake-up call. Without that, we would've gotten buried, and ruined a great season. With a little attitude adjustment, we got back to playing Michigan football, and that's all we ever had to do.

Keep doing the same things, and you're going to get the same results. If you want different results, you better do something different.

Listening to your coaches and changing your game plan isn't a sign of weakness. Sticking to a *failing* game plan is a sign of weakness! All it requires is the confidence to change course.

26

Turn Mistakes into Momentum

The first twelve pages of that blue Michigan Wolverine football binder we handed out to everyone at our first meeting covered all of our basic values and policies. Right after those twelve pages, we devoted the next three pages to something we called Sudden Change, one of the most important concepts of our organization—and maybe yours, too.

Sudden Change was our term for how we respond to unexpected problems. Do you collapse, like most teams do? Or do you rise to the occasion, and turn the tide?

Almost any organization can keep rolling when things are going well. But mastering Sudden Change is the real test of a great team: the ability to transform a sudden setback into your finest hour.

Obviously, every person and every organization is going to face unforeseen troubles. Could be anything from a crashed computer to a broken copier to a sudden drop in your stock price.

I don't care what it is, you're going to have to handle it. Your people are going to have to know what to do, how to fix the problem *fast,* and how to turn things around on a dime. If your organization can do this on a consistent basis, there isn't much else out there that can stop you from achieving your goals.

For Michigan football, Sudden Change refers to our ability to respond after our offense coughs up a fumble or an interception, and gives our opponent a great opportunity to take advantage of the situation and grab the momentum. Now, this isn't going to happen often—it better not, if we're going to be any good—but no matter how sharp an outfit you have, these things are going to happen sometimes. And when they do, we're going to *seize the opportunity* and make something good out of it. We're going to run right back out there and *shut them down,* and steal the momentum right back.

During that first meeting, this is how my Sudden Change speech went, word for word:

"It's a sunny, hot and humid day in early September 1984, and you are playing the number-one-ranked college football team in the country, Miami of Florida. On offense alone, they have three All-Americans—Willie Smith, Eddie Brown and Lester Williams—not to mention Alonzo Highsmith, Stanley Shakespeare and their great quarterback, Bernie Kosar. They are absolutely loaded. You will probably not face a more explosive offense your entire career.

"You are on defense, battling against those guys all day. Miami is not able to score a single point against you and your teammates the entire first half. In the second half, we take the lead, 6–0.

"In the third quarter, Miami pulls ahead, 7–6, on a time-consuming, 65-yard drive. You are sweating, you are tired, you are spent, but at least you know you are now assured of a few minutes to get some water and a breather, while our offense takes the field.

"But on the very next series our quarterback throws an interception and Miami gets the ball back on our 45-yard line. Everyone in the stadium thinks Michigan has just blown it, that the top-ranked Hurricanes are bound to take over now. Everyone, that is, *but you and your teammates on defense*! This is what we call SUDDEN CHANGE. Against the highest-scoring team in America your defense stops them on three straight plays and forces them to punt. WE ARE SUCCESSFUL!

"After you stopped them in a Sudden Change situation, we took the momentum back and the lead, too, 12–7. You have stopped the vaunted Miami offense again and again that day, including four interceptions off the great Bernie Kosar, and you justly believe you've done your part to secure a huge victory for your team and your school.

"But in the fourth quarter, with 10 minutes left in the game, our offense turns the ball over *again*. Once more, just when you thought you were going to get some relief, you're forced to cut your break short, drop your water, grab your headgear and get out there to stop the most powerful offense in the nation—or fail, and watch your entire effort go down the drain. Miami is talented, you're dog-tired, but you do not complain. You do not point fingers. *You go out and do your job.*

"Miami is driving into Michigan territory for the winning touchdown. But just when it looks like the Hurricanes are going to take the lead for good, you and your defense come up with *another* big play to stop Miami by intercepting Kosar for the *fifth time that day*. Once again, you and your defense have converted a Sudden Change situation into a momentum builder for your offense, which then goes down the field for the final touch-down. Thanks to you, Michigan has just beaten the top-ranked team in the country!

"It is more than a great victory. It is a *textbook demonstration* of how a great team masters Sudden Change.

"Now, what happened out there?

"In a Sudden Change situation, your *opponents* are thinking:

"'What a great break.

"'Our defense did a great job to get the ball back.

"'We have them on the ropes now.

"'Their defense will be tired.

"'Let's hit them quick!'

"That's bad enough. Making it far worse, most teams that *suffer* a Sudden Change are thinking:

"'What a lousy break.

"'Our offense sure put us in a big hole. How could they do that to us?

"'It just isn't fair.

"'I'm tired. I don't know whether I can hold out again.

"'Boy, I hope *someone* out here comes up with a big play to save us.'

"I think you can see why it takes a great defense to overcome a sudden change situation. It's not just a matter of *playing* great defense, it's a matter of *changing your attitude completely, at that instant,* with no warning! Your opponents will be mentally up, and unless you prepare yourself, you will not be!

"So this is what you must do:

"Always huddle up with your coach before you go back into the game.

"Gain control of your thoughts and get yourself ready to play defense again.

"Realize that you must get yourself *and your teammates* up mentally—and immediately!

"Go all-out to make the big play YOURSELF! Don't wait for anyone else to do it for you.

"RECOGNIZE THAT THIS MOMENT IS THE TEST OF YOUR DEFENSE, YOUR ABILITY, AND YOUR CHARACTER. *ACCEPT THE CHALLENGE!*

"Remember: When you stop your opponents after giving them a break like that, your team will have an *even greater* psychological advantage over them than you had *before* the turnover.

"WHEN YOU DO THESE THINGS, THE SUDDEN CHANGE IS *OURS*!"

It worked! And I have the proof. Every game of every season I coached, we kept track of how many times we turned the ball over, and how many times our opponents scored on us because of it. In other words, how many Sudden Change opportunities we faced each season, and how often we came through and stopped them.

Our success rate was 63 percent—and that is pretty damn impressive. That means *two-thirds of the time* we gave our opponents a break, we took it right back, and came out of it with more confidence and momentum than they did. If you can handle Sudden Change that well, that often—well, I've got news for you: You're going to be a helluva tough team to beat!

When we turned the ball over, we didn't see it as a setback, but as an *opportunity* for us to BREAK THEIR BACKS. Sudden Change became a *rallying cry* for us. Instead of moping and complaining after our offense turned it over, we started yelling, "Sudden Change! Sudden Change!" all up and down the sidelines. Guys got into it. They got more excited about our turn-overs than the other team did!

Nothing will break an opponent's spirit better than that.

And more importantly, nothing will boost your team's confidence like turning a crushing blow into a triumph. Nothing!

27

Stay Focused Under Fire

You could say our coaching staff was *determined* to cover every possible contingency before kickoff. But that does NOT mean we quit coaching after the ball was in the air. No way!

I've heard some coaches—and executives and politicians, too, for that matter—say, "After I've prepared my people, all I've gotta do is wind 'em up and let 'em go. Then it's up to them."

Well, to me, that's just ridiculous. If you're responsible, you've got to be involved, every step of the way.

I remember one time we were scouting a high school player here in Michigan, but I couldn't take my eyes off his head coach. The guy was just standing there on the sidelines, his arms folded, with no clipboard, no headset. Nothing! And he'd always stand twenty yards away from everyone else. If their opponents had the ball down by his 10-yard line—which seemed to happen a lot—he'd be standing out by the 50. His poor assistants—and why they worked for this guy is a mystery to me—had to keep running back and forth to him just to let him know what they were doing.

I couldn't believe it! Honestly, what the hell is that? Why are they paying that guy? Why does he even show up for the games? Needless to say, his team was awful—undisciplined, unfocused, uninspired. But what would you expect, with no leader?

The guy who says, "Once the hay is in the barn, there's nothing you can do"—well, that's a guy who's going to make no contribution to his team when the pressure is at its greatest and they need you the most.

Don't believe anyone who says you can't coach during games. You have to! If you don't lead them, who's going to? They *want* you to coach them.

Crunch time is not only what you're paid for, it's also one of your best opportunities to teach your people, because they're alert. They may have a hard time paying attention when you're making them sit through films or push tackling sleds around all week, but they don't seem to have any difficulty at all when they're finally playing against the team they've been hearing about since Monday, and the crowd is roaring. When they're under pressure, that's when they learn best.

Their eyes and ears are wide open, so take advantage of it. Everything you were trying to hammer home during training you can reinforce now, and it'll sink in. I think our guys sometimes improved more during a single game than they did in a week of practice.

When your employees are finally facing the customers, or actually working the machines, or traveling to meetings around the country, that's when they realize what you were talking about all that time. That's when you hit 'em again to make it all stick. Just a few words to your people when they're under pressure will go a long way.

It's also important to set an example. My players need to see that I'm into the game, that I'm paying attention to every little thing out there and that I clearly believe every play matters. And trust me, they're watching you, all the time—even when you're oblivious to it.

They say the only decisions a football coach has to make are when to go for it on fourth down and when to punt. I guarantee you this: Whoever said that never coached football—or wasn't any good at it. I made a decision on every single play. You've got to coach up a storm from the second toe meets leather until the whistle blows.

And when you're facing a big decision and you don't have much time to make it, you've got to pull the trigger. *Not* making a decision is the *worst* thing you can do. So long as you feel you made the right decision based on the information you had *at that time,* there's no need to fret about it. If it fails, you'll know what to do next time.

In 1971, my third season at Michigan, we'd gone 11-0 before getting upset by Stanford in the Rose Bowl on a last-gasp field goal, 13–12. The next season, we were hell-bent to make that right. After 10 games, we were undefeated, ranked third in the nation, with an offense that featured quarterback Denny Franklin and a great running attack, and a defense that allowed fewer than five points a game. That squad was as good as any team I coached.

The Buckeyes came into our 1972 grudge match ranked ninth, because they'd lost to Michigan State. As the favorites, we came into the game knowing we had a clean shot at everything we had dreamed of the year before: the Big Ten title, another trip to the Rose Bowl, and a national title.

It's November 25, 1972, when Michigan and Ohio State teed it up again down in Columbus in front of 87,000 insane Buckeye fans.

Late in the second quarter we were behind, 7–3, with 4:30 left in the half. We took the ball over on our 20-yard line and marched it all the way down to the Buckeye one-yard line, with four downs to score. We had no doubt we were going to do it.

On first down, we sent our tailback Chuck Heater up the middle. One-yard loss. We tried it again, and Heater got the yard back, but now it's third-and-goal from the one. So we gave the ball to our big fullback, Bob Thornbladh, who launched himself into the Buckeye line—and landed just a foot, *maybe,* from the goal line.

Now we were looking at fourth-and-goal. We called a timeout to think about this one a little more, but honestly, it didn't take that much deliberating. For cryin' out loud, we were moving the ball like the Cowboys on those guys—we'd just covered 79 yards in a few minutes—and we only needed *a foot* to take a 10–7 lead into halftime. I didn't see the point in going 79 yards to settle for a lousy field goal.

We sent the play in to Denny—but on the snap, the ball bounced out of his hands, and he had to recover the ball on the ground. Play over, drive over, first half over: 7–3, Buckeyes, at the half.

In the locker room, we were a bit frustrated, sure, but we were still confident. Hell, all the statistics were on our side—except the score. We just figured it was a matter of time before we wore down Woody's boys.

Well, damn it all if the Buckeyes didn't score on the first possession of the second half, so now we were down, 14–3, which is not where you want to be against Woody. The man knew how to hold a lead! We knew we needed to get some points on the board, and fast, or else we'd never get back in the game.

We got the ball back and drove it right down to the Buckeye five-yard line, setting up another first-and-goal. Three plays later it's fourth-and-goal on the one-yard line—again! This time, it was an even easier decision, because we were so far behind. Denny handed off to Big Ed Shuttlesworth, who pounded his way into the Ohio State end zone. Ohio State 14, Michigan 11—and we've got the momentum.

A bit later we had *another* fourth-and-one decision, this time on the Buckeye 20-yard line. Again we decided to go for it. And again we got stuffed! That made three times we'd gotten into the red zone, with only one touchdown to show for it. That'll drive you insane.

But we weren't done. Randy Logan, our All-American defensive back, made a clutch interception at the Buckeye 29-yard line, and we figured this is our chance to take the game over. Man, it's just gotta happen, right?

A few plays later we've got first-and-goal—again—from the Ohio State four-yard line. After a couple runs that didn't go anywhere, we had third-and-goal from the one, when Franklin handed off to Harry Banks, who plunged off-tackle. Sure as I'm sitting here, that guy got into the end zone. But the ref doesn't signal it. What the hell's going on? What the hell are they waiting for? No touchdown? Rotten call!

Incredibly, unbelievably, amazingly, that left us with fourth-and-goal from the one—*again*! We were still behind, 14–11, and we were well into the fourth quarter by this point. A field goal would have tied the game, which might have knocked us out of the national title picture, but it would have secured the Big Ten title and sent us to Pasadena.

Well, my philosophy had not changed. If you can run the ball all day on their defense and get the ball to their one-yard line, and you can't knock it in from there, you don't deserve to win. This might surprise you, given my reputation for conservative play calling, but I was tired of getting stopped when we had such a great offense, and I was afraid that turning the ball over again would give them too much momentum. Besides, *we* were the undefeated team, not them!

We went for it. Franklin dove in on a quarterback sneak—but that son of a gun Randy Gradishar got in there somehow and stopped Denny cold.

We never threatened again, and Ohio State won, 14-11. Another painful loss to Woody. God I hated that!

Every leader must face big decisions loaded with great consequences. My good friend Jerry Ford (You may have heard of him: He was not only a Michigan Wolverine All-American but also the thirty-eighth president of the United States of America.) once told me that the hard thing about being president was that all the easy decisions, all the small problems, were always handled by someone below you. Only the tough ones made it to the top. Well, that's what you're paid for.

In that Ohio State game, we had six—six!—fourth-down decisions, three of them fourth-and-goal. Heck, you usually don't get that many in a whole month, sometimes not in a whole season. For different reasons, we went for it every time. We scored a touchdown, got a first down, threw an incomplete pass and got stuffed three times. Two for six—not too good, by our standards.

But, from a leader's perspective, it's not the results you have to focus on when you evaluate those decisions. By my book—

and that's ultimately the only one that mattered to me—five of those six calls were good decisions, and only one—when it was fourth-and-10 on their 37—would I do differently.

Do I think about that game? Hell yes! Of course I do. And I wish to God we'd been able to get Franklin or Banks in the end zone—or the ref had made the right call. But I can honestly say I had no regrets about those decisions then, and I have no regrets about those decisions to this day.

Only one of our six fourth-down plays worked, but five of them were the right calls. I made those decisions based on the best information we had at that time, so I can live with that. And that's why I didn't hesitate to make big decisions the next year, either.

VI

Face the Facts

and Ignore the Rest

28

Rebuild with the Basics

If you lead long enough, sooner or later you're going to suffer through a disappointing year.

When that happens, get down to the core problem immediately—and fix that, and *only* that! Too often I see leaders panic, and throw away all the things that got them there in the first place. The *worst* thing you can do is abandon all the things you were already doing right, and make everything else a lot worse.

No, you need a surgical strike. And usually, that's simply a matter of figuring out what's gotten out of whack, then getting that aspect of your organization back in line with the same fundamental values you built it on years ago.

I had two tough seasons that stand out—1979 and 1984—but for completely different reasons. Nineteen seventy-nine wasn't the worst season of my coaching career—1984 earns that dubious distinction—but it was probably the most *trying.*

We started out the year ranked seventh in the country, but

we lost our second game to Notre Dame, 12–10, on four field goals. Then we got on a roll, winning our next seven games before losing three in a row, to Purdue, 24–21, Ohio State, 18–15, and North Carolina, 17–15, in the Gator Bowl. Four losses by a total of 10 points—pretty heartbreaking.

We finished the season 8-4, third in the Big Ten and 18th in the country—all the lowest marks since my staff and I had arrived in Ann Arbor eleven years earlier.

That was bad enough—but it wasn't the worst part of it for me. After the season ended it came to my attention—as it always did when something was wrong—that some of the guys on the team were smoking pot, and one or two of them might have been dealing it.

The guy at the center of the whole thing was a highly successful athlete—he started in the defensive backfield for us—a nice kid and a handsome guy. This is someone who had everything going for him. But when I found out about his role in all this, I went *after* him! And you know what happened? Once he knew I was on the warpath, he disappeared, just vanished from the campus. When the police finally found him, they arrested him.

All right, one's gone. But I still had a problem on that team, and I didn't plan to wait around to see if it was going to solve itself. No point in that. Problems like that never do. If you discover a serious problem in your organization, I say it's time to take swift, decisive action, and move on.

As soon as we got back from the Gator Bowl, I called a team meeting in the old cinder block football building on State Street for one purpose, and one purpose only. I stood before them and said, "I'm going to tell you guys one thing: I'm straightening this squad out *right now*!"

Then I called one of the guys up front and said, "You're coming with me. The rest of you guys sit right here." I took him into a room off to the side, I told him what I'd heard, that I wasn't going to tolerate it, and that, as of that moment, he was no longer a member of the Michigan football program. GONE!

Then I went back out to the meeting room and called for the next guy to come up, and took him to the back room. Same thing. GONE!

The players sitting back in the meeting room figured out what was going on soon enough. I was the judge, jury and executioner, all in one, and they're sitting there wondering, "Who's next?"

Now, you have to understand: I did *not* like doing this. I was not on some power trip. I never got my thrills by kicking guys off the team. I *hated* doing it.

But we had a problem on that team, and I was going to fix it.

After I'd finished kicking five guys off the squad—and that was front-page news the next day—I told the remaining players that we were obviously not messing around. "I tell you guys in our first team meeting every August what our drug policy is—zero tolerance—and it certainly hadn't changed *during* the season, and it's not going to change *next* season, either. So if you don't like it, you should do everyone a favor and get off the team right now. You don't belong here."

We instituted random drug testing immediately. And I was probably even sweeter during spring ball that year than I usually was. Well fine. I'd had it.

I never called it a crisis, though, because I knew exactly what we had to do. It was just something that needed to be straightened out. And we did exactly that.

The next season, after a rocky 1-2 start, we rattled off nine straight wins for the Big Ten title and my first Rose Bowl victory. THAT was satisfying!

It all started when we were faced with a problem, and we

weren't afraid to fix it. As my old boss, Don Canham, used to say, "Never turn a one-day story into a two-day story."

Don't let it linger. Take your medicine, take action, and get the mess behind you.

If you're faced with an emergency, like we had in 1979, clearly my advice is to identify the cancer, cut it out immediately and get back to work.

On the other hand, if your team's on a losing streak, but you're still getting the effort, the attitude is good and you're doing things the right way, then stick to your guns, get back to basics, and things will turn around.

That's what we did after our 1984 season, when we finished 6-6—my only unranked team, and the Wolverines' worst season, to this day, since 1967. That's not a record you want to have. But I've got it, and it looks like I'll probably have it for a while yet.

But unlike the 1979 team, the '84 squad's problem wasn't a few bad apples. We just didn't have enough talent—and I think we could have done a much better job coaching! We took our fundamental values for granted, and we paid the price—all year long.

We started the 1984 season with a bang by beating number-one-ranked Miami of Florida, 22–14, at our place. The polls rewarded us by vaulting us from 14th to third in the country—which we promptly gave back the very next week by losing to Washington at home, 20–11. A couple weeks later we were 3-1, heading into the Michigan State game. Just when it looked like we were on our way to another good season, we fumbled the ball, and when our quarterback, Jim Harbaugh, dove for it, the Spartans hit him and he broke his arm.

With Harbaugh out for the season, we had a hard time beating anyone. We lost that game to Michigan State, 19-7, we took care of Northwestern, 31-0, but then we went to Iowa and suffered the most embarrassing loss of my career, 26-0. We just got killed. Just terrible. At this point we're 4-3, and you had to wonder if we were going to throw in the towel or not.

But the next week we came back and beat Illinois, the defending Big Ten champs, 26-18. Our guys really went after them! I'll be honest: I don't know how we did that. That was one of the greatest wins I've seen, because we didn't have a lot going for us. Those guys just played their absolute best, really gutted it out. After that debacle at Iowa, that Illinois game showed me everything I needed to know about those guys in terms of character.

The only thing I was really mad about, after Jim went down, was my inability to prepare the type of quarterback who could win games for us. That's not *their* fault—the kids we put in there did an admirable job—that's *my* fault. That's recruiting. That's preparation. As a coaching staff, we just didn't get the job done—and that starts with me!

So what do you do? For the rest of the 1984 season, we kept right on coaching our way, figuring maybe we could win the next game. We didn't suddenly try a lot of gimmicks to fool the opponent since it was difficult for us to go up against them man-to-man in the first place. I believed then—and I still do, today—that playing football our way got us some victories that we might not have gotten had we left our game plan and tried to get too fancy.

Although we lost five of our last seven games, the 1984 season wasn't nearly as hard for me as the 1979 season. And you know why? Because that was a 6-6 team. They were busting their butts just to get to 6-6! And you have to respect that.

You want proof? We got invited to the Holiday Bowl, and went up against undefeated, number-one-ranked Brigham Young. Our defense made one of the best offenses in the country turn the ball over six times. We were ahead, 17–10—in the fourth quarter—when Brigham Young drove twice for touchdowns, the last one coming with just 1:23 left in the game. They were crowned the national champions, but we were *unranked,* and almost beat 'em! Can you believe that?

I sure wasn't thrilled with our record, but you only start worrying if you see your people giving up when the going gets tough. But if you're getting the effort, you don't have any problems you can't fix. And that's the situation I faced.

But just in case you start thinking 1984 was just dandy with me, let me clarify: Six-and-six is NOT Michigan football, and I had no intentions of going through another season like that again. When I look at that season in the media guide—ahhhh! It kills me.

How bad was it? A few weeks after we returned from the Holiday Bowl, I was driving along I-94 toward Detroit on a nasty January night—all snow and slush and bitter cold—when my damn car breaks down. I get out to hitchhike, thinking someone's got to recognize me—I wasn't too far from Ann Arbor—but everyone's passing me by. Even three state troopers blow past me—and those guys tend to be pretty big football fans!

Finally, someone pulls over—and it's Jon Falk, our equipment manager. I jump in the passenger side, covered in ice, and I'm still so cold I can't stop my hands from shaking. "Where're you going, Falk?"

"Coach, I kind of have plans."

"Well, you've got new plans now! You're taking me back to Ann Arbor." On the way back, I tell him my story. "Falk, a hundred cars and *three state troopers* flew past me when I was standing on the side of the road. Can you believe that?"

"Well, Coach, we did finish 6-6 last year."

Now that's a man with too much job security.

I just shot him a look.

Our challenge the next season, as I saw it, was to get back to the principles that we used to win all those Big Ten titles. Nineteen sixty-nine all over again. I decided to start over from scratch.

The first thing I did was set up a coaches meeting. After everyone was sitting down at the table, I scanned my coaches' faces, and finally said, "You are all fired." I let that sink in for a bit. "And I'm fired, too! We are *all* fired, and every player on this team and every employee in this office is fired, too! From now on, *everyone* gets evaluated—EVERYBODY! You've all been put on notice that your jobs are up for grabs—including mine! Another season like that, and I could be gone anyway—and then we're *all* on our own. You want to keep your job, you have to prove that you can *do* your job. NO EXCEPTIONS!"

Well, that pretty much set the tone for *that* off-season!

First on the docket was yours truly. You already read about the hotshot speaker I heard during that off-season at the coaches conference—the guy from California with all the answers. That shook my confidence—then restored it, when I realized that, despite all his fancy schemes, he couldn't get the job done. I decided then and there that the game, at least, had *not* passed me by.

Had I lost the desire to coach? Based on the fact that I was willing to fire every single person working for Michigan football—including myself—I had to conclude that, no, I had not.

Had I gotten soft? I doubt anyone on that 1984 team would call me soft—but I had to concede that I had not sufficiently reinforced all those things that make a Michigan football team a Michigan football team. My fault!

I realized the solution was simple. Not *easy,* mind you, but simple. I decided that in 1985 we had to do what we'd always done before, just do it better. A LOT better!

We didn't adopt that California coach's defensive schemes or any other gimmicks. What we did instead was hit *every single day* in spring practice, the first time we'd done that since 1969. First day of spring ball, Falk marches into the locker room and yells, "Full pads! Full pads!" And he kept it up every day of spring ball.

"We were too soft last year!" I told them. "So I'm toughening you up! You see how it's going to be. If you can't hack it, get out *now*!" Unlike the '69 team, though, no one dropped out, because they knew how good we could be. They stayed.

We also had to rededicate ourselves to the importance of The Team, The Team, The Team! Now, we'd been preaching that since 1969. But they'd heard it so often, maybe they took it for granted. Maybe I did, too. But starting that spring, we hammered that home like it was a brand-new concept. I was determined to keep that ringing in their ears until they were waking up in the middle of the night repeating it to themselves!

To be honest, I think it took only three weeks of spring practice to get back to where we wanted to be. By the time we got to the blue-white scrimmage in Michigan Stadium—which marks the end of spring ball—I could already tell we had great senior leaders and a hungry group of players eager to redeem themselves. We were getting our edge back.

Right after spring ball I met with every player, just like I always did. But this time, I wasn't giving anybody anything. Jamie Morris had one hellacious spring—the little guy had been cutting through our first-team defense like a guided missile—and I knew damn well he wanted me to tell him, right then and there, that he was going to be our starting tailback as a sophomore the next season. Another year, I might have. But not in 1985. No sir! I was in no mood to promise anything to anybody. You want to start? Fine. Keep showing up and *earn it.* Don't like it? Well, let me ask you: Who was 6-6 last year? That's right: We were!

So all I told Jamie was, "You had a good spring. Keep in shape, and we'll see you in the fall." That's it. Maybe it ticked him off a little. Well, good! Because he came back three months later on a *mission*!

We had the players stay in town that summer, too. Everyone does that now, but that team was one of the first. We just had too much ground to make up. So we were going to stay out of trouble, work out as a team every day and come together.

Because, dammit, we're not going 6-6 again!

That off-season everybody was saying Michigan isn't Michigan anymore, Bo's lost it, and the 1985 Wolverines haven't got any talent. Well, we were going to see about all of that.

At the end of the summer I was already starting to think we might have something special, but you never know until toe meets leather—and our schedule that year was just brutal. In 12 games we were going to play *six ranked teams,* including our first three nonconference opponents. Holy smokes! NOT what you need when you're unranked and you've lost five of your last seven games. That schedule would have *crushed* a lesser team.

We opened against 13th-ranked Notre Dame—and we beat 'em, 20–12. It wasn't even that close, either. Next up we had South Carolina, Bobby Morrison's team. Those guys were good, ranked 11th, and they played in one of the toughest stadiums in the nation. Those men down in South Carolina, they know how to take the field. We were already on the field when I told my guys, "I want you to see this!"

The speakers boomed the theme song from *2001: A Space Odyssey,* which builds really slowly. Then they started pumping a thick fog by the players' tunnel, and the crowd started going nuts as the anticipation built.

Our guys were getting jacked up just waiting for them to come out. "C'MON! WHATYA—SCARED? *GET ON OUT HERE!*" Until finally the Gamecocks came flying out of that tunnel—dressed all in black! I'm not kidding, I lost my hearing for a few minutes from that music blaring and the crowd screaming. God, that was great. *That* is how you take the field. THAT is college football!

We started the game with the ball and sent Thomas Wilcher on our standard off-tackle play. Their linebacker came in from out of nowhere, and Wilcher's helmet flew off—and he was ready to go! I'm telling you, from the opening kickoff, the entire atmosphere in that stadium just was *electric.*

That set the tone—and then we just went out and flat out kicked their butts, 34–3. No matter how successful you are, you don't get too many like that. I loved that game!

We had no time to pat ourselves on the back, though, because we had Maryland next, another top 20 team, with Bobby Ross coaching and Boomer Esiason throwing.

Didn't matter. We whooped up on them, too, 20–0.

By the time we went to Iowa City to take on the Hawkeyes in the sixth week of the season, we were ranked second, and they were ranked first. We played our hearts out, but lost 12–10, on four field goals, the last one with just two seconds left on the clock. If you want to know why I hate field goals, there you have it!

Two weeks later, we went down to Illinois to play a team we just didn't like very much. That rivalry had turned pretty nasty for a few years there when Mike White was coaching the Illini. He even painted their locker room Maize and Blue! We didn't like them, and their fans just *hated* us. Wow!

They had been the Big Ten champs two years earlier, but now they weren't even ranked—and they tied us, 3–3. It felt like a loss to us—and a bitter one.

We were pissed! But I wasn't mad at my players. I felt horrible for them. So in the locker room afterward I stood up on a trunk to talk to them. "I love each and every one of you guys. And I will *promise* you this right now: NO SONUVABITCH IS GOING TO GET THE BETTER OF US AGAIN THE REST OF THE YEAR. EVER! *PUT THAT DOWN!* WE . . . WILL . . . NOT . . . LOSE . . . AN-OTHER GAME!"

I believed it!

They believed it!

And we didn't lose another game the rest of the year!

We just *blew* through the rest of our schedule, just like we did starting with that Minnesota game in 1969. After we beat Nebraska in the Fiesta Bowl with that great second half, we finished 10-1-1, second in the nation, the highest rank of any team I coached.

Here's the great part. When we were rededicating ourselves to our fundamental values during that long off-season, we had no—and I mean NO—preseason All-Big Ten or All-America candidates. Not one. A no-name defense? We had a no-name team! Only time that ever happened when I coached at Michigan.

But once the season started, we gave up only 12 points to Notre Dame, three to South Carolina, zero to Maryland, six to Wisconsin, and zero to Michigan State. Five games, and our opponents could manage only 21 points against us. The media started to look at our defense, and they figured *someone* had to be doing something on that side of the ball. So they all decided to home in on our defensive tackle, Mike Hammerstein. But I'm telling you, sure as I sit in this chair, *no one knew how to spell Hammerstein's name before the season started*!

At the end of the year, we'd given up only 98 points in 12 games. So when they named Mike an All-American, what did the rest of the defense say? We *all* made All-American! Mike just represented that defense. For us, that was a team award!

When I look back on those two seasons, 1984 and 1985, I realize the secret was, there was no secret. We just remembered how we do things around here. Then we went back to doing those things better than anyone else. That's all.

And that's how we went from being unranked one year to number two the next.

I don't care what anybody says: THAT is a comeback!

29

Ignore Your Critics

A few weeks ago, Cathy and I were walking through a bookstore—I love bookstores—and she shows me a paperback some guy wrote, saying Michigan football isn't what it's cracked up to be. He said the main indictment against Bo Schembechler is that he lost 22 games in his career at Michigan by two points or less.

Now, I thought about this for a moment. We won 194 games and lost only 48 in my 21 years coaching at Michigan, and almost half of those losses were by two points or less. Well, hell! I don't know if you construe that as bad coaching. You could argue we never got blown out—and maybe we weren't very lucky, either! Shoot, if we made just 11 more field goals, and our opponents missed just 11 more, then we'd have 22 more victories—and probably a half-dozen national titles.

And poor Fielding Yost—who didn't lose a single game in his first FOUR YEARS at Michigan—this guy ate him up, too. I'm thinking, this son of a gun is nuts!

Hey. You can take any coach you want—I don't care if it's

Woody Hayes or Ara Parseghian or Joe Paterno, all giants—and you can pick apart their career and find that, sure, they lost some games, probably a few they shouldn't have. Every one of those three guys won a national title, but every one of them had losing seasons, too—usually when I was on their staff, it occurs to me! And these are some of the best coaches the game has ever seen. What does that mean?

I'll tell you what it means: Nothing!

Everyone's got critics. And if you're in charge, you're going to have more than the people working for you do. Well, I had 101,001 critics every Saturday, and millions more watching on TV—screaming at me to pass more, to blitz more, to go for it on fourth-and-one from our own 40-yard line. Let me tell you something: I fundamentally did not give a *damn* what the press, the administration or the alumni thought about my coaching. Fritz Crisler said it best. "If you're winning," he said, "you don't need them. And if you're losing, they can't help you."

So, you block them out!

To me, those are just people trying to interrupt what you're doing. You can't be beholden to anyone not directly connected to your organization, because you've got enough to worry about just doing your job. You're going to need lots of help running any organization, but not that kind. You just have to shut out the noise, because if you let some outsider talk you out of what you think is right, I'll bet you a hundred dollars right now you'll regret it.

If any outsider tries to tell you how to do your job, particularly if they're advocating methods you *know* are wrong—kick 'em out of your program! You've got to establish right away, that none of this goes. You are in charge.

If you make it clear from the get-go that you're not to be messed with—as I did with a few unscrupulous alumni in my first year—they figure that out pretty fast, too, and they'll back down. And word gets around. A little fear among outsiders isn't necessarily a bad thing. "*I'm* not gonna talk to him! *You* talk to him!"

That's okay with me.

That's the problem with business these days: Your shareholder doesn't care about the company's long-term vision. He just wants a quick return on his investment. And that's what these overpaid CEOs give them—then leave the mess for the next guy to clean up.

In America right now, we have the worst debt in the history of this country, and the only reason is because no one has the *guts* to cut any of these pork programs and entitlements. They know how to get reelected, and when it comes time to pay for all those things we don't need, they'll be long gone!

I'm sorry, folks, but THAT is not leadership!

Shutting those people out is one of the most important things any leader must do. Doesn't matter if you're working in front of a hundred people or a hundred thousand. You've got to be so *engrossed* in what you're doing that you can make the right decisions without being distracted.

What does it take to ignore 100,000 critics? It takes one thing: *confidence.*

Where do you get confidence? Simple: through *preparation.*

Before a big game, if I know I've worked hard, I've listened to my coaches, and I've done everything I could to prepare my team—well, if I did all those things, why in hell should I have to worry about what some guy in Section 23 is yelling at me? He didn't do any of those things, and therefore he has no idea what he's talking about.

If someone wants to criticize me after I've done all those things, I don't care what he says—because I'm right! And by God, I am not going to let someone who didn't do *any* of those things convince me otherwise.

I love Ann Arbor. I've lived here almost half my life. But I've gotta tell you, because everyone's so highly educated here, it can be a town of experts. I like to think we did pretty well in my time here, but for the guy in Section 23, it was never enough. "Why do they run that same play up the middle again and again?"

I'll tell you why: because it *wasn't* the same play! Depending on what our opponents' defense was trying to do to us, we'd run the off-tackle play differently. We weren't trying to fool their linebackers or their defensive backs. We were trying to fool their *defensive linemen*!

We could block that "basic running play" a half-dozen different ways, so their linemen couldn't tell which way we were going with it. In a typical sequence of running plays, the first thing I'm going to do is knock the defensive lineman on his butt, straight up. The next time, I'll have my lineman block his man inside. If his man tries to play down inside, our tight end comes in and wipes him out. The next time, he thinks we're going inside again, so I have my guy take one step outside of him, then have my guard step up to trap him.

The same way a pitcher tries to fool you with different pitches, we could mix up base-blocks, gap-blocks, lead-blocks, pass-blocks, draw-blocks and double-teams to get the defensive lineman's head spinning. Once he's confused, he's easy to get around.

Don't know all those blocks? Don't worry—neither does the guy in Section 23!

That's how we beat Indiana in 1979 on the last play of the game. The score was 21-21, we had the ball on Indiana's 45-yard line, and only six seconds left on the clock. Instead of just throwing the bomb, like everyone expected us to do, we sent Anthony Carter across the middle, *between* their linebackers and the safeties. And that's where John Wangler hit him with a pass.

The only reason that worked is because we'd been handing off the ball all day, but on that play we faked the handoff, which made Indiana's linebackers run up to stop what they thought was going to be a run. Can you imagine? A run, at the 45-yard line, with no time left? Even I'm not that conservative! Regardless, they bit, and came up to the line when they should have been backpedaling to cover Anthony.

Now, at the same time, I'm sure the Indiana coaches were telling their defensive backs, "Whatever you do, don't let Carter get past you," so those guys are *way* back there, leaving a huge gap for Anthony to run through, behind the charging linebackers and in front of the backpedaling defensive backs.

And that's exactly what happened. That's why you see that play, over and over on TV, of Anthony cutting behind those linebackers and past those defensive backs and dancing in the end zone, with no time left on the clock. Wow, that was great!

When Anthony scored, I didn't look up at the stands after that play—I never did—to see if the guy in Section 23 suddenly approved of my play calling. But when the whole place was going insane, something tells me the guy in Section 23 wasn't criticizing Bo Schembechler—and it wouldn't have mattered if he was!

Teddy Roosevelt was right: It's not the critic who counts, it's the man in the ring.

My players knew I didn't give a damn about the press or alums or anyone else outside our building, but just to be sure they knew where I stood, I still made that crystal-clear to them in our first meeting every year. It's right there in my speech.

I'd tell 'em straight up: "Here you will be judged only on your performance and your attitude. The only people who will influence my thinking will be your coaches. You need to understand that, other than the assistants, nobody, but *nobody* influences my decisions on who should start, what plays we should call, anything. So don't think for a second that any sportswriter or your mom or dad or some guy on the street is going to get in my ear and influence my thinking. Nobody. That's just not going to happen.

"And if one of YOU starts getting booed or hounded by the press or the alums or your classmates, keep in mind there is only ONE person you have to please, and it's ME. Got it? No one else!"

If you are the man in charge, you are only responsible for one thing, and that's the people in your organization. If you do what's right by them, you can ignore everything else, because nothing else matters.

VII

Overtime

30

Loyalty Counts

If you really want your people to perform for you, they can't just fear you. They have to respect you, and feel a real sense of loyalty to you that goes beyond the task at hand.

Now how can you get that kind of loyalty?

There's only one way I know of: You have to give it to them first.

Not just as employees, but as people—and later, as friends. I hope it goes without saying, this far into the book, that getting a better performance is not the *only* reason you do anything for your people—or even the most important one. You do it because it's the right thing to do—and as a bonus, you'll make a lot of great friends for the rest of your life.

At each of our reunions, about 90 percent of the guys I coached come back, and I bet I see almost that many in my office or my home every year. It's one of the best things about being retired. I don't have to yell at them anymore—but sometimes I do anyway, just for old times' sake. You know, so many of those guys are successful businessmen and lawyers and TV stars—but when I tell them they're late, even when they're not, they still jump a little! Don't worry: They get me back.

The hardest time to earn their trust is when you're new. You don't know them, they don't know you, and they don't owe you anything. I think about that 1969 team—talk about a leap of faith. So I feel I owe those guys a lot.

Garvie Craw, the great running back on that team, he can't go a week without calling me. I've got Caldarazzo in here every fall, and now I'm looking out for his son, who's a student at Michigan. I just can't get rid of those guys, no matter how hard I try!

We play golf in Florida every spring, and boy am I a lousy golfer. The only thing I can teach those guys on a course is new and creative ways to swear. But I do it because I love being around those guys. Dan Dierdorf, Jim Betts, Frank Gusich—they all still come around.

When I was still coaching, those guys would stop by practice and I'd introduce them to the team. The players could tell how much I respected the guys who came before. They could tell it was special to be a Wolverine alumnus in good standing. The current players saw me honor that by making calls for the alums, writing them letters, making recommendations and visiting them in the hospital, too, when necessary.

If you played for Michigan, you'll always have an ally in Ann Arbor: Bo Schembechler.

If you earn my trust, I will be loyal to you. I will help you whenever I can, I won't keep score, and when things are tough, I'll come running. But that doesn't mean I won't be aware of what you've been up to—and if I think you're screwing up, I'm going to let you know!

The vast majority of my players have done very well, but I've had a couple players go to prison, and that's nothing you want to see happen.

Billy Taylor was one of those great players I inherited from Bump. The man remains the only Michigan player to average over 100 yards rushing a game, he scored one of the most famous Michigan touchdowns against Ohio State in our 10–6 victory in 1971, and he left Michigan as an All-American, with his degree. Not bad.

But when his pro career ended, he fell in with some bad guys, and one day he found himself sitting in the driver's seat of the getaway car for a bank robbery. He told me he drove around the block a few times, while the heist was going on, debating whether he should just take off. Well, he went back, they got caught and he served two and a half years in prison.

When I got the news, I was shocked. To say I was disappointed in Billy is to understate the case quite a bit. When I was coaching him, we'd had a few run-ins, but nothing significant—and he certainly never struck me as the kind of guy who might help someone rob a bank!

That's why I was so devastated—and ticked off! But I wasn't going to forget him, or ignore him. I visited him in prison, in Wisconsin and Milan, Michigan. We talked. And I repeated what I said when he played for me: Okay, you got knocked down, but the question is, will you get back up? If you want to stay down, there is nothing I can do for you. But if you want to get back up, I'll help.

Billy got his master's degree in prison, when it would have been so easy to join a gang and all that. That impressed me.

In his book, Billy gives me a lot of credit for helping him, but honestly, I was no savior. All I did was let him know I'm still here—I wasn't running away—that I cared about him, and if I could help, I would. But he did all the work. That's always how it is. And that's how, when he earned his PhD a few years ago, he became Dr. William Taylor. How about that?

Mike Smith played for us a few years after Billy graduated. He's a nice kid from Kalamazoo with good parents, who sent him to a Catholic high school. He was always dressed like an Ivy League student, and the guys on the team nicknamed him 'Zoo. He roomed with Max Richardson, who's now an attorney in Atlanta, and he became a good friend of Jimmy Hackett's, the Steelcase CEO, who played with Mike on the demo team. Those three guys were from very different backgrounds, but they've stayed in touch long after graduation. That's what college teams can do for you.

In 1987, Mike starts living two lives, working nine-to-five at IBM, then at Faygo, but at night he's running around with the wrong crowd, and ends up transporting cocaine for some drug dealers. Not smart, to say the least. Of course, the police eventually caught him, and the state's mandatory sentencing laws—which have since been repealed—meant he got life in Coldwater State Penitentiary with no chance of parole. As tough as it gets.

Now I admit, the first few years Mike was in there, I was so mad at him that I didn't lift a finger to get him out. But his teammates—especially Max and Hackett—thought the penalty didn't fit the crime. Mike wasn't selling drugs on a schoolyard, he wasn't a repeat offender, he wasn't some drug kingpin.

Mike's family and friends lobbied me to help out, and by 1995 I came around. I went to visit Mike in prison, and I leaned forward, and I said, "Mike, if I find out you're lying to me about what you did, and didn't do, I'm out of here." But it became clear pretty quickly that he was on the level. After Mike had served ten years in prison as a model inmate, I felt that was enough. Problem was, the sentence was nonnegotiable, so it would take nothing less than a pardon from Governor John Engler to get Mike out. We would need to put together one heck of a case.

Max worked his tail off assembling everything we needed. Mike's teammates visited him in prison, wrote him letters, contributed money for his release effort and provided character testimony for Mike's brief. Hackett testified that he would hire Mike the day he was released, which had to help. Even Mike's warden said, in his forty years on the job, this was only the second time he advocated the release of a prisoner.

My duty was to lobby Governor Engler, who eventually set up a hearing for us. So many of Mike's coaches, teammates and friends from U-M and Kalamazoo showed up for his hearing— over a hundred made the trip, by car, bus and plane—that they had to change venues to fit them all in one place. If nothing else tells you about the loyalty we feel for each other, that does.

When I testified, I told them how furious I was when Mike first got arrested, especially because he had always been such a solid citizen at Michigan. But whenever I visited him in prison, he never made any excuses, never complained, never said, "Why me?" He only asked how the team was doing. That said something to me about his character.

"Mike messed up, big-time," I said in closing. "And he needs to pay the price. But I need to ask you this: If this were your son, and he made a mistake like that, can you honestly say this punishment fits the crime? I don't think so.

"And let me guarantee the parole board that I will personally see to it that Mike Smith will NOT be in trouble ever again—no drugs, no guns, nothing—and if he does, you will not have to deal with him because I will get to him first!"

Governor Engler granted Mike a pardon in 1998. Boy, what a relief that was. He's working for Cintas now in Grand Rapids—and what a sight to see Mike back at our reunion in 2004, looking good, just like he should.

I'm proud of him.

Where does this loyalty come from? That's easy. It started with my old college coach, Wayne Woodrow Hayes. Woody was no picnic to work for, but he passed the true test of loyalty by looking out for you long after it was in his self-interest to do so.

When I became Michigan's head coach, it's fair to say Woody wasn't exactly thrilled—and probably a lot less so after we beat the best team he'd ever coached in 1969.

During the Ten Year War, we communicated just two times each year—at the Big Ten coaches preseason meeting in Chicago, and at midfield before our game in late November—except for two other occasions.

The first occurred after I had my heart attack at the 1970 Rose Bowl. One of the first letters to arrive at my home in Ann Arbor, when I was recuperating in my bed upstairs, was from none other than Woody Hayes.

Now, this was just a few weeks after we'd given Woody the most bitter loss of his career. And this was a guy who hated Michigan so much that, the story goes, he once made his assistant coach push his car over the Michigan state line: He refused to buy gas in this state because he couldn't stomach the idea that a few cents of the state gasoline tax might trickle down to the University of Michigan. Brother, *that* is a rivalry.

But there was his letter, waiting for me on a small table right next to my bed, when I couldn't do much more than just lie there.

> Dear Bo,
>
> If you were going to have a sick spell, why didn't you have it at our game, for your team didn't look the same without you. On television it appeared that they stuck in there real well, but they lacked the coordination that they had against us.
>
> Anne [Woody's wife] is always accusing me of practicing medicine without a license, but even at that hazard I'm going to offer a little free advice . . .

Woody went on to describe people he knew, some my age or even younger, who had come back from their heart attacks better than before by exercising and eating right. He mentioned a thirty-two-year-old guy whose doctor had just told him he could play tennis again.

> I'm not trying to suggest that you go back to handball for you never were very good at it.
>
> All I'm trying to say is: If you won't get stubborn and heroic you can be in better health than ever.
>
> I'll see you next November 21.
>
> Your old coach and longtime friend,
>
> Woody

When you're forty years old and the Grim Reaper is already introducing himself to you—well, let's just say, I needed that. From that old warrior especially, that meant something to me.

The only other time during the Ten Year War I communicated with Woody outside official business was at the other end of that span. This time he needed me. In the 1978 Gator Bowl, Woody punched a Clemson player, and it created a great furor. The national media was going berserk. A lot of people were calling for Woody's head, and it wasn't clear what Ohio State was going to do about it.

A few days later I got a call from Dr. Bob Murphy, the Buckeyes' team physician, God bless his soul. He told me, "Woody hasn't come out of his house since he got back from the Gator Bowl. Bo, I'm worried about him. You've got to get Woody out of the house." So we arranged to meet at Doyt Perry's house in Bowling Green—neutral territory

Now, this took place in the middle of recruiting season, but some things are more important. We talked for a long time—hours—the longest conversation we had, by far, since I had quit working for him back in 1962. Doyt and I tried, as best we could, to convince Woody to apologize to save his job, but he wouldn't budge. Stubborn as a mule.

Later that week he was scheduled to give a speech in Columbus. Normally this wouldn't be any big deal—Woody gave dozens of speeches every year—but he hadn't talked to the media since the incident, so it became a national affair.

"Now Bo thinks I ought to apologize for what happened in the Gator Bowl," he said, "but Bo doesn't know everything. You want me to apologize for all the good things I've done?"

And in his own way, he considered that an apology, but it was too little, too late, and Woody lost his job. Would my life be easier without having to battle Woody Hayes every November—let alone having to fight him for every recruit we wanted twelve months a year? Hell, yes! But it broke my heart.

I heard he'd been fired right as I was heading into a coaches meeting. Woody wasn't dead, of course—he lived another eight years—but I'd already lost something, I knew that much. As soon as I told my assistants the news, I broke down. I couldn't help it.

I don't think there have ever been two rivals more hard-nosed than the two of us were. Man, we were after it! But when the game's over, it's over. And we're friends. Good friends. And we remained good friends until the day he died—which happened the morning after he introduced me at a banquet. That was loyalty, too.

In 1982, Texas A&M offered me $2.25 million for ten years, which would have made me the highest-paid coach in the country. At the time I was making $60,000 a year at Michigan—about a quarter as much. That, you probably knew. Of course, I decided to turn down the money and stay at Michigan. But you haven't heard this part.

I called all the assistants over to my basement rec room, right there at 870 Arlington Road. I went around the room, asking all of them what they thought I should do. The vote was about even. It was a lot of money, after all, Texas A&M was a serious program in a big-time league, and as one of them said, "No one would ever blame you for doing this."

And that's when I cut off the discussion.

"That's easy for you to say. But you don't have to stand up in front of those players—players you've known since high school, whose homes you've been in and whose parents you've met— and look them in the eye and tell them you're leaving."

And that's what settled it—loyalty.

If your men are not more important to you than your money, then you didn't really care about them in the first place.

If I wasn't loyal to the people who worked so hard for me—the players, the coaches, the staff—I just couldn't live with myself.

Gary Moeller is to me what I was to Woody—except Gary and I have never been rivals. Gary played for me at Ohio State—he captained my last year there, 1962—and assisted me at Miami and at Michigan, where he did a bang-up job as our defensive coordinator until Illinois came calling. He coached some of the best defenses we've ever had here.

Illinois hired him as their head coach in 1977, and promised him five years—then canned him after three. Just ridiculous. I called him up immediately afterward and told him he should come back to Michigan.

"But you don't have any jobs open," he said. "You've got Bill McCartney running your defense, and he's doing a hell of a job."

"True, but Don Nehlen just took the job at West Virginia, so you can run the offense." He did, and his first year back we won 10 games, including my first Rose Bowl.

We were never in the habit of running up the score here at Michigan, but Gary's firing by Illinois ticked me off so much I didn't feel too badly about putting 45 on them Gary's first year back, and 70 the next.

When I decided to step down in 1989, I was the athletic director, so I could name my successor. That was another no-brainer. Gary Moeller. And he'd still be the head coach today if I was still the athletic director in 1995.

Now, Gary is not a real big drinker—he'll have a glass of wine with dinner, maybe a beer after a game—and that was the problem one night he was at some restaurant near Ann Arbor. He had had too many, he made a scene, and he spent the night in jail.

When this happened, I was in Mexico on a fishing trip, oblivious to the whole thing. When I got back to the hotel, I had a message from one of our staffers to call the office. The guy was out, so I left a message, but I don't know if he ever got it. I waited a couple days, then called again to find out the Michigan administration had decided to let Gary go.

Boy, was I hot! I hopped on the next flight, but when I got back, there was nothing I could do. It was too late. I remember yelling at a staffer about it, trying to win a fight we'd already lost, then just collapsing in the chair of my office. I was spent, defeated. It just ate me up that they were going to let a great man go over one mistake, and there was nothing I could do about it.

One bad night—that's all it was. But when you're the head coach at Michigan, I guess you can't afford that.

Well, Gary took it pretty hard. After he left here, he coached the Detroit Lions—he was one of the few guys who ever had a winning record there—but he stayed away from the football building, and that hurt, too, because you knew it was killing him. Even at our reunion in 1999, he didn't come back.

When I spoke at the end of the event, I told the coaches and players that this was a great night, and I thanked them for it. I loved it. "I don't know another team in the country that could pull this off," I said. "But there's one guy missing tonight, you know who it is, and that needs to be rectified. He needs to be here next time. And I'm putting *all of you* in charge of making sure he never misses another one."

We had our next reunion in 2004, and enough guys got to Gary that he had no choice but to show up. That's all I asked for.

After we introduced all the players—about 400 of our guys were there—and all the coaches, we introduced Gary Moeller.

Or, we tried to. The second Jimmy Brandstatter, our emcee, said, "Gentlemen, please welcome Gary"—you couldn't hear him! Everyone jumped to their feet—I mean jumped—and *erupted* in applause. They gave Gary a five-minute standing ovation, clapping, chanting his name—"MOE! MOE! MOE!"—and carrying on. And folks, five minutes of that is a very long time! You've never seen so many big guys crying. Guys who played in Super Bowls, guys who never got into a game for us—and they had tears streaming down their faces. "MOE! MOE! MOE!" Gary pulled a few tears himself. How he got up and spoke after that, I have no idea. I'm not sure I could have.

I do know this. I've been to thousands of banquets, award ceremonies, hall of fame inductions, weddings and funerals. But I have never seen *anyone, anywhere* get the kind of reception Gary got that night.

Since I retired, nothing has made me feel better than seeing that.

The sad thing is, when you coach as long as I did, you're going to lose some people. And I have. Cecil Pryor, a great guy from that 1969 team, died in the fall of 2005, while we were working on this book. Dave Brown, a two-time All-American, just flat-out collapsed a few months later. You just can't imagine a thing like that happening to people in their prime.

You meet these guys when they're swashbuckling young men, with everything going for them. They're strong, they're sharp, they're confident, and they've got their whole lives in front of them. And somehow, you think they'll always be that way, because you meet a new class every fall.

But they graduate and get old, too, just like the rest of us. Just like me. And you see it when they come back. Of course, they see me, too—I'm getting old! So maybe we're all a little surprised when we see each other again. But that's life. We talk about all the usual things, and I still like to give them a hard time. That's just part of the deal.

But when I hear one of them is sick, or even dying—well, it's never easy. It never seems right. I've never gotten used to it. But you do everything you can for them.

I think of Bobby Baumgartner. He was an offensive guard with Caldarazzo on that 1969 team. He was the guy who stayed in town that summer just to beat the six-minute mile—and did it, finally, on the last day. Those guys were great—the core of a team that pulled off our greatest win, that famous game against the Buckeyes.

Baumie had a great job out in San Francisco as a banker, he had a wonderful wife, a couple of good kids. Everything was going his way. Then the cancer hit.

This was about eleven or twelve years ago. I was out of a job, my kids were out of the house, and my wife, Millie, had just passed away. So I was alone. And, I suppose, I was kind of feeling sorry for myself, too.

But I figured, one thing I can do to help someone else is run out and see Baumie. I knew he was dying, and he knew it, too. And I knew if I didn't get out there fast, I was going to kick myself for not spending some time with him. So I got on a plane and went out to San Francisco, and spent a day with him in his hospital room.

Baumie and I had a few laughs, reminiscing about everything we'd gone through—the first time I told them they were all going to live in Ann Arbor, the slap-and-stomp drill, the celebration of Olympic proportions after he and his buddies finally broke the six-minute mile. The amazing feeling on that team flying home from Minnesota, when we knew before anyone else did that we had greatness in us. The upset over the Buckeyes.

We talked all day, Baumie and me, about his teammates, his friends, his family. It got emotional for both of us. Right before I left his room, I turned to him and said, "Keep going, Baumie."

He seemed to respond to that, but he couldn't live much longer. I knew that was going to happen, and he did, too—but it still hits you.

What a man he was. A big, tough guy, but as sweet as can be, with this little voice—so high. A wonderful man. And we lost him.

You feel powerless. It's so unfair, and there is so little you can do. But you do what you can—because you love him. I never said it, but he knew. They all do.

And they know it, because it's true.

Don't tell me it was about national titles.

31

Know When to Leave, and How

Someday someone is going to take your job, and you're going to have to let them. If you became a leader for the right reasons in the first place, you'll be able to pass it on and feel good about it.

When I announced my retirement in 1989, I knew we had a hell of a team coming back the next season. And I'm not going to lie to you: I would have *loved* to coach that team. We had everything! And if it wasn't for my ticker, I would have. But my doctor made it clear I was pushing it as it was, and if I wanted to spend some good years with my family, I had to get out. Lord knows, I owed them that.

But I didn't just say goodbye, and walk out the door. Like Bump did for me, I left the cupboard full. I wanted to set up my successor, Gary Moeller, for success. So I prepared our people to make that transition work.

Before we made it official, Gary invited me to stay on as the front man while he and the other assistants did the actual work.

That was a very generous gesture, to say the least. But I couldn't do it because it wouldn't be honest. I can feel good that every day I was on the job, I gave it everything I had. I never wanted to compromise that, or the program we all had worked so hard to build up. It was time for me to go.

By promoting Gary, we not only got a great coach, we got to ensure that everyone else could stay on, too—the assistants, the trainers, the secretaries. Everybody. In fact, that was the *only* condition I had when I left: If I step down, only one guy is leaving—and his name is Schembechler!

Yes, I still had an office in the football building, and Gary's office was at the other end of the hallway, but I can assure you: *That* was a one-way corridor. I was never going to walk down uninvited to see the head coach.

Gary always had my full support. I wasn't going to second-guess him in the papers or anywhere else. I was available to talk if he wanted to, but if he didn't, that was his decision—exactly the same courtesy Bump had given me. Gary chose to keep his own counsel, which was his prerogative, and I respected that.

Lloyd's approach is different. We talk just about every week. In fact, when Lloyd first got the job—as an interim head coach, a few months before our opening game in 1995—I knocked on his door, and asked if I could come in.

Lloyd looked a little surprised—it had been the other way around for years—but he said, "Sure, come in." I closed the door behind me, and sat down. I said, "You know, right now, you've probably got a lot of doubts, and you're wondering if you're up to the task."

Lloyd nodded, but you could tell he was wondering where I was going with this.

"I know how you feel," I said, "because that's exactly how I felt when I became the head coach at Miami, and at Michigan."

Remember, Lloyd first started coaching for me in 1980, when we were already up and running. And I'm willing to bet he didn't see a lot of doubt from me during our ten years coaching together. But I told him my first year as head coach at Miami of Ohio, we started out 2-3-1, and in my first year at Michigan, we were 3-2 after we lost that Michigan State game. Both times I had plenty of critics, and plenty of doubts.

"So here's what you do," I told him. "Block all those doubts out! Get rid of them! And remember why they named *you,* and not someone else, to be the head coach of the University of Michigan Wolverines. You already know everything you need to know to succeed here—and you will!"

Three years later, Michigan won its first national title in fifty years, and Lloyd was named Coach of the Year.

So which way is better, Gary's or Lloyd's? Well, Gary won three Big Ten titles in five years, so you'd have to conclude his way worked. And Lloyd has won five Big Ten titles in eleven years—so his way has worked, too.

The point is, it doesn't matter. Whatever your successors decide to do, it's your job to respect their decision—and then get the hell out of their way!

Around here, that's kind of enforced. A couple days after I started working for the Detroit Tigers, I came back to the football building here to work out—but my name had already been removed from my locker. I said, "Falk, what the hell is this?"

And he just shrugs, and gives me that line from *The Natural*: "They come and they go, Hobbs. They come and they go."

Don't forget that.

Even if you thought you were a great leader, once you're out of the limelight, you get down to earth pretty fast. The guys who have a hard time dealing with that are guys with big egos. Those are the guys who aren't satisfied with their lives or their careers, and their egos still have to be fed. And that's too bad, because they're not going to feed your ego all your life. They move on to the next guy. And you need to move on, too.

I don't sit and stew that I never won a national title, or that I have the world's worst record in the Rose Bowl. And I don't sit and bask in all the Big Ten titles we won, either. No. If I had won all those Rose Bowls or national championships, I probably would have been impossible to live with! So do I have any regrets? I can honestly say I don't. None whatsoever.

After you step down, don't look back. It won't do you any good.

If you gave everything you had, and you left the right way, you're going to have a lot of fun in retirement. I know I have.

In 1992, a few days after the Tigers fired me, Millie died. I was devastated. I didn't do anything for a while, for almost a year. I looked gray and flabby, and my friends were worried about me.

Months passed. Finally, a few friends invited me down to their home in Florida, and took me out to a party where everyone knew me.

Well, everyone except Cathy Aikens—who just happened to be the most beautiful woman in the room! Turns out she'd lost her husband five years earlier, and I was sure she had plenty of guys after her.

I left the party early to watch Michigan's Fab Five in the NCAA tournament at another friend's house, but I guess it got back to a few folks that I was asking about the attractive blonde on the other side of the room. They called me during halftime—they knew I wouldn't answer during the game—to arrange a date.

Nice try, but I was going to the Bahamas for a fishing trip the next day, so I didn't see how I could swing it. They were hearing none of it. "Okay," they said, "we're going to pick you up at eight o'clock for breakfast, and she's going to be there."

Now, I've got to confess: I didn't know anything about this dating business. I actually showed up for that breakfast in my fishing gear! I couldn't have been too much to look at—but she looked gorgeous, even at eight in the morning.

There was another catch: Cathy knows a lot more about literature than linebackers. At one point, she asked me if I had been a basketball coach.

"No," I said, "your scouting report is a little off. I was a football coach."

Then she asked me, "Is that all you've done?"

I had to laugh. "Lemme tell you something. *That* was a full-time job!"

We hit it off that morning, but afterward I guess I kind of stalled. Hell, I admit it: I was scared! Three weeks later, when my plane stopped in Minneapolis for a two-hour layover, I told myself, "If you're a man, you'll call her!"

I did. We met again two weeks later at her house in Florida. We were supposed to go out to dinner, but instead we sat on her couch and talked—and talked and talked—until it was midnight. And then I told her: "I came down here to see the ocean, and it's right out that door. If you've got a gut in your body, you'll put your swimsuit on and we'll go swimming in that ocean."

Well, she did it! I was splashing around in the water. I felt like a kid again!

I slept on that couch that first night—and the next night, and the next night—five in a row! Man, we talked about everything. We discovered we have a lot of the same interests, and we think alike. She's well-read, she knows a lot about a lot of things. And she's even more conservative than I am.

Now, I may not know much about dating, but I do know recruiting. I know if you're in that house for five days, something good is happening.

We got married, of course, and we've traveled everywhere together—Australia, South Africa, Europe, New Zealand, you name it. What a hoot! You've got to realize, I never had time for any real vacations when I was coaching. And to have this second chance at life, with this smart, beautiful woman—it's more than a mortal man could ask for.

If there's a downside, it's my diet, which now consists of skim milk, no sugar, no butter, no fun. But hey, you can't blame her. She's keeping me going. She's got me eating right, working out every day, and looking like some kind of magazine model—or at least a lot sharper than I looked in the 1970s, when I was wearing all that blue-plaid polyester!

I'm now 197 pounds of blue twisted steel, and I feel great.

Everyone asks what I'm doing these days, and it seems that I'm just as busy as you people with jobs.

I've raised a lot of money for the Millie Schembechler Foundation, the Heart of a Champion Cardiac Center, the University of Michigan Hospital, the athletic department and any former player who asks. I still give speeches around the country, but what I like best is just going down to the football building and seeing who shows up.

You have to realize, most places, a guy leaves his job, he can't go back to visit. That's especially true in coaching. In fact, it's true just about everywhere but here. So, I'm very lucky.

And when I go into the office, I promise you it's going to be an interesting day.

I still get my mail here, my calls here, and my visitors here. Everyone seems to know when I'm in town.

I can come down here anytime I want, and I see all my friends who are still working here—like Lloyd and Falk and Mary Passink—and all my friends who stop by to visit, like Hanlon and Burton and just about every player I coached, including all the folks you've just read about.

Sometimes I'll just call out, "Hey, MARY! Get in here!" And she'll come in, sit down, and we'll just tell stories for hours. That's fun.

You see, my memories are not in a plaque, or a trophy or a ring. You won't find any of those things displayed in my office, in my home, or on my fingers.

No, my memories are running into someone I coached or worked with. That's the best way to have memories. So when I come in, there's a stack of mail waiting for me, a list of calls to return—and then the phone starts ringing, and guys start knocking on the door. You can't get rid of these guys, no matter how hard you try!

Of course, I love it. Wouldn't you?

In 1985, the year we came back from that 6-6 season and finished 10-1-1, ranked second in the country, we'd had such a good season, with such a good feeling in that locker room, that our quarterback, Jim Harbaugh, was nervous that maybe the team wouldn't live up to all that the next year, when he was a senior. So that spring, he went up to Jerry Hanlon and asked him what kind of team we were going to have that year.

We get this question a lot—from our players, the press, fans, our neighbors. Everyone wants to know what next year's team is going to be like. Well, Hanlon gave Harbaugh the best answer to that question I have ever heard.

He said, "Jim, come back in twenty years, and I'll tell you. Only then will we know how you and your classmates turned out. Did you get good jobs? Are you hardworking and honest? Were you good husbands and fathers? Did you contribute to your community? *Did you make the world a better place?*"

During my thirty-nine years as head coach, my teams won 234 games, thirteen Big Ten titles, two MAC titles and five bowl games. We coached thirty-three All-Americans and 126 All-Big Ten players.

But Jerry's right. That's not what matters.

What matters is you grew up. You became men. And now you're raising your own children to do the same.

Guys like Don Moorhead, my first quarterback at Michigan, who is a teacher in Portage, Michigan, and a good family man, whose students don't even know he played football for the Wolverines, let alone led them to the greatest upset in team history.

Or Rob Lytle, who never complained when I moved him from tailback to fullback, and who went on to a great career with the Denver Broncos. He's a successful businessman now, whose kids have all graduated from college, but he still loves the game so much he works the chains for his old high school team in Freemont, Ohio, on Friday nights.

Or Stefan Humphries, who was an All-American guard here and a two-time academic All-American who played in the NFL before becoming a doctor at the Mayo Clinic.

And the list goes on. And on. And on. Hundreds of guys like that: hardworking, honest, *good* men.

And I love every one of those guys. And if I never told them to their faces, I'm telling them now.

I love you guys, and I wouldn't trade a day with you for anything.

So, Jim—and you better be reading this book, because if you don't, who will?—it's twenty years later, and now we know the answer to your question.

Yes, Jim. You had a great team. You all did.

32

If I Could Have One More Week

I probably spent a couple hundred hours answering Bacon's questions, just to put this book together—far more time than any coach should *ever* have to spend with a sportswriter—and most of the time, I could see his questions coming. Maybe he could see most of my answers coming, too, I don't know. You'd have to ask him.

But one day, he asked me a question, out of the blue, that surprised me. And I think maybe my answer surprised him, too. "If you could have one more week as Michigan's head coach," he asked, "in the prime of your career, what would you ask for?"

Maybe some former coaches, in their heart of hearts, would want to be in the limelight again, at a press conference, or giving a speech to their adoring alums, or on TV talking to ABC during halftime. That's not me, and anyone who really knows me knows that.

Maybe Bacon thought I'd ask for another shot at the Rose

Bowl, or a national title—or even a chance to replay that great Michigan–Ohio State game in 1969. Now those things, maybe I *would* love another crack!

But if you granted me just one more week as Michigan's head coach, I wouldn't hesitate. I know exactly what I'd want.

First, I'd want to be in touch with my sons, and have my wife in town. As I've gotten older, this has become even more important to me. Maybe I've gotten a little perspective, a little balance. I don't know. But that's my first request.

Next, I wouldn't ask to coach another game. No. Give me one more week of coaching *in preparation* for the Ohio State game. And make it against the great Wayne Woodrow Hayes. Just give me a week—from our film session on Sunday to my pre-game speech on Saturday—to get our guys ready for that game against that old general on the other side of the field. That would be it.

The game would just be icing for me, because if you're a real coach, a real leader, the preparation is the thing. You work all week to get ready—that's what a coach does. That's when you put your game plan in place, see what you've got, sense how your team is feeling—and sense what they need from you—as you get ready for game day. Like I said, the game would be the icing—but it's not the cake.

Then on Friday night, when I've finished handing out the hot chocolate and cookies during the bed check with all my players, and I knew we were ready—and I mean really *ready*—I'd return to my room, I'd sit on the corner of the bed and I'd just go, Ahhhhh.

And I'd be satisfied.

Epilogue

Bo Schembechler died on the morning of Friday, November 17, 2006, the day before the undefeated Wolverines were to play the undefeated Buckeyes in the most anticipated college football game in years.

The previous Saturday, Bo's youngest son, Shemy, a scout with the Washington Redskins, had been up at Michigan State to watch the Spartans play Minnesota. But Shemy knew Bo hadn't fully recovered from the heart procedure he had undergone a month earlier, so he left East Lansing at halftime and drove to Ann Arbor to watch the Michigan-Indiana game on TV with his father. He wasn't sure how many more games they had left.

"Dad, I'm on my way."

"Shem, you eaten yet? How about a pizza?"

They ordered two mediums with "too much meat," in Shemy's words. He could not deny his dad this minor indulgence. They sat in Bo's basement, ate their pizza and watched their last Michigan game together.

"As usual," Shemy said, "Dad was coaching up a storm." Late

in the first half, Michigan's Morgan Trent intercepted a Hoosier pass in the end zone. When Trent wavered between running it back or downing it, Bo started yelling, "Go down! Go down!"

"Dad always hated that," Shemy said. At last, Trent seemed to hear the old coach, and took a knee.

It was a satisfying Michigan victory, a 34–3 whitewashing, the kind Bo used to put on his Big Ten foes with regularity. The Wolverines were 11-0, ranked second in the nation and heading into Columbus with high hopes.

The next evening, Sunday night, Tom Slade, one of Bo's old quarterbacks, died of cancer at the age of fifty-four. As a sophomore, Slade had led the 1971 Wolverines to an 11-1 season, losing only to Stanford in the Rose Bowl, 13–12, on a last-second field goal. Despite his virtually spotless record, Slade spent his last two years backing up Dennis Franklin and Larry Cipa. Another man might have become bitter. Another coach might have forgotten him. Neither happened.

Slade became a well-known dentist whose clients included his former coach. They grew close, and stayed that way to the end. When Slade needed a bone marrow transplant, Bo organized fund-raisers and mass testings for a match, but none could be found. Slade's body began to deteriorate. During a particularly difficult day in the hospital, Slade woke up to see his former coach sitting in a chair against the wall. They looked at each other but said nothing, and Slade fell back to sleep. When he awoke again five hours later, Bo was sitting in the same chair, looking right at him.

Bo took Slade's death hard, but he got himself to football practice on Tuesday, just the same. Shemy drove back again to join him. It wasn't quite like the old days, when Bo would chase his players from one station to the next, yelling "On the hop! On the hop!" waving the yardstick he used to measure the space between their feet, and snap it across their backsides when their feet were too far apart. This time he just said, "Shem, you probably better get me something to sit on." Jon Falk, the equipment manager who had known Bo for almost four decades, quickly produced a stool. They spent the afternoon watching practice and shooting the breeze, two of Bo's favorite pastimes.

When practice ended, Bo and Shemy found themselves walking out alone. Bo was not given to sentimentality, and neither were his sons. But on this day, something told Shemy to break the rule. "I just told Dad I loved him," he said. Then he walked toward the stadium by himself, and broke down.

On Thursday, Bo and Cathy attended Tom Slade's funeral. Afterward, Coach Carr told Bo he didn't need to spend himself giving the team his traditional Thursday night pep talk, but Bo would hear none of it. He stood up in front of the team and told them who Tom Slade was, on and off the field.

"When I visited Tom Slade these last days of his life, we talked about everything—his work, his kids, his church—but the conversation always came back to Michigan football. You men are going to go out and do a lot of great things in your life. But you are never going to have as great an experience as you have had and will have playing football here at Michigan."

The next morning, shortly after Bo arrived at a TV studio to tape his weekly show, he collapsed, and died instantly. The cause of death was not a heart attack but heart failure. Bo had simply used up all the beats he'd been given.

We all knew Bo had cheated death for years. Yet when we got the news—and it traveled fast that day—we were stunned. I lost a great friend. But, amazingly, thousands of people could say the very same thing—and mean it. He was that big.

Within the hour, ESPN was running the news constantly, adding reactions from Bo's many admirers as they came in and playing retrospectives of his career. University of Michigan Web sites received more hits on that single day than they had all year. *The New York Times* ran Bo's photo and story on the front page. And *The Ann Arbor News* printed its headline in six-inch letters.

That night, several students organized a vigil on the Diag, Michigan's town square. A thousand young people came out in the cold to listen to Bo's former players speak from the steps of the library. In the candlelight, you could see the tears streaming down their cheeks. They were not paying homage to a coach— they were born about the time Bo left Michigan's sidelines—but to a leader.

At the official memorial service three days later, 20,000 mourners returned to Michigan Stadium to hear Dan Dierdorf talk about Bo's famous saying, "Those Who Stay Will Be Champions."

What that really meant, Dierdorf finally decided, was "that if you stayed with Bo, you would be a champion not just while you were wearing the winged helmet of the Michigan Wolverines, but for the rest of your life. The way you would be a husband, the way you would be a father, the way you would be a responsible member of your community. I think this is what Bo really meant. What we did away from this town was more important to Bo than what we did when we were here.

"We will be those good husbands, those good fathers and all those things, Bo, that you wanted us to be.

"We stayed. We are champions.

"And it's all because of you."

Reflections

Because Bo died right as this book was being completed, we felt it would be appropriate to solicit a few memories from his former coaches, players, staffers, friends and family. Not surprisingly, everyone we asked came through—often with pages. They usually included a story or two, and listed a few of the bedrock values Bo taught that they've carried with them the rest of their lives. Naturally, many of Bo's values they retained were quite similar, some even verbatim—Bo's values didn't change over the years—so to avoid repetition, we've stuck to the stories here, and reduced even those substantially, just for space considerations. However, to give you some idea of what Bo's protégés took with them, Fritz Seyferth's rendition speaks for many:

"Bo left those he touched with three life lessons I'll never forget: One, be a man of your word. If a man's word has no value, he has no value. Two, do not worry about short-term consequences. We are in this game of life for the long term. And three, touch all of the people you can to make a positive difference in their lives. Do this, and your rewards will be immeasurable."

I'll let the rest speak for themselves.

NOTE: To keep things simple, I've listed the person's official connection with Bo (teammate, assistant, and so forth), and in the case of the players, the last season they played for Bo.

BILL GUNLOCK, Miami of Ohio Teammate; Assistant with Bo at Ohio State

Bo and I met in 1947 at the Ohio High School North-South All-Star Game in Canton. The organizers thought it would be a good idea for a North player and a South player to room together, and so began my lifelong friendship with that squat, bow-legged, cocky offensive tackle from Barberton, Ohio. Bo made fun of the extensive toiletries I had brought to Canton, and I reminded him that I was a starter in the game and he was not. That was the first of thousands of good-natured ribbings we shared.

At times he was a stubborn SOB, but he was always honest, dedicated and contagiously passionate. He always told it like it was, whether it was politically correct or not. I even named my fourth son after him. I loved that man for what he was. I always will.

TOM REED, Miami Player, 1966; Assistant to Bo

When I was playing at Miami, Bo and Jim Young came up with this great idea to keep us on campus during spring break: two-a-day practices. We walked across the street that Friday afternoon carrying our helmets while all our friends waved goodbye as they hopped in their cars for Fort Lauderdale. "Those Who Stay Will Be Champions." He didn't say it then, but he did make us stay—and we were champions, in 1965 and 1966.

KENNY ROOT, Miami Player, 1968

I spent five seasons playing for Bo at Miami. I'll never forget the fiery and emotional locker room pre-game speeches that made me want to tear the hinges off the doors to get to the field, but I will always remember Bo for another day, years later. In the mid-1980s, about twenty years after I graduated, I was in Columbus for a Michigan–Ohio State game with my son Ryan, who was ten years old. It was a great game, and because Michigan had won in the fourth quarter, I decided to try to show Ryan the locker room. When we arrived at the door, my good friend Jon Falk, the equipment manager, said he would try to get us in as soon as possible, but the locker room was a zoo, packed with reporters.

At that same moment my old coach Gary Moeller saw me and took us right inside. After Moe introduced us to some of the players, and I said hello to some of my old coaches who had followed Bo to Michigan, Moe led us into this small dressing room, packed with two or three dozen reporters forming a huge semicircle around Bo, who was answering their questions rapid-fire in the corner of the room. Moe pushed Ryan and me through the crowd so we were standing at the front of the group. When he saw us, Bo raised his hand to halt the conversation and walked right over to Ryan, put his arm around him and walked him back to where he'd been standing and sat Ryan on a bench. "Now who are you, young man?" After Ryan mumbled his name, Bo asked, "Did your father tell you that he was a heck of a player for me? No? Well, he was!" Bo and Ryan sat on that bench and talked about the game, Ohio Stadium, Ryan's football team, his school, his brothers, his mother. The conversation lasted maybe ten minutes, but the whole time no one spoke except Bo and Ryan. It was a great moment for me, and as I watched this, all I could think was, "This is why I love this man so much."

DICK CALDARAZZO, Michigan Player, 1969

In 1969, during Bo's first hellish spring ball, I pinched a nerve in my neck in a one-on-one hitting drill. I let out a scream that nearly stopped the practice session. As I was kneeling in the grass being attended to by our trainer, Lindsey McClain, Bo walked by, looked at me and said, "Son, that probably would've killed an ordinary man!"

GARY MOELLER, Ohio State Player, 1962; Assistant

In 1969, after we beat Iowa, 51–6, to set up the showdown with the undefeated Buckeyes, the players stood in that locker room, holding their helmets and jamming them into the air, chanting, "Bring on the Buckeyes! Bring on the Buckeyes!" I said to Bo, "These guys are getting too high." And he said, "Let 'em go, Moe. They're just going to keep getting higher, and we're going to need that on Saturday." He read that team, and he read it beautifully. That was one of his great gifts.

GARVIE CRAW, Michigan Player, 1969

I remember coming in to work early on a Monday a few years ago, when I found a message on my desk that Bo had called the previous Friday at about 5 P.M. When I called him back, he said, "Where the hell were you when I called on Friday?" Now we live about fifty miles south of New York City, and the traffic to the Jersey Shore on Fridays can be a nightmare. I said, "Hey, Bo, I got out a little early to beat the crowds on the highway." He was quiet for a second and despite being well into my forties, I could feel the rebuke coming. When he finally spoke, his tone was low and disappointed. "But, Craw, THAT'S for OTHER GUYS!"

His message was loud and clear. No shortcuts, 110 percent, whatever it takes for as long as it takes. God do I miss that.

DAN DIERDORF, Michigan Player, 1970

At the end of pre-game warm-ups, our offense would always get together and run a couple of plays, then go in. One time we were in the huddle and all of a sudden this guy shows up from ABC, which was broadcasting the game. He walks into the huddle and says to Bo, "Coach, can you get your team off the field? We need to bring out the band."

Now, as a player, these are the kind of moments you can only dream about. For once, we were going to see somebody else be on the receiving end of the Bo we knew and loved.

That guy got the proverbial foot in the you-know-where, and he landed about six feet outside the huddle. And man, what a sweet moment that was!

JIM BETTS, Michigan Player, 1970; Academic Advisor

After some initial friction between us, we figured out we had a lot in common. There were many days our discussions had nothing to do with football, but about life. We talked about the racial strife and social unrest on campuses across the country. Some coaches were making their players sign contracts professing their loyalty to their coach and their school. Bo wouldn't have anything to do with that. I remember Bo told me, "If any of my players boycott the program, I'll resign, because I'd know I'd already lost them."

Most of the time you don't even realize you're getting an education until you're much older, when you have to deal with one of life's challenges, and it seems so intuitive, you ask yourself, Where did that come from? It came from Bo, of course.

REGGIE McKENZIE, Michigan Player, 1971

He was demanding, and he was unyielding. It was his way or the highway. You appreciated Bo more after you left. When I got to pro ball, I knew that nobody would ever be tougher on me than Bo Schembechler had been. He was the greatest coach I ever played for. I loved him, and I'll never forget him.

FRITZ SEYFERTH, Michigan Player, 1971; Assistant

In the summer of 1985, Bo was getting a heart catheterization. His wife, Millie, had been trying to get him to stop coaching because it was "killing him," she said, so he didn't tell her about this procedure, but he'd told me. When I visited him in the hospital, he'd had a spinal block for the procedure and was not supposed to lift his head, so he asked me to feed him his dinner. So there I am spoon-feeding the man who could put the fear of God into anyone, and he was as appreciative and as humble as could be. Bo had a lot of sides the average fan would never guess. Do I ever miss him.

DONNIE WARNER, Michigan Player, 1973

Bo asked no more and no less from the walk-ons than he did from the All-Americans. There were quite a few walk-ons when I was playing, and not one of us was ever asked to turn in our gear for lack of skill, size or speed. I really appreciated the fact that the walk-ons all received Big Ten championship rings, just like the rest of the team. I have three myself. There has never been a class distinction between the walk-ons and the scholarship guys—not when we were playing, and not during our reunions. I'm sure that's because of Bo.

DAVE BRANDON, Michigan Player, 1973

I first met Bo in early 1970 at his home in Ann Arbor. I was in the midst of my official recruiting visit and Bo was at his home recuperating from the heart attack he suffered at the Rose Bowl following the 1969 season. I stood at the foot of his bed while Bo lay there in his pajamas and robe, passionately explaining the importance of the Michigan football tradition. He explained that those who were tough enough to stay would be champions. He told me how committed he was to running a program that played by the rules. He explained how he would make no promises to any player about starting, playing time or the position they would play on the field. Everything would be earned by performance on the practice field.

The amazing thing about this experience was the fact that it took me only about thirty seconds to forget I was standing in the bedroom of a guy who just had suffered a heart attack! He was as intense, committed, enthusiastic and passionate in that circumstance as he proved to be at every meeting, practice and game I participated in over the following four years as one of his players. I knew immediately that I wanted to prove to this guy I was tough enough to stay . . . and be a champion.

I will forever be grateful for the lessons he taught me about leadership. He taught me how to prepare. He taught me to compete at the highest level and WIN. And he helped shape my education, my career and my leadership style. I am one of the many guys whose life was made better by Bo Schembechler.

JON FALK, Equipment Manager

I first met Bo Schembechler in 1967 when I was a freshman working in the equipment room at Miami of Ohio. He seemed like a very gruff guy, so I stayed away from him. I graduated from Miami in 1971 and stayed on as the football team's assistant equipment manager. I lived at home with my mother and grandmother and took care of them. In 1974 Bo invited me to interview in Ann Arbor. I had never lived anywhere else but Oxford, Ohio, so I was a little apprehensive at the prospect of working at a place so large.

When I returned from Ann Arbor I told my mother and grandmother that I was going to turn down Coach Schembechler because I did not want to leave the two of them by themselves.

That night, around four in the morning, my mother came into my room crying. She said it hurt her to tell me so, but Bo Schembechler was right and I must go to Michigan. "I know Coach Schembechler will take care of you."

I ate many, many dinners in Bo's home. As I look back, my mother was right. Bo Schembechler took care of me—and he did so for thirty-three years.

JIM HACKETT, Michigan Player, 1976

I talked to Bo two days before he died. He wasn't telling me about his operation to implant a new pacemaker three weeks earlier. He was telling me how disappointed he was that he couldn't do more to help Tom Slade find a bone marrow donor before Tom died that week.

Hollywood is adept at fashioning stories of imaginary heroes. I was lucky to know a real one.

MIKE SMITH, Michigan Player, 1977

During my official recruiting visit with Bo, he leaned toward my parents and said, "I will be his father away from home." And that is exactly what he was to me. After the meeting with Bo, my family and I immediately bought into becoming "True Wolverines." We still are today.

JOHN ROBINSON, Former Head Coach, University of Southern California

As I go through airports, people constantly come up to me and say, "I'm a Michigan man. I played for Bo." I always sensed that they felt they were special because of it. The rest of us can say, "I loved Bo."

BRUCE MADEJ, Michigan Sports Information Director

Bo always said he was "just an old curmudgeon," but the times never passed him by. He taught me how to deal with people, especially the media, and he loved to laugh. He would laugh at a joke, at you or himself. He was not afraid to laugh at his own foibles.

When we were discussing careers one day, I told Bo that he was one of the people that helped me hone my craft as a PR person. He smiled, then looked back at me. "Now I finally know why you are such a lousy PR guy." He then roared with laughter at his own line, cracking up both of us.

Bo was no curmudgeon. He was a class act.

BRAD BATES, Michigan Player, 1980

"Seniors up!"

After every Michigan victory Bo invited—really, commanded—all the seniors to stand on the nearest chair, above the underclassmen and even the coaches, and lead the team in singing "The Victors."

Imagine that. Our prize for all the pain, the time, the anxiety, the effort and the commitment was merely to sing a song. But oh, on so many levels, it was the sweetest of rewards. The last time I did this, on January 1, 1981, we got to do what no Bo Schembechler team had ever done before: sing "The Victors" at the Rose Bowl. Everyone in that room would tell you then and now: We sang it for Bo!

Now that I'm the athletic director at Miami, Bo's alma mater, not a day goes by where I do not draw on something I learned from Bo.

JIM HARBAUGH, Michigan Player, 1986

My impressions of Bo started when I was nine years old, and my dad was a secondary coach on his staff. During practice, the coaches' kids played our own game of football, and whenever an errant kick or pass landed on Bo's field, he'd blow his whistle and scream, "Get those damn kids off my field!"

When he would see me in the hallway he'd say, "You're a cocky little guy, aren't you?" I'd say, "Sometimes, I guess." No matter what he had to say to you, it always felt great to be noticed by Bo.

To this day I remember almost all of my encounters with Bo in great detail, but the most memorable occurred in his office a few days after the 1985 Ohio State game, which we won, 27-17. He stood up and put his fists on his desk and told me that I had played one of the finest games he had ever seen a Michigan quarterback play. I thanked him. Then he leaned back in his chair and looked up at the ceiling. "What it must feel like to have a son play the way you did! To stand in that pocket with the safety bearing down on you unblocked and hit Jon Kolesar on the post to seal the victory. UNBLOCKED!" He then let loose his familiar chuckle. "I'm proud of you, Jim." I felt as loved and appreciated as I have ever felt, like I was one of Bo's sons. In reality I was one of Bo's thousands of sons.

JAMIE MORRIS, Michigan Player, 1987

I will miss being called "The cutest little running back"—even though I hated it at the time. I will miss being told, "Morris, you know *nothing* about football!" I will miss hearing, "You are the dumbest American in America"—because we were talking about politics, and I'm one of *them*—a Democrat!

I will miss talking with him about the good old days—and not the days when I played, but the days when *he* played football and baseball, and when he coached with Woody.

Most of all, I will miss hearing how much love and pride he felt in being a Michigan man.

MARY SUE COLEMAN, Michigan President

Bo Schembechler did not receive an honorary degree because of his won-loss record, remarkable as it was. He was not honored for his Big Ten championships or consecutive appearances in a bowl game, or the number of his players who made it to the NFL. Bo was awarded an honorary degree from the University of Michigan because he was a man of integrity. It is an ideal we expect each and every student, employee and graduate of this university and our faculty to uphold and demonstrate.

MARY PASSINK, Michigan Secretary

I first encountered Bo when I interviewed for the job. I was twenty-nine years old with a husband and two kids, and a little rusty getting back into the daily work routine. The anticipation of meeting "The Big Guy" created a couple of days of self-doubt.

Bo immediately put me at ease with several minutes of questions and answers. I actually felt very comfortable with him. Then Bo laid a "what-if" on me. He said, "Suppose [former U-M quarterback] Rick Leach walked into your office and asked you, 'Honey, what are you doing tonight?' What would you say?"

"I'd say I'll probably be changing diapers and doing dishes."

He gave me one of his big belly laughs. "Good answer. You're hired!"

My desk was right outside his door and I learned so much by witnessing the interactions of Bo with his coaches and players. He was the best storyteller and I will miss that the most. There will never be anyone, ever, who has had more of an impact on my life or my children's lives as Bo Schembechler has.

LLOYD CARR, *Michigan Head Coach, Former Assistant to Bo*

Of all Bo's qualities, his tremendous willpower is the one that I admired the most. He had an incredible will to win, to live and to make a difference. As Rudyard Kipling said, "If you can talk with crowds and keep your virtue, Or walk with kings—nor lose the common touch." That was Bo's magic. He never lost the common touch.

SHEMY SCHEMBECHLER, *Bo's Son*

I would like to thank John Bacon for his efforts in putting together this book with my dad. He truly captured my dad's passion and spirit; it was as if Bo was sitting at the kitchen table reciting the stories to me again as he had done so many times before. It means so much to me that this book can share the wonderful traits of my dad to those who never had the chance to know him personally.

If I had to sum up what really drove my dad, I'd say it was his belief that he could make the world a better place. He loved coaching because he had an opportunity every day to make an impact on a kid's life, and he did not take the weight of that responsibility lightly. My dad's selflessness and desire to do whatever he could to help those around him leaves me in awe every time I reflect upon him. Even with his heart trouble, diabetes and neuropathy, he put all of his ailments on the back burner because his mission in life had been set, and nothing was going to stop him from carrying it out.

Bo told his players, "Those who stay will be champions." I think it can also be said that those who live like Bo will be champions.

CATHY SCHEMBECHLER, *Bo's Wife*

Having met Bo after his retirement, I knew a different man than most. I never realized until after his death how far-reaching the effect he had on people really was. People from all over the world contacted me—from New Zealand to England to Poland to a soldier in Iraq. They all had such kind words, and plenty of stories to tell. He touched so many.

Bo had a full life after coaching, and he never stopped learning. He always had several books going at once. We had the great fortune to travel quite extensively. Ballooning over France, riding shotgun on a photo safari in Africa, or hiking glaciers in his beloved New Zealand, he took the time to ask everyone we encountered about their life and he always left them laughing.

Bo's attitude was amazing. He met every day as a challenge even though the last few months of his life were very painful. Each morning he hit the floor whistling or singing—EVERY DAY! He taught me great lessons and gave new meaning to the word *faithful.* I have a huge hole in my heart now. My best friend is gone. But remember this: God picked the most beautiful flower in the field that day—My Bo!

Acknowledgments

Every author incurs dozens of debts in the course of writing a book, but due to the sad circumstances of November 2006, I incurred more than most.

In addition to losing a great mentor and friend, I lost my co-author. Although Bo had already answered just about every question I could think of, I would have loved to ask him a few more, and get his reaction to the final manuscript. Of course, he would say, "You see? That's your problem, Bacon. You always have one more question!"

I relied on his players, his coaches and his friends to verify the stories you've just read. As always, whenever you say it's for Bo, they come running. So thank you, Brad Bates, Jim Betts, Dave Brandon, Jim Brandstatter, Tirrell Burton, Dick Caldarazzo, Garvie Craw, Dan Dierdorf, Don Dufek, Jon Falk, Mike Gillette, Bill Gunlock, Jim Hackett, Jerry Hanlon, Jim Harbaugh, Rich Hewlett (who also handled Bo's legal issues), Bill McCartney, Mark Messner, Gary Moeller, Jamie Morris, Bubba Paris, Scott Passink, Tom Reed, Kenny Root, Fritz Seyferth, Paul Seymour, the late Tom Slade, Mike Smith, Scott Smykowski, John Wangler, Donnie Warner and Craig Wotta.

Inside the Michigan athletic department, I've long known sports information whizzes Bruce Madej, Dave Ablauf, Barb Cossman, Jim Schneider and Tara Preston are the best in the business, and they proved it once again. Greg Kinney of the Bentley Historical Library runs the most impressive sports archives in the nation, but he was never too busy to lend his expertise. In the football office, Lloyd Carr's secretary, Jennifer Maszatics, was her typically helpful self throughout. Bo's former secretary Lynn Koch came out of retirement to pitch in cheerfully once again.

My biggest debt is to Mary Passink. As Bo's trusted assistant, she guarded his time because she knew how much difficulty Bo had saying no to anyone—so I'm grateful she nudged him to say yes to me. She provided tireless help—including printing out a dozen copies of the second draft for the insiders to proofread before they left for the Rose Bowl—even though I'm officially an outsider. She's the greatest ally any Bo-ologist could have, and a great friend. Without Mary's cooperation this book would not have been possible. As Bo often said, "Mary, you're the best." I agree.

In the fall of 2006, Lloyd Carr was pretty busy coaching the Michigan football team, but he still found time to talk with me and regale my students with his stories. I'm certain his was the most popular lecture on Michigan's campus that semester. The late Don Canham was also generous with his time and insights, many of which you'll find here.

Cathy Schembechler has been a valued friend for over a decade, and never was her support more important to me than it was after Bo passed away. Her trust and resolve have been invaluable, and she kept Bo going longer than he ever could have by himself. Shemy Schembechler's stories and feedback greatly improved the book. His friendship has been a bonus.

My agent, David Black, is a writer's best friend, ably aided by Dave Larabell. My editor at Hachette, Rick Wolff, has been wise, patient and encouraging throughout. He and our publisher, Jamie Raab, stood by me and the project after Bo died. Thanks also to Rick's assistant Sean Jones.

I must give a special thanks to Charles Eisendrath and the folks at the Knight-Wallace Journalism Fellowship at the University of Michigan, who awarded me the first Benny Friedman Fellowship in sports journalism. I told them I intended to study the uniquely American phenomenon of college athletics—and I actually did it, resulting in the course I now teach at Michigan and the book you've just read. Neither would have been possible without the eight months they gave me to pursue my dreams.

My father, Dr. George Bacon, spent a few weekends helping me organize Bo's papers. Randy Milgrom helped iron out the contract. Jay Nelson, Tim Petersen, Peter Uher and Bob Weisman, great friends, all provided helpful critiques of the manuscript. During our weekly meetings, John Lofy and Jim Tobin not only nurtured this idea from its inception, but they also helped develop the pitch to my agent, the pitch to the publisher, and the manuscript itself. They are two of the best writers and editors out there, and two of my best friends. They seemed to get as big a kick out of the project as I did, and that's saying something.

Above all, I thank Bo, for everything. I cannot tell you how much I wish he was still here.

Index